the cinema of ANDRZEJ WAJDA

DIRECTORS' CUTS

Other titles in the Directors' Cuts series:

the cinema of EMIR KUSTURICA: *notes from the underground*
GORAN GOCIC

the cinema of KEN LOACH: *art in the service of the people*
JACOB LEIGH

the cinema of WIM WENDERS: *the celluloid highway*
ALEXANDER GRAF

the cinema of KATHRYN BIGELOW: *hollywood transgressor*
edited by DEBORAH JERMYN & SEAN REDMOND

the cinema of ROBERT LEPAGE: *the poetics of memory*
ALEKSANDAR DUNDJEROVIC

the cinema of GEORGE A. ROMERO: *knight of the living dead*
TONY WILLIAMS

the cinema of TERRENCE MALICK: *poetic visions of america*
edited by HANNAH PATTERSON

the cinema of DAVID LYNCH: *american dreams, nightmare visions*
edited by ERICA SHEEN & ANNETTE DAVISION

the cinema of NANNI MORETTI: *dreams and diaries*
edited by EWA MAZIERSKA & LAURA RASCAROLI

the cinema of MIKE LEIGH: *a sense of the real*
GARRY WATSON

the cinema of KRZYSZTOF KIESLOWSKI: *variations on destiny and chance*
MAREK HALTOF

the cinema of
ANDRZEJ WAJDA

the art of irony and defiance

edited by
john orr & elżbieta ostrowska

 **WALLFLOWER PRESS** LONDON & NEW YORK

First published in Great Britain in 2003 by
Wallflower Press
4th Floor, 26 Shacklewell Lane, London E8 2EZ
www.wallflowerpress.co.uk

A catalogue for this book is available from the British Library

ISBN 1-903364-89-2 (paperback)
ISBN 1-903364-57-4 (hardback)

Book design by Rob Bowden Design

Printed in Great Britain by Antony Rowe, Chippenham, Wiltshire

CONTENTS

Notes on Contributors   vii
Foreword: Cinema: Past and Present   ix
Preface: The Importance of Andrzej Wajda   xviii

1   At the Crossroads: Irony and Defiance in the Films of Andrzej Wajda   1
     John Orr

2   Wajda's Imagination of Disaster: War Trauma, Surrealism and Kitsch   15
     Paul Coates

3   'He Speaks To Us': The Author in *Everything For Sale*, *Man of Marble*   30
     and *Pan Tadeusz*
     Tadeusz Lubelski

4   Dangerous Liaisons: Wajda's Discourse of Sex, Love and Nation   46
     Elżbieta Ostrowska

5   Changing Meanings of Home and Exile: From *Ashes and Diamonds*   64
     to *Pan Tadeusz*
     Izabela Kalinowska

6   Wajda's Filmic Representation of Polish-Jewish Relations   76
     Michael Stevenson

7   Remembering and Deconstructing: The Historical Flashback in   93
     Man of Marble and *Man of Iron*
     Maureen Turim

8   'Visual Eloquence' and Documentary Form: Meeting *Man of Marble*   103
     in Nowa Huta
     Bjørn Sørenssen

9   Catastrophic Spectacles: Historical Trauma and the Masculine Subject   116
     in *Lotna*
     Christopher J. Caes

10   Wajda, Grotowski and Mickiewicz: The Dialectics of Apotheosis   132
     and Derision
     Michael Goddard

11   Andrzej Wajda's Vision of *'The Promised Land'*   146
     Ewelina Nurczyńska-Fidelska

12   *As the Years Pass, As the Days Pass...* – An Ironic Epic   160
     Tomasz Kłys

13   'Ojczyzno Moja': Adapting *Pan Tadeusz*   172
     Lisa Di Bartolomeo

Filmography   190
Bibliography   194
Index   201

Christopher J. Caes is a graduate student in Slavic Studies at the University of California, Berkeley. He holds a BA in German and an MA in Russian from Ohio State University. He is currently working on a dissertation on the film, culture and politics of the post-Stalinist 'Thaw' in Poland during the late 1950s.

Paul Coates is Professor in Film Studies in the School of English and Film Studies at the University of Aberdeen, Scotland. His publications include *The Story of the Lost Reflection* (Verso, 1985), *The Gorgon's Gaze* (Columbia University Press, 1991), *Lucid Dreams: The Films of Krzysztof Kieślowski* (ed.) (Flicks Books, 1999) and *Cinema, Religion and the Romantic Legacy* (Ashgate, 2002).

Lisa Di Bartolomeo received her PhD in Slavic Languages and Literatures from the University of North Carolina at Chapel Hill. Entitled 'Other Visions: Krzysztof Kieślowski's 'Trzy Kolory Trilogy', it has won the Kazimierz Dziewanowski Mem-orial Award. She has studied at the University of Łódź on a Fulbright Scholarship and her research interests include folklore and carnivals, and the Holocaust in film and literature.

Michael Goddard is a PhD candidate in the Department of Art History and Theory, University of Sydney, currently researching a thesis on the relations between Witold Gombrowicz's work and Gilles Deleuze's philosophy. He has published articles on New Zealand cinema, film theory, Polish modernism and continental philosophy.

Izabela Kalinowska is Assistant Professor in the Department of European Languages, Literatures, and Cultures at SUNY, Stony Brook. Her most recent work includes 'Nineteenth-Century Notions of Exile and Modern Polish Cinema: From the Polish School of Cinematography to Kieślowski's *White*' (in Dominika Radulescu (ed.) *Realms of Exile, Diasporas, Nomadism and Eastern European Voices.* Lexington Books, 2002).

Tomasz Kłys teaches film history and theory at the Department of Media and Audiovisual Culture in the University of Łódź. He published *Film fikcji i jego dominanty* (*The Fiction Film and its Dominants*, Wydawnictwo Naukowe Semper, 1999), and has written film reviews and theoretical articles on film for Polish magazines and anthologies. He is presently preparing a work on Dickens, Thackeray and other literary sources of narrative film.

Tadeusz Lubelski is a film critic, cinema historian, Professor at Jagiellonian University in Cracow and deputy editor of the periodical *Kino*. His recent publications include *Strategie autorskie w polskim filmie fabularnym 1945–1961* (Rabid, 2000) and *Nowa Fala: O pewnej przygodzie kina francuskiego* (Universitas, 2000). He is working on a biography of Andrzej Wajda.

Ewelina Nurczyńska-Fidelska is Professor at the University of Łódź in the Department of Media and Audiovisual Culture. Her main research interest lies in the history of Polish cinema. Publications include *Andrzej Munk* (Wydawnictwo Literackie, 1982), *Edukacja filmowa na tle kultury literackiej* (Łódzkie Towarzystwo Naukowe, 1989), *Polish Cinema in Ten Takes* (editor) (Łódzkie Towarzystwo Naukowe, 1996), *Polska klasyka literacka według Andrzeja Wajdy* (Wydawnictwo, 1998) and *Czas i przesłona: O Filipie Bajonie i jego twórczosci* (Rabid, 2003)

John Orr is Professor Emeritus at the University of Edinburgh where he teaches film. He has published several books on cinema, including *Cinema and Modernity* (Polity Press, 1993), *Contemporary Cinema* (Edinburgh Uuniversity Press, 1998) and *The Art and Politics of Film* (Edinburgh University Press, 2000). His recent work includes essays on Kieślowski, Lynch, Dogme95 and Terrence Malick.

Elżbieta Ostrowska teaches film in the Department of Media and Audiovisual Culture, University of Łódź. Her recent publications include *Przestrze filmowa* (Kraków, 2000), *Gender in Film and the Media: East-West Dialogues* (co-editor) (Peter Lang, 2000) and *Gender w kinie europejskim i mediach* (editor) (Rabid, 2001).

Bjørn Sørenssen is Professor of Film and Media Studies at the Norwegian University of Science and Technology, Trondheim, Norway. In addition to several articles on documentary, film history and new media in international film and media journals, he has published books on film and television, most recently, a study on the history and theory of international documentary, *Å fange virkeligheten-Dokumentarfilmens århundre* (*Catching Reality*, Universitetsforlaget, 2001).

Michael Stevenson is a Lecturer in the Department of Film, Theatre and Television at the University of Reading, UK. His research interests include Polish, British and Third World Cinemas. He is joint editor and contributor to *Gender in Film and the Media: East-West Dialogues* (Peter Lang, 2000).

Maureen Turim is Professor of English and Film Studies at the University of Florida. She is the author of *Abstraction in Avant-Garde Films* (UMI Research Press, 1985), *Flashbacks in Film: Memory and History* (Routledge, 1989) and *The Films of Oshima Nagisa: Images of a Japanese Iconoclast* (University of California Press, 1998). She has published over sixty essays in anthologies and journals on theoretical, historical and aesthetic issues in cinema and video, art, and comparative literature. Her latest book project is entitled *Desire and its Ends: The Driving Forces of Recent Cinema*.

Cinema: Past and Present

Andrzej Wajda

As I thought about my speech for today, I chose not to give a lecture. Never in my life have I confronted so many experts on my work and I do not think it will happen to me again. So my anxiety is greater than ever and I have decided this should not be a speech but a confession.

I shall try to answer the question, what is national cinema today? Everything seems to show that national cinemas will survive and I have no doubt they will. But can they replace American cinema? For sure the influx of American film makes all European artists uneasy ... but I do not think it can be replaced. American cinema will continue to play the same role it always has. Can national cinemas, then, develop alongside it? I think they can. And I believe they will survive. What makes me think so? First of all, production techniques have advanced and are much easier than they used to be in my day. It is impossible now to erect barriers of any kind preventing people from making films they want to make, whether it is through studies in film school, problems of financing or censorship. Anyone, director or cinematographer, can get a digital camera and make a film, just as the principles of Dogme95 proclaim, on what is happening around them. If what they have to say turns out to be interesting, the film will be distributed, maybe only to a handful of cinemas, but experience teaches us that such cinemas still want to show such films.

Since such a film will be shot in the native tongue, does language therefore play a fundamental role? This is another problem that should be considered for I have an impression that the world will not successfully unite through one language. People want to speak different languages, and attempts to impose a common language have been futile. Poland regained independence in 1918. The three partitioning powers taught in two languages. Some officers in the army – I still remember that – spoke two foreign languages. This entire body switched to Polish in no time, and it was not a problem to create a Polish administration. Our historical experience proves that a language cannot be imposed. Tradition and literature encourage people to watch national films, in national languages. I do not think, however, that we in Poland want to make amateur or semi-amateur films that are shown for a small audience in a few cinemas. I believe we should aim higher than that. Polish cinema after the war won the recognition of the world. Could it be similarly successful now? I have an impression that time, if you like, has formed a loop since 1945 and we have returned to the starting point. The Polish cinema of the last decade is in my opinion a bit like pre-war cinema. This judgement may be a bit harsh but since I make films too and my perception of my work over the last ten years is similar, please let me make such a comparison. It is so easy to compare *Quo Vadis* (2001) with Jósef Lejtes' pre-war picture *Under Your Protection* (1933). Cezary Pazura's role in contemporary cinema is parallel to that of Adolf Dymsza's before the war.[1] There are no films about elegant salons, but then there are no elegant salons. Instead, there are gangsters and films about gangsters nowadays in a way that corresponds to pre-war films about elegant salons.

So if this situation is typical, then is it indeed our desire to make national films, shown only in one country, for the people who want to see themselves on the screen and to hear their own language? Interestingly, the French, whose minds are much more Cartesian, have chosen not to defend national cinema on the principle of the free market but on the principle of a language quota. A bill has been adopted stipulating that only 60 per cent of all distributed films can be in any one language. The language was not specified but the 60 per cent restriction sets up a distinct barrier. Yet any attempt to restrict the role of the English language fails and I refuse to believe it can succeed. At the same time, when I look at united Europe and all its activities, I see a new Tower of Babel with a confusion of languages coming into being. Sometimes I have an impression that all Eurocrats get together at night, speak English and agree on what they will say in their native tongues in the morning. This means that national cinemas will continue to exist. The war in the Balkans, internal conflicts in various countries prove that people still want to speak languages that no one else knows and they believe it is of utmost importance.

Lately attempts have been made, especially because such things are profitable, to make films in co-operation with other countries: Germany and France, France and Poland, Poland and someone else etc. Special EU legislation has allowed for joint financing of such movies, yet also permitted their release as films of a given country. Soon, however, such films were being dubbed 'Euro-puddings': a kind of meal that is totally unpalatable. I have wondered whether the problem is that actors in such films often speak a language that is not their own. It seems to me, however, that we have a different problem here. It is not the problem of the language in which the actors speak but the language in which the director thinks. The director loses his footing when he is outside his own world and his own circle. He does not know whom he is talking to, does not know what his audience thinks. If I think in Polish, then I try to make what I do coherent. In a nutshell: I want to talk about myself. I have an impression it is the only way for the art of film.

Let me tell you briefly what the world was like when I was a child. It was very different. Constructivism and Futurism, great artistic movements, thrived; avant-garde art groups like Rytm and Blok were active. Representatives of these movements believed that they would root out irrationality, introduce sense into human existence and create a better future world. Yet soon after World War One, the demons of Fascism emerged, quickly followed by Stalinism, which did promise a better future though real life soon shattered such hopes. I am proud that Polish cinema addressed these two matters. It spoke out against the Nazi war and made films that challenged the lie of Stalinism. Let me tell you what my generation concentrated on. I remember that Jerzy Andrzejewski,[2] who was always interested in all sorts of catchphrases and used them for his works, drew my attention to a saying that was popular in 1955 and 1956. When asked 'How are things?' you'd answer 'Disastrous'. Our cinema made a subject out of those disasters.

Let me quote Alfred de Musset's poem *Ode to Poland* at this point:

> Until that day, brave Poland, when you show us all
> some disaster greater than all the ones before
> and wake us up – Poland, you will not find strength,
> you will not wipe out indifference from our face.

It is your time, heroes, but fight on your own,
Europe never seems too eager to give help,
It prefers excitements that do not haunt at night,
Then fight, Poland, or perish – we are blasé.

I experienced this blasé indifference when my second film, *Kanal* (1957), was shown at Cannes. The festival was very different from what it is now. The resort was half empty in the spring season before the summer influx began, and the festival had to attract rich, suave French audiences. Unlike today when no uniform style is required, ladies had elegant dresses and diamond jewellery; men wore dinner jackets. This was the audience who saw my film. What appeared in the *Nice Matin* newspaper the following day was more of a warning for the festival organisers than a critical review. The reviewer claimed that films in which people waded in the sewers must not be shown. The festival was addressed to elegant people who wished to see great art and did not want to wade in the sewers with Polish insurgents. The poem just recited and this story complement each other. We simply believed that as long as we had a message for the world, we had to expose our wounds, and to make it the subject of our films.

What did we think of pre-war cinema? We already knew what to think about it when we were at Film School. We still did not know what films we wanted to make but we knew full well we did not want to make the films that had been made before the war. We rejected the cinema represented by Dymsza or other pre-war trends on all counts, and we viewed critically the people who had created Polish pre-war cinema. I am thinking here about Wanda Jakubowska and Aleksander Ford:[3] we perceived them as pre-war directors, not to mention Allan Starski's father,[4] who wrote scripts for Dymsza. We chose to create cinema from scratch. Of course we had our models. We watched the films of Italian Neorealism and were inspired by them. That was the world we wanted to show on screen, the world of poor people, because we were poor. It was very important that our voice was heard on the other side of the Iron Curtain too. We felt then that the Polish cinema had a duty not only to speak about itself but also to communicate with those on the other side in the Cold War. We wanted to speak with the voice of our neighbours who then still did not have their own cinemas or at least were not yet accorded recognition. I think our mission succeeded. Our war films showed the truth about the Polish 'October' in 1956 to those on the other side of the Iron Curtain, and later our films in August 1980 let the world know that something fundamental was happening in Poland.

The rhythm of a film was another thing that seemed important to me as a young director. We did not like Soviet cinema, not because of what it said but because of its slow tempo. Polish audiences felt the same. Unfortunately, great Soviet cinema, born in the 1920s, did not develop in the way its great directors expected it to. Hence we wanted our films to adopt the rhythms of Western films, because we thought it would keep us alive. And that is why Western audiences could watch our films – the rhythms were more animated and they captured the reality of our lives. Our national cinema was greatly supported at that time by other national cinemas or by outstanding people who had begun to create world cinema. American cinema was not at the top of all great achievements then. Fellini, Bergman and Kurosawa were the big names, and we watched their films wanting to find their Polish equivalents. The audience for our films was the intelligentsia, the highly educated, as it was for the films of Bergman and Kurosawa. Even if someone like me did not have a full education, he tried to catch up by seeing those films. Communication was easy because our shared knowledge allowed us to make easy reference to history or to Greek mythology. There was a high degree of understanding between artist and audience. I have an impression things are different today, and it is more difficult to ascertain how to communicate with an audience. Then we reached out to the world, the world reached out to us, and intellectual audiences were the basis of our communication, and the aspirations of Polish cinema at that time clearly reflect this. In the 1960s Jerzy Kawalerowicz made *Pharaoh* (1966), a beautiful, original film which won worldwide acclaim, while Wojciech Has made *The Saragossa Manuscript* (1965), which Buñuel considered to be one of the best films in the world. There was a kind of community of cinephiles – film-makers and audiences alike who sought to understand the world. We worked hard for such an audience then and, unless one realises this, it is difficult to understand the situation of the cinema of that time.

Today most national cinemas are partly financed by the state. Even though funds may be rare, all European countries with their own film industries operate some system of subsidy. It is interesting that often the state used to have specific requirements in return for its money. Today, on the whole, the state gives the money but does not demand anything. Things should be better but, strangely, they are worse. What is more, cinema is at the mercy of television, which produces films but then relegates them to off-peak viewing times. On the one hand, it assists cinema: on the other its assistance is inadequate. The success bestowed by film festivals and awards, increasingly numerous, is illusionary. More and more frequently, films with awards are not put into distribution and there is no chance for audiences to see them. Next, more and more films are made in unknown or almost unknown languages, which breaks up even further what used to unite world cinema. Cinema has become a pastime. In Poland, young people between 15 and 25 are the largest audience. Those people are generally contented. They do not go to the cinema to share their pain in the way that the Polish intelligentsia of the previous generation watched our films. They are not burdened with the past. It is difficult to make historical films because these young people hardly have any sense of the past and are surprised to learn about some of the things their parents experienced. These young people have been brought up stress-free. But, equally important, cinema tickets are expensive so only the prosperous go to the cinema. A film about social problems requires a large audience because one would like to appeal to as many people as possible and to move them. But why should anyone make a social problem film today if only the well-heeled go to the cinema? To tell them that poverty exists? They know that and will not be moved by it. A new audience has arisen, creating a new kind of situation.

Let me move onto the saddest thing I want to say today. It turns out that Poles prefer to go to movie theatres in city centres. There is, for instance, a very good cinema dating back to the 1950s in Nowa Huta[5] but no one goes there because everyone goes to see a film in one of the movie theatres in the centre of Cracow. But this cinema must bring in money, just like a supermarket, because otherwise the cinema will be knocked down and a supermarket will be built in its place. So if cinema owners want to stay on in the market, there is no way out for them. It is not only the matter of their personal preferences or that they do not like our films: if they want to have a cinema theatre in the city centre, and people only go to such cinemas, they must show films that would attract audiences. Meanwhile, let me return to the more general problem. The intelligentsia is in retreat. The ethos of the intelligentsia is disappearing. Educational qualifications are also different and require something different from young people. They do not unite them in the way they united us. Cinema for the well-heeled is a pastime and does not draw on the past or history. But this only means that things have become normal. This is what cinema audiences should be like. So why are we resentful then? Isn't it what we fought for? I wonder, however, whether we have come back, so to speak, to the beginning, to the starting point. I wonder, and it is a sad thought, whether the Polish film school in 1956 came into being only to settle the accounts with the past and whether this painful confrontation about which the poem earlier speaks is not the only way for the art of Polish cinema; whether the disasters and suffering of our nation are not the only subject that we can share with the world outside and grab its attention? Yet maybe Polish cinema was born only to speak about the disasters of this nation.

I must say a few words about American cinema, even applaud it, as I think a war with American cinema is based on a misunderstanding. Firstly, the term 'American cinema' should not be used at all because it is too general. Americans make a great deal of films that may have something in common; some are splendid, magnificent productions whose message appeals to us all, while some are pure entertainment. I do not think those two trends should be confused. We should draw our own conclusions from it. American cinema has united that big country. Its diversity has made it possible to show individual endeavour and the need for self-reliance. It has illustrated the slogan 'Act or perish'. Yet at the same time, American cinema also takes in European ideas. I can see references to European literature and thought in Spielberg's latest film, *A.I. Artificial Intelligence* (2001). The fairytale magic that he exploits so beautifully also has European roots. This film is for me, I am ashamed to say, more European than Patrice Chéreau's *Intimacy* (2000). American films teach me one important lesson: the audience may disagree with the concept that the director offers but they must understand what the director has to say. Unfortunately, a great majority of European films are lost somewhere along the line between director and screen because the director thinks that his confused, unintelligible language is part of his message. In fact, it makes it impossible to understand the director's ideas and as a result we only know that he is desperately trying to tell us something. That is why when I started working on *Ashes and Diamonds* (*Popiół i diament*, 1958), John Huston's *The Asphalt Jungle* (1950) was my inspiration. Few remember this film now but it is worth seeing. These were the films we wanted to make. It was beautiful; we were impressed by it. The final scene, when the gangster on the run returns home, lies down on the grass and the grazing horses come near him, is brilliantly unique. I have never seen such a scene. But I also mean the entire film, the way it was made, the inspiration it gave me. That is why I believe that I have to applaud American cinema – I owe it a great deal.

Let us, however, return to the situation at home. I have read Ryszard Kapuściński's essay in Gazeta Wyborcza.[6] Kapuściński writes, 'Man cannot live in the atmosphere of marginalisation, contempt, sense of inferiority but has the need for identity, identification, which is, in turn, difficult in a world that enforces migration as a result of inequality.' Later on he says, 'Our world is at a crossroads. A certain tendency seems inevitable: we will live in a multicultural world.' In a way, we have always lived in a multicultural world but we were not aware of it because never before has the system of communication – via television, telephone or the internet – been so efficient. I draw a certain conclusion from the quotations I have given. As long as we really want to hold onto our place and our language, we must not renounce national cinema…

Cinema is not only spoken language. It is also an art of images. Here is an example I frequently use: the sequence showing Maciek Chełmicki's death on a rubbish tip brings *Ashes and Diamonds* to a close. I have often been asked how it was possible that the film was released at all. Jerzy Andrzejewski's party membership definitely helped; it would not have been possible otherwise. Regardless of that, for the censors who examined the film the message in the final scene could well have been that whoever rebels against the communist authorities ends up on the rubbish dump of history. Yet when the film was distributed the audience may well have thought, 'Who are these authorities who kill our boy, a resistance fighter, on a rubbish tip? This isn't right.' Both interpretations were possible and that is why the film was released with this amazing scene. Still, a censor phoned me early in the morning of the release of *Ashes and Diamonds* and suggested the sequence should be cut out. I knew, however, that I could hold out a few more hours and then we would see. We made it, the sequence stayed. I am saying this because I believe it is proof that national cinema, which speaks a verbal language no outsider would understand, may speak a language of images with such force that even censorship could not cope. I believe that the cinema of our times, a digital camera in the hands of the director, the Dogme rule that demands a film be contemporary and speaks to the living moment, the quest to use naturalistic language, are all powerful and make sense. Monopolies of both the state and the film industry lose their meaning as this contemporary type of film production develops. Our hopes for European cinema must surely go in this direction. This cinema will not become homogeneous because the audiences will remain diversified and certain films will be addressed only to certain groups. So original, often strange films will be made because artists will want to make them. Language will not play a major role because a film addressed to everyone will be in English, just as it was with *Joan of Arc* (1999) by Luc Besson, the French director who made his film in English to ensure a large audience. On the other hand, it is interesting that *Schindler's List* (1993) is the only film about the Holocaust that has been seen throughout the entire world. We in Poland had made films about the same subject much earlier. They may not have been that bad and may have seized the attention of their audience but only a film made in English could give the world an abiding image of the Holocaust.

So what do I hope for as my life is coming to an end? I believe we should work on European films, national films. Ryszard Kapuściński says that our European world will grow old but young, healthy barbarians will learn our language, fall in love with our past and our culture, and because of them our work is worth our while. As long as we bequeath to them what we should, those barbarians will create beautiful Polish art. I wholeheartedly count on it…

Andrzej Wajda
Łódź, October 2001
(Translated by Joanna Kazik)

Notes

1   Adolf Dymsza – one of the most popular pre-war comic actors.
2   The author of the novel *Ashes and Diamonds* and a co-author of the screenplay of Andrzej Wajda's film based on the novel.
3   Members of the pre-war leftist Society of the Devotees of the Artistic Film, START, who played a significant role in post-war Polish cinema.
4   Ludwik Starski – scriptwriter of both many pre-war and post-war popular films.
5   A town constructed after the war, now a district in Cracow; a symbol of Stalinism in Poland. The action of *Man of Marble* is set in Nowa Huta.
6   The best-selling Polish daily newspaper.

PREFACE

The Importance of Andrzej Wajda

John Orr & Elżbieta Ostrowska

The veteran Polish director Andrzej Wajda has proved himself one of the great figures in European cinema during the second half of the twentieth century. This volume of essays by international scholars is a celebration of that achievement. It follows on from a commemorative conference on his work in cinema and theatre held at the University of Łódź in October 2001 and also from his special Lifetime Award at the 2000 Oscar ceremonies in Hollywood. It is a studied retrospect that proceeds from the famous wartime trilogy of the 1950s through to his recent version of *Pan Tadeusz* (1999), the epic poem of Poland's foremost poet of the nineteenth century, Adam Mickiewicz. His long career reminds us, in a post-Cold War situation, of that tangled relationship between cinema and politics we now sense in countries as diverse as Iran and China, yet was for over thirty years an everyday feature of cultural life in much of Central and Eastern Europe. The foreword to this volume is in fact Wajda's own assessment of some aspects of his career, made in his address to the Łódź conference. But it is also more than that. It is a set of speculations that centres around Poland yet moves beyond it, addressing the general fate of European cinema, past, present and future.

The critical essays that follow all address key aspects of his work, and his continuing importance for us all. John Orr outlines the constant play on irony and defiance that builds into Wajda's film aesthetic his continuing confrontations with Polish history and the cultural constraints of the communist state under which he lived for so long. His essay also highlights the fertile hybridity of Wajda's aesthetics, his ability to harness different traditions of realism, romanticism and modernist reflexivity in forging a coherent filmic vision of his native country and its modern predicament. Using Freudian analysis to great effect, Paul Coates looks more specifically at the impact of war traumas on Wajda's variations in film form and on his respective fascinations, too often neglected by critics, with surrealism and kitsch in his 1959 war film *Lotna*. These complex fascinations, when linked to the traumatic events of Poland's wartime experience that he re-fashioned on cinema screens a decade later, give him, Coates argues, a special place in the twentieth-century revival of European romanticism that builds on modernist aesthetics.

The key essays by Polish critics Tadeusz Lubelski and Elżbieta Ostrowska offer us other insights. Lubelski looks at Wajda's self-fictionalisation at key points in his career, where he consciously inserts himself as author into his films. He gives three key examples: Wajda's 1968 film about the making of a film that was also a memorial tribute to one of his favourite actors, Zbigniew Cybulski, *Everything For Sale*; his landmark 1976 fable about Polish politics and image-making, *Man of Marble;* and his 1999 epic *Pan Tadeusz* where the voice-over narrative links the author of the text, Mickiewicz, to the author of the film, Wajda himself. Ostrowska has a different focus. She examines the vital relationship between the micro- and macrocosmic that radiates through his greatest films, between the intimate dilemmas of sex and love and the broader issues of Polish nationhood that always seem to frame and enclose them, and at times to oppress them. Here she explores in detail the two great films set in the immediate post-war period where that relationship is most manifest, *Ashes and Diamonds* (1958) and *Landscape After Battle* (1970); and a later wartime film about Polish-German relations, *A Love in Germany,* shot as a co-production in 1983 from the novel by Rolf Hochhuth.

Izabela Kalinowska and Michael Stevenson examine singular themes that recur repeatedly throughout Wajda's career. Kalinowska looks at the Polish meanings of home and exile in Wajda's cinema, seen as a function of repeated human dislocation throughout recent history and of its psychological fall-out. She focuses on the sense of homelessness prevalent in the post-war generation that Wajda's films had brought so powerfully to light. Yet she also explores the mythical world of home in Wajda's history films, particularly the manor house, or gentry home, of *Promised Land* (1974). In this film, she contends, it functions as a myth of original wholeness for a lost intelligentsia in a communist Poland of the 1960 and 1970s. Stevenson, by contrast, deals with the enduring problem of Polish-Jewish relations and the Holocaust experience in Wajda's work, right from his startling 1954 debut *A Generation*, a film of wartime resistance unjustly neglected, to his controversial work in the 1990s, the feature films *Korczak* (1990) and *Holy Week* (1995). He sees Wajda's concern with Holocaust experience as consistent and conscientious, despite the adverse criticisms he has often encountered and shows the durability of his concern from his earliest to his most recent work in examining Polish-Jewish relations in all spheres of life.

After his wartime trilogy, the most widely known of Wajda's films internationally have been the *Man of Marble/Man of Iron* diptych. Arguably the most political of Wajda's films, they are also artistic markers between 1976 and 1981 of the rise and fall of Solidarity as the major opposition movement to the Polish communist state. From these two films Maureen Turim singles out the use of the historical flashback as a key narrative form. Inspired by *Citizen Kane,* Wajda, Turim contends, takes the historical flashback to new levels of complexity in its use of documentary footage, filmic reconstruction and montage. As a device it operates on several levels at once as a filmic challenge to the dominant political ideology of the time. Analysing in more detail the relationship between framing narrative and documentary form in the two films, Bjørn Sørenssen also records at first-hand the audience reaction to *Man of Marble* in 1977 at a cinema in Nowa Huta, the new industrial town that features so heavily in flashback during the film. He concludes that by focusing on the past more than the present, *Man of Marble* has a rhetoric of greater subtlety, and through focusing on the present more than the past, *Man of Iron* has a rhetoric of greater urgency.

Two contrasting forms of Wajda's revisionist romanticism are analysed by Michael Goddard and Christopher J. Caes. Goddard examines Wajda's dialectic of apotheosis and derision by comparing it with that resonating through the theatre of Jerzy Grotowski and in particular his staging of Mickiewicz's *Forefathers' Eve* (*Dziady III*). In Goddard's view, Wajda's films, especially *Man of Marble* and *Pan Tadeusz*, show greater continuity with the spirit and the romantic motifs of Mickiewicz than do the distancing devices of Grotowski's stage experiments. In contrast, Caes looks closely at the relationship between romance and masculinity in Wajda's war cavalry film *Lotna*, highlighting the traumas of the clash between Polish romantic tradition and military modernity at the start of World War Two. He argues that the film re-presents military spectacle with a central ambivalence: on the one hand it is an authentic form of homo-social bonding; on the other, it is an emblem of historical failure with deep psychic consequences for the post-war generation.

One of the great skills of Andrzej Wajda has been his flair for adapting screen narratives from different written sources, fiction, drama and poetry. Ewelina Nurczyńska-Fidelska provides us a with a detailed case-study of *Promised Land*, made in 1974 and recently re-edited by Wajda in a new revised print. She elaborates the many differences between Wajda's history narrative and its literary source, the turn-of-century novel by Władysław Stanisław Reymont that deals with sexual, financial and political intrigue in the new industrial Łódź of that period. Tomasz Kłys looks at Wajda's adapting in a different context, television. His popular 1980 television series of Kraków life, *As the Years Pass, As the Days Pass...*, was adapted from texts by Polish modernist writers created between 1883 and 1919. Kłys argues that the television period-drama marks Wajda's original contribution to an important history genre, the ironic epic that produces a 'fascinating dialectic of the sublime and the trivial, of exalted affirmation and caustic satire, of authentic emotion and buffoonish affectation'. Finally, Lisa Di Bartolemeo looks at Wajda's last feature-film of the century, based upon one of the true classics of Polish writing, Mickiewicz's *Pan Tadeusz*. She argues that Wajda uses all his filmic powers here to recreate Mickiewicz's sensibility, his deep feeling for nature and nationhood and his lament in Parisian exile for a lost world that he had left behind.

This volume, then, is more than just a collection of critical observations. We believe it is the first English-language commentary on Wajda to cover the major aspects of his work from different critical points of view. We see it as complementing and updating the excellent 1970s monograph of Bolesław Michałek, but also of going much further. The advantage of hindsight allows for reflection in depth on a variety of topics and controversies that Wajda's work provokes, and to see that work taking its course over a full half-century. The volume also makes use of general advances in film theory and criticism so that Wajda can be seen in a fresh light as a figure both truly national and international in the context of world cinema.

For making such a volume possible special thanks must be extended to the Department of Literature, Theatre and Film at the University of Łódź and to all those who participated in the Wajda conference of October 2001.

We would also like to thank the following for permission to use the stills in this volume: SF 'Oko', SF 'Kadr', 'Perspektywa' and Filmoteka Narodowa in Warsaw; special thanks to Grzegorz Balski, Jerzy Buchwald, Henryk Czepek, Janusz Morgenstern, Aleksandra Myszak, Zbigniew Stanek and Adam Wyżyński for assistance with the illustrations.

John Orr and Elżbieta Ostrowska
October 2003

CHAPTER ONE

At the Crossroads: Irony and Defiance in the Films of Andrzej Wajda

John Orr

For most of his career, Andrzej Wajda made films in a Poland that was a Party-State contained in its exercise of power by recurrent forms of popular defiance; in 1956, in 1970, in 1980 and again in 1989 when Party demise spearheaded the wider collapse of communism in Central and Eastern Europe. Wajda's films too were defiant, but continuous rather than sporadic, subtle rather than open, making use of greater freedom (or less censorship) in cinema than in politics. They can be seen now as an intrinsic part of that wider politics of defiance, at the very core of its shifting discourse. His films only make sense in that context, which is a politics of paradox. Polish Communism could be deeply unpopular, yet appealed openly to popular sentiment and not without success. It appealed, within the limits of its class ideology, to the sovereignty of the nation and the social unity of its people, values Wajda himself adhered to in a different way, and which had coloured the Polish romantic tradition communists would denounce as bourgeois ideology. In the post-war period, the discourse of Polish Romanticism was embedded in Wajda's defiance of the new state, yet it was also a tradition in politics, as he well knew, that had previously failed. The irony of his predicament was not lost on the son of a

Polish Cavalry officer who had perished not in the futile war of horses against German tanks in 1939 but in the Katyń massacre the Party later covered up during its troubled reign of over thirty years.

In Wajda, cinematic irony bespeaks the limit of defiance, of its ambition and its vanities, its frailties and its failures. Yet defiance constantly renews and reinvents itself because it has no other option. It has to challenge not only through protest. It must work with irony, fable, allegory and daring and show through the nuance and tone of the moving image the multitude of unjust things that remain unspoken. Only thus can it embrace popular cause. Yet the romantic legacy brought its own limitations. Coloured by attachment to an outworn tradition of the collective, to a sense of heroic doom and the eternal victimhood of the nation, romantic aspirations to popularity are always in danger of bombast and vanity. In Polish history, grand defiance of the state of things always has to take into account past failures in the grand defiance of the state of things. For much of Wajda's career this would seem a vicious circle in Polish history that was never to be broken, an absurd metanarrative nowhere to be found in the unwritten laws of the Enlightenment said by so many to govern the path of European history.

From his debut feature *A Generation* (*Pokolenie*, 1954) right up until *Danton* (1982), made in France during the period of Poland's martial law and often viewed as an allegory of doomed resistance, this symbiosis of irony and defiance had been fleshed out in a diversity of forms. Indeed the forms often seem so diverse as to be perverse. His films combine so many narrative and stylistic elements he is sometimes viewed as a hybrid director, not easily classifiable, and for some of his detractors too loose and eclectic in his approach to film. Out of pure necessity, however, the entanglements of irony and defiance forced Wajda to fuse very disparate aspects of film language, of narrative and *mise-en-scène*, into an aesthetic unity. For that reason it is never really easy to label him a realist, a modernist or a romantic because nothing quite fits. At times he can be all of these things for the simple reason that conviction entailed telling complex stories and telling them in particular ways. Whether invented or adapted from fiction or a mix of both, such stories have a formidable agenda. From the death of Stalin to the start of martial law in 1981, Wajda's role was that of a national figure too easily caricatured as the keeper of the nation's conscience. There were too many great artists and thinkers in Poland in this period for that to be the case, yet there remains a stark singularity about his artistic signature. Within the European spectrum his concern with the pitfalls and agonies of national identity place him, in film, alongside Jean Renoir of inter-war France and a group of directors emerging in the 1970s each with a specific imprimatur for their own nation: Theo Angelopoulos in Greece, Rainer Werner Fassbinder in Germany and Andrei Tarkovsky in Soviet Russia.

This central role was enhanced by other factors: the avoidance of war-cinema by his great contemporary Wojciech Has, the untimely death of another great contemporary Andrzej Munk, and then the early migration of talented newcomers like Roman Polanski and Jerzy Skolimowski. The premature absence of the latter three left major gaps in Polish film-making. Munk's scepticism was more corrosive than Wajda's while Polanski and Skolimowski were more attuned to the new modernisms sweeping Western Europe. While Wajda professed his admiration for Luis Bu el, it was Has' surreal epic of 1965, *The Saragossa Manuscript* (*Rękopis znaleziony w Saragossie*) that remains the most Buñuelian of all Polish films and surely influenced in turn the later films of the Spanish master. Yet the continuing boldness of Wajda's vision over 25 years was a tribute to his powers of endurance in a Party-State that censored film heavily for its politics and continued to have a tense relationship with a civil society whose autonomy it was reluctant to admit. Wajda's vision is more complex than many allow, and here we can be precise. The elements releasing the contrapuntal flows of irony and defiance could well be dubbed the synthetic style of the three R's: the *real*, the *romantic* and the *reflexive*. If realism is the closest, most obvious form of defiance, not only in Poland but elsewhere in post-war Europe, then Wajda's residual romantic impulse adds on an inverse image of the social collective, offering an altered imaginary unity to that officially prescribed. Yet the *limits* of that imaginary unity were something Wajda creatively explored throughout his career, deconstructing through his filmic self-conscious, through his reflexive powers, a romantic impulse that could overwhelm him. At his sharpest, he refuses to believe in any propaganda, including his own. At his best, film form turns full circle. Appearing at one moment to be at the crossroads of style, uncertain which way to turn, Wajda magically chooses the path that leads to aesthetic unity. Realist, romantic and reflexive in turn, Wajda triumphantly fuses irony and defiance.

Truly mimetic in one sense, with his sharp eye for detail, Wajda is never completely naturalistic. In his war films there are key forms of absent presence: only a handful of German soldiers in *Kanal* (*Kanał*, 1957), few Soviets in *Ashes and Diamonds* (*Popiół i diament*, 1958), and of course no Warsaw, the old Warsaw that is being torched by Nazis in the documentary footage that begins *Kanal*. Yet old Warsaw and the foreign armies who occupied it in turn are a brooding out-of-field presence. *Landscape After*

Battle (*Krajobraz po bitwie*, 1970) begins with the American liberation of a concentration camp after the Germans have disappeared. Wajda also cut his flashback sequence of a female SS unit abusing the film's hero Tadeusz (Daniel Olbrychski) so that when Tadeusz later spots one of them in civilian clothes commemorating the war dead, her appearance becomes an uncanny return of the repressed. It is a surprising aesthetic of absence at a time when Nazi extras were strewn across the film studios of Europe, and replete with irony: atrocity everywhere but no Germans in uniform. In *Promised Land* (*Ziemia obiecana*, 1974) Wajda faithfully echoes industrial turn-of-the-century Łódź by filming in textile factories still functioning in the 1970s, and by restoring to their former grace the city's merchant houses the Party has allowed to decay. But his precise makeover of both is a sign of cinematic vision, not documentary reconstruction. It is his world as well as Poland's past. Later, in *Man of Marble* (*Człowiek z marmuru*, 1976), censorship had a beneficial effect when direct reference to the 1970s Gdańsk riots in which Birkut dies, is forced out of the final cut. Again, absent presence, the brooding sense of a repressed and buried history that will later return, as it did so powerfully in *Man of Iron* (*Człowiek z żelaza*, 1981). Yet *Man of Marble* is also an unfolding of previous omissions. Instead of shattered cityscapes and shattered communities, Wajda's mobile camera confronts the brute modernist architectures of Nowa Huta and the new Warsaw he had previously evaded. In this vision of the real, mimesis is delayed representation, the insertion of previous omissions in previous films. And this, in his battle with the censors, was an experience involuntarily close to Wajda's heart.

While Wajda's romanticism, analysed throughout in this volume, is a legacy of nineteenth-century Polish culture, I want to take comparison out of the Polish context and look at two contrasting Americans with whom he shares much and nothing at all – Orson Welles and Terrence Malick: Welles for his match-up of the real and the reflexive and Malick for his detached fusion of realism and romance. We know that Wajda had been impressed by the epic narratives and landscapes of John Ford but here there are more specific connections. The first is long acknowledged. Stylistically Welles was a prime inspiration for the war trilogy, and narratively for the format of *Man of Marble* and *Man of Iron*. In the former case we have the use of deep-focus and its different planes, alternation of montage and the long take, backlighting, low-angle shooting and high contrast photography. There is also the Wellesian flair for the acting ensemble that started with the Mercury Players. While Wajda's career went the other way, from film into theatre, the acting power of the ensemble is crucial to the films of both directors. *Man of Marble*, no mere remake of *Citizen Kane* (1941) but one of the most inventive films of its time, takes the Wellesian time-image into new dimensions in the 1970s. In *Citizen Kane* we had the earnest yet banal investigator mulling over multiple images of the fallen idol. But Wajda's young cine-investigator, Agnieszka, is anything but banal and Birkut, her toppled idol, her 'man of marble', seems strangely un-fallen. The Wellesian connection here is nothing like the endless and obsessive pastiche of Hitchcock that is now so common in the film world, but inter-text as a fertility rite that is ever fruitful, a sign of Wajda's openness to cinema on the broadest scale.

The Malick connection is more surprising, and in a way the exact opposite. Style-wise they are worlds apart, Malick with the alienation effect of naïve voice-over and his long-lens shots, his tactile feel for landscape and wilderness and often, *contra* Wajda, his draining out of drama and conscious lack of affect. While Wajda is a compulsive film-maker and a celebrity in his own country, Malick seems a reclusive loner. Yet both cineastes have a romantic dimension that taps into the dangerous romance of their respective nations. Both set the naïve aspiration to happiness without compromise against the human capacity for evil and thus set in train the push-and-pull of romantic urge and post-romantic irony. Both have forged narratives conveying in filmic detail the diurnal rhythms of work and war. Often they have a like cinematic subject, the loner-idealist on the wrong side of authority who drifts and is doomed. Both resource in the service of a tragic vision the national past and collective memory, and as artists both are part of the vision they create. Both are reflective, poets of visual meditation on the remembered past. While Malick's is a cinema of reverie, however, Wajda's remained for most of his life one of defiance and urgency. Reverie was a luxury under Polish circumstances that Wajda could not afford.

In the post-war period the trilogy conjures another key connection, an intriguing precedent. Wajda has spoken of his debt to John Huston's *The Asphalt Jungle* (1950) for the ending of *Ashes and Diamonds*. But recent remarks by Roman Polanski suggest another lacuna. Polanski, who fled capture by the Nazis in occupied Poland then acted the role of a young partisan in *A Generation*, has mentioned *Odd Man Out* (1947) as the film captivating him most as a teenager in the desolation of post-war Poland and prompting him into movie-making (Boorman 1995: 160–1). For Carol Reed's Irish melodrama and its fugitive theme, an IRA man on the run, won over a boy who had already experienced, quite precociously, the fugitive life. Indeed this and Reed's other landmark film *The Third Man* (1948) are films that capture the wider maelstrom of flight in the aftermath of European war. In both, Robert Krasker's photography fills out Reed's neo-Expressionist vision of a fugitive city under occupation with its dark streets and dim passageways. The unforgettable Krasker look surely prefigures the *mise-en-scène* of *Kanal* and *Ashes and Diamonds*; nocturnal, glistening, claustrophobic.

There are narrative parallels too: in Wajda as in Reed, the heroic fight is fiercely unequal, the few against the many; the botched robbery and killing that sparks the doomed flight of IRA hero Johnny MacQueen (James Mason), and the botched assassination that sparks the doomed subterfuge of Maciek Chełmicki (Zbigniew Cybulski). Both directors use time-compression as a model of suspense, the long day's journey into night, starting late afternoon, as tragic sign. Towards the end the wounded MacQueen hallucinates in his lover's arms on Belfast streets: the dying Korab (Tadeusz Janczar) does likewise at the barred exit to the sewer in *Kanal*. In Reed and Wajda, expressionist technique lies at the intersection of the romantic and the real. *Odd Man Out* and *Ashes and Diamonds* both display baroque images of crucifixion, the former in the bizarre studio of Lukey the painter who tries and fails to turn the wounded MacQueen into an image of Christ, the latter in the sequence where Maciek and Krystyna (Ewa Krzyżewska) see the upturned crucifix in the old chapel just before Maciek discovers at rest the bodies of the two workers he has mistakenly killed. Saturated in Catholic culture, both heroes are thus mirrored as perverse imitations of Christ, icons of romantic agony. Yet Wajda's portrait of Maciek runs much deeper than Reed's one-dimensional fugitive. Maciek is a deeply ironised figure steeped in the existential and the absurd, caught at the meeting-point of the ideal and the real, the transcendent and the immanent, the abject and the exalted.

The war trilogy also charts the journey to that point of no return through its changing configuration of heroism. In *A Generation,* half-trapped in the codes of socialist realism, the main hero Stach (Tadeusz Łomnicki) is a stern young partisan rewarded by romance with Dorota (Urszula Modrzyńska), the youth organiser and prime mover of militant action. Jasio Krone, the doomed romantic, is a secondary plot figure played by Tadeusz Janczar who reprises a similar role with Korab in *Kanal.* In both films, however, Janczar stands out as the prime iconic figure where love, romance and death intersect: in the first instance in the Warsaw suburbs, in the second in the Dantesque sewers under the city. Wajda's first figure of doomed romance, he is then superseded by the second, more complex and existential figure of Cybulski in the final part of the trilogy. Here the trope of doomed romance is transfigured, in effect made transcendent through banality. It is Maciek's transient affair with Krystyna in the Hotel Monopol that bears the tragic weight of time, passion with a

The killing goes wrong: *Ashes and Diamonds*

barmaid born out of propinquity and the knowledge of a pressing, murderous fate. The extreme close-ups by which Wajda, using some diffusion, evokes their brief intimacy, and where the camera glides over their uncertain faces, is as powerful as anything Bergman achieved in his modernist chamber pieces. (Note that *The Silence* (1963) with its transient hotel intimacy in an Eastern European city follows only five years later.)

The affair triumphantly bears the weight of a deeper abstraction – the brief encounter of the tragic and the stoic: Krystyna as the stoic survivor outliving her murdered parents, Maciek as the fugitive from the sewers whose dark glasses protect him from sunlight and who still has unfinished business, his target a different kind of patriot and veteran of the Spanish Civil War, whose life will not outlast the celebrations of this war's end. Unlike Rossellini, Wajda's response to the ruin and tyranny of war was not immediate but retrospective. The Polish Revolt of 1956 has interceded and Maciek is just as much a student of that aftermath as he is a doomed resistance fighter of the earlier aftermath. Through dress, speech and mannerism Wajda allows reflection to double back on itself in the kind of double reading that defined many of his films: one eye on the past, one eye on the present. The term 'allegory' is a misnomer here: the term 'ambiguity' much too loose. Often in watching a Wajda film about the past, a second reading about the present seems to run in tandem and in shadow. From this point of view, aftermath of war remained the key source of time remembered in the most powerful of his later films, *Landscape After Battle* and *Man of Marble*. For both are also meditations on time present.

Wajda's response to the modernist innovations of Western European film in the 1960s, and to a changing Poland, seemed to be mixed and uneasy. *Innocent Sorcerers* (*Niewinni czarodzieje*, 1960), *Love at Twenty* (*Miłość dwudziestolatków*, 1962) and *Hunting Flies* (*Polowanie na muchy*, 1969) are films that are uncertain in tone and often whimsical, easily surpassed by the new features of Polanski and Skolimowski. Wajda's absorption of modernist style verged on the edge of kitsch, closer to Claude Lelouch than to Godard, Truffaut or Fellini. The immediate present seemed to confound him, even in his ambitious, autobiographical *Everything For Sale* (*Wszystko na sprzedaż*). A film-within-a-film that is also a meditation on film-making, it is about the accidental death of a famous film actor that has, curiously, no centre to it. For Wajda cannot decide who is at the centre: the dead actor (modelled on Cybulski), or the director (modelled on Wajda himself) or the actor (Daniel Olbrychski) playing the dead Cybulski in the director's film about his life or the respective wives, Beata and Elżbieta, of the director and the dead actor. This may be an ingenious *film à clef* but it is also diffuseness run riot. In a curious paradox the film's only centre is he-who-is-absent, namely Cybulski. Yet this shows up a major defect since no one in the film has the physical presence of the absent Cybulski to carry the narrative in the way that Marcello Mastroianni carries Fellini's cine-biography, *8½* (1962). The past remembered (Cybulski's death in a freak train accident was in 1967) is, one suspects, too close, too recent. Wajda's version of movie bohemia, of the circle of cineastes and actors he frequented, verges with its overdressed women, garish colours and self-conscious partying, on bohemian kitsch. There seems an impulse here to obliterate the greyness of socialist Poland by mimicking the music and fashion of the 'swinging sixties' in London and Paris and thus being *à la mode* at one stage removed. The temptations of surfeit and excess are too great for Wajda to resist. For all its reflexive ingenuity, the film seems weighed down by the conceit of this imitation. In truth Wajda had not been able to place its finger on the pulse of the Polish present, which still seemed to elude him. He had created instead, and doubtless with some sharpness and irony, the pastiche of a vacuous world.

His great contribution to European modernism in the 1970s comes in two films where he returns to the recent past and newly brings it to life. In doing so, he resurrects his own sense of the present. *Landscape After Battle* returns to the aftermath of war in adapting the story-memoirs of Tadeusz Borowski, who had survived the concentration camps only to commit suicide in 1951, a tragic victim in a generation 'contaminated by death' (Michałek 1973: 124). It is the most liminal of Wajda's films with its Polish subjects freed from one camp and dumped into a holding camp, a former SS barracks now under American guard, for Displaced Persons. The inmates no longer enslaved but not yet free, are literally in limbo. Are they to go back to Poland and its uncertain future under Soviet occupation? Or are they to turn their backs on their country and try to head west? For Wajda, filming in 1970, the uncertain future had now become the uncertain present. For this reason the sense of narrative time is changed so utterly from that in the trilogy. In the holding camp time hangs suspended between the extremes of recurrent hysteria among bored yet traumatised inmates and a dead time when nothing seems to happen. On one level the camp, with its blasé American guards and bombastic Polish officers, could seem like a Marxist parody of Polish tradition and Western capitalism. On another it works as a mirror image of something more immediate, the crude itic patriotism in communist Poland of 1969 with Soviet soldiers watching on. Uncannily, Wajda allows the oblique, forbidden reference to play off the obvious, explicit one. The film is thus both, a doubled narrative that takes a radical approach to history all the while using material seen as the stuff of documentary to forge an anti-naturalistic film.

Here Wajda can be placed in the modernist idiom of the new history film at the turn of the 1970s. Among the most inventive are Jean-Pierre Melville's dark fable of the French Resistance *L'Armee des Ombres* (1969), Bertolucci's oneiric encounters with Fascism in *The Spider's Strategem* (1969) and *The Conformist* (1970), Altman's reworking of American myths in *McCabe and Mrs Miller* (1971) and *Thieves Like Us* (1973), and finally Bergman's tragic dream-history *Cries and Whispers* (1972). What unites these films are the following: the past as immediacy, as presentness but also as phantasmagoria, the history-narrative neither as costume-drama nor docudrama but as reverie, a dreamed past relived as the contingent moment of the present. In terms of tone, theme and period, Melville's film seems closest but Wajda's film stands out alone because of its Polish predicament. It refers the existential absurd, a modernist trope of later decades, back to a mythic origin, the post-traumatic calm of release from the fear of genocide. Tadeusz, the author-poet Wajda inserts into his narrative of Borowski's original story, is both survivor and observer, semi-detached not only from the horrors he has witnessed but also the trauma inflicted on its escaping victims. The ties that bind in classical plot, taut linkages of situation, motive and action all slacken in true Deleuzian fashion. Nothing much seems to work out in terms of cause and effect, and Wajda's *mise-en-scène*, with its slow panning and incessant zooms, seems out of character, unhurried, Altmanesque. Yet for its troubled subject matter it is precisely right. Its oneiric qualities will in turn inspire the two great history-films of Polish directors in the next two decades – Ryszard Bugajski's dark expressionist fable banned under martial law, *Interrogation* (*Przesłuchanie*, 1982) and Agnieszka Holland's ironically picaresque *Europa, Europa* (1991) that charts a survivor's role-playing strategies used by a German-Jewish boy fleeing eastwards to join the Soviet Komsomol and then, after Nazi invasion, the Hitler youth.

A tempo that is frenzied one moment, meandering the next, conveys in Wajda's film the uneven experience of liminality. At the centre is Olbrychski's brief dalliance with a young Jewish woman, Nina (Stanisława Celińska) in which eternally distracted, he fails to acknowledge the identity of the sexual other even after sex and then seems to connive in the tragic incident where she is accidentally shot by an American guard. This looks at times like Wajda's update on the Hamlet–Ophelia relationship, given special resonance in the Polish context by Jan Kott's cogent argument that Shakespeare's hero should be played as a troubled existential figure in a political age. Impulsive, play-acting, ironic, inattentive, the figure of Tadeusz embodies the mood-swings of an egocentric poet obsessed by the relationship of Self and Nation with little time for passionate engagement. Nina's Jewish identity gives the relationship an added frisson. With his loose backpack and tight-fitting clothes, Tadeusz seems like a contemporary figure as does his Jewish lover, survivors of a student revolt in 1968 that went unsupported by Polish workers yet still provoked an anti-Jewish purge spearheaded by General Moczar and saw many of Poland's Jewish intellectuals driven into exile.

In this oneiric double reading where Nina's sudden appearance at the holding camp is never really explained, the past echoes the present, and the present is transported into the past. The lovers are agonistic motifs of then and now, of persecution repeated in a lesser key but with the question of complicity (in 1970) raised anew. Wajda takes the brave decision to make the affair sensual without being overwrought but also to show Olbrychski distracted in the church, with Nina at his side, by the sight of his former SS tormentor, the Aryan blonde on whom he still casts an anguished, erotic gaze. After Nina's accidental killing, which can be read from a Marxist standpoint as callous American stupidity, the shock of death and mourning triggers in Tadeusz a survivor's guilt. It is as if his cramped and crouching figure, torn by grief beneath the resting-place of his dead lover's body, had viscerally absorbed the knowledge of genocide soon to permeate throughout post-war Europe. The crouching position is a brute and vivid signifier of Polish survival and Jewish destruction in a war in which, nonetheless, over a million Poles had also perished. In the end the balance is not between survival and extreme suffering but between degrees of extreme suffering. As survivor Tadeusz is flayed by guilt, his witnessing of Nina's death after the war's end almost a compulsion to repeat the horror of death he must have earlier witnessed and perpetuating its trauma. Wajda's hero-survivor, compulsively play-acting, mutely hysteric, is thus locked into the endless trauma of witnessing the fallen (Caruth 1996: 10).

Wajda's second great modernist triumph comes seven years later in *Man of Marble*. Here Wajda is able once more to reinvent Welles for his own purpose, but without the curse of déjà vu. Its investigation into the life of a fallen idol follows the narrative pattern of *Citizen Kane*. Its quest narrative about a forgotten post-war 'hero' of socialist labour pursued as an elusive image by student film-maker Agnieszka (Krystyna Janda) making her diploma film in 1976, seamlessly interweaves past and present, as Agnieszka prompts her subjects, one by one, into flashback reminiscence to create a composite picture of a life beyond the image. It also signifies the one film in which Wajda successfully absorbs the legacy of the French New Wave. In matching *Citizen Kane*'s narrative form to the fast and fluid *cinéma vérité* of the New Wave, a technical feat for which director of photography Edward Kłosiński deserves much credit, a key dimension of Polish history seems to crystallise before our eyes. From Birkut, the man of marble who turns against his Stalinist patrons to his activist son in the Gdańsk shipyards, Maciek Tomczyk (both played by Jerzy Radziwiłłowicz), Wajda charts a lineage of defiance at a time when Poland seemed, deceptively, to be entering an age of growth and prosperity. The knowledge of Birkut, and then of Tomczyk, that Agnieszka gains opens her eyes to Polish politics and foretells the rise of Solidarity.

The quest itself, with Agnieszka framed by low-angle tracking shots, owes more to *Touch of Evil* (1957) and *The Trial* (1962) than it does to Truffaut or Godard. Yet the lyricism, the fluency, the banter, the existential tone and finally the reflexive saga of Agnieszka's two-man film crew all show the mark of French modernism. The film has a third reflexive source, however, this time within the Soviet orbit. The mirroring of past by present, the precise use of documentary footage and the film's doubling of the central role all bring to mind Tarkovsky's great cine-biography, *Mirror* (1974). Radziwiłłowicz doubles up in the role of Birkut and Tomczyk, *père et fils*, just as Margarita

Terekhova had doubled the generational roles of mother and spouse for Tarkovsky. Both films cue a fluid interchange of past and present between 1970s socialism and the age of Stalin when all things political remained unspoken. Both thrive as great art-works in polities that have tried at different times to bury the past. In *Mirror* much remains enigmatic and unspoken because even in the Soviet 1970s, so little could be said. By contrast Wajda was able to take advantage of the greater critical stance possible towards the politics of the past in Poland. For Tarkovsky time became poetry through enigma and meditation; for Wajda, it became poetic through the dynamics of unmasking.

Like *Ashes and Diamonds*, *Man of Marble* is a film that perfects the iconography of the figure. In every frame every movement of the hands, the eyes, the body is made to count, to be precise, to dominate the screen – except that there are two different figures and two different styles. Agnieszka and Birkut, one in the present, one in the past, one female, the other male, one impatient and hyperactive, the other calm and exalted. This binary opposition, this polarisation of the look is crucial. While Maciek had been set off against a variety of others, Agnieszka and Birkut, dwelling in different time frames, are set off against each other. For this is, after all, a long-distance affair of the living and dead, the sceptic and the naïf, the flesh and the image. So it is of course one-way love, and inseparable from Agnieszka's fascination with the forbidden. While the flesh is forbidden by time and death and surfaces in surrogate form as the son that Agnieszka will marry in *Man of Iron*, the image, both marble and celluloid is forgotten by the state and by history, stored away in vaults to be conveniently forgotten.

This is a film, too, in which film mirrors politics in its ruthless use of power. No shrinking violet, Agnieszka cajoles and manipulates to get her forbidden material on Birkut just as Burski, the Wajda-like veteran she interviews, had ruthlessly coached Birkut in his commodified movie image as a hero of labour. In flashback the young Burski is doubled by a look-alike zealot from the secret police who in present time turns out as the owner of a strip-joint, presenting us with a different kind of flesh-image. In Wajda's dizzy interweaving of bona fide footage and faked footage, it became as impossible to tell where Birkut's persona ends and where his image begins as it does to tell where documentary ends and propaganda begins. Dizzily objectified, the smiling shock-worker ever on the move is frozen in his image. Except that history moves on and melts him down. For, in a familiar Wajda trope, disillusion sets in. The naïf loses his political virginity by seeing through his image and the false effect it creates, thus turning into someone else the Party wants forgotten, a militant killed in the 1970s Gdańsk riots, a sequence the censors forbade Wajda from leaving in his final cut. In the film, the Party had wished to excise Birkut from the public memory. In reality it wishes to do the same with his fictional death. Four years later, making use of a greater yet passing freedom Wajda duly reinstated the event in *Man of Iron*, where protestors parade the body of the murdered Birkut on a door through the streets of Gdańsk.

With its novel gender inversion of male object and female gaze, *Man of Marble* may be read as Wajda's *Vertigo* (1958). Agnieszka falls in love with the image of Birkut and her investigation, reaching the point of obsession, brings him back from the dead through progeny. The son, of course, is not the father anymore than Judy Barton is Madeleine Elster. The obsession, though relentless, is not the pathology that it was in Hitchcock. Yet it is a spiral, a spiral seen through limitless mirrors, a reflexive vertigo in which *contra* Hitchcock, and since it must defy the political, the romance is identified with life and not with death. The contrast of endings could not be greater. The defiant son trudging the long corridors of the Warsaw television station with Agnieszka is a resurrection, not a sacrifice. In a final irony of Wajda's film, which may well be a comment on his work as a whole, romance can only triumph by converting the sublime back into the mundane.

It was too much to ask, perhaps, that Wajda could repeat his artistic triumph in the sequel *Man of Iron*, whose strength and weakness both lie in the attraction to the immediate present. In shooting his film in Gdańsk, Wajda knew that he was filming militant Polish workers decisively making history. Indeed, his documentary footage has a power it could not have in normal documentary. In the scenes in the Gdańsk shipyards, his dynamic montage makes the film part of the fate of Polish history in the making. But as in *Everything For Sale,* he faced thorny reflexive problems, problems of narrative diffusion in glossing the past while being too close to the history he is witnessing. Bombarded by the assault of the moment, perspective becomes a challenge that threatens to outrun its witness, and Wajda overreaches himself by attempting too much. He continues the story of Agnieszka and Tomczyk in flashback, which then climaxes with the kitsch sequence when Lech Wałęsa is an actual witness at their fictional 'marriage ceremony'. Yet at the same time he profiles in depth the complicity of the drunken media hack, Winkiel (Marian Opania), blackmailed by the Party into smearing Tomczyk and Solidarity; and as the narrative whole becomes less than the sum of its parts, the actual history threatens to outrun him. That it never does is down to his extraordinary powers of recovery. But there is a thin dividing line and one senses in this film that Wajda is poised at times too precariously at its edge.

At the same time, the 'moment' of Solidarity is also the moment that allows Wajda to switch romantic impulse (and its built-in ironies) from tradition to modernity, from exile to inclusion, from doomed heroes to a practical collectivity, to a social movement encapsulating, as he saw it, the true aspirations of the Polish people. In the foundation of the new Polish State, Wajda indeed played his part as a senator for Solidarity in the Polish parliament, thus fulfilling a wish denied him from 1945 onwards, to feel part of a true collectivity that had real power and purpose and hope for the future. Yet just as Wajda had used cinema to ironise history, history was to have its incidental revenge. In the push and pull of democratic politics, Solidarity proved short-lived as a party with mass appeal, perishing almost in its hour of triumph. During his brief term as Polish President Lech Wałęsa, charismatic leader of Solidarity, proved to his electors to be anything but charismatic. Looking back at *Man of Iron* where Wajda had ironised history but also expressed his fulsome praise of Solidarity, we can now see that history has in turn ironised Wajda and dated his film 'document'. Paradoxically, *Man of Marble,* freed from this burden of history in the making, though full of history-as-made, remains as fresh as it was when first released 25 years ago.

In the new Poland, moving towards his career's end, Wajda was finally able to cast aside the heavy cloak of defiance without shedding his flair for irony. In his 'path towards the light' as he put it (Wajda 2000d: 226), he brought to the screen his own version of Mickiewicz's epic poem *Pan Tadeusz.* His sense of history and of irony, here quite delicate, was as strong as ever but is matched by something else, supreme detachment in style and deep harmony in its view of the order of things. The film was a burst of aesthetic renewal that still marked him out, late in life, as one of the great living directors in European cinema and showed him completely worthy of the honorary Oscar awarded in 2000 for lifetime achievement as a creative artist. It proved him a European master of the epic closer in sensibility to Visconti than to John Ford, and it was also his greatest excursion into the Poland of the nineteenth century so close to his heart. Indeed as the twentieth century came to a close it could be said that, for the benefit of us all, Wajda has saved something of his best until last.

CHAPTER TWO

Wajda's Imagination of Disaster: War Trauma, Surrealism and Kitsch

Paul Coates

The Polish School and the Image of War

On its emergence, 'the Polish School' was associated primarily with filmic treatments of the trauma of the Polish experience of World War Two; with such films as Andrzej Wajda's *A Generation* (*Pokolenie*, 1954), *Kanal* (*Kanał*, 1957) and *Ashes and Diamonds* (*Popiół i diament*, 1958), Andrzej Munk's *Eroica* (1957) and *The Passenger* (*Pasażerka*, 1960), Jerzy Kawalerowicz's *The True End of the Great War* (*Prawdziwy koniec wielkiej wojny*, 1957), or Wojciech Has's *How To Be Loved?* (*Jak być kochaną?*, 1963). This association justifies efforts to interpret the movement in the light of the various theories of trauma that have documented the frailty of the mind's defence mechanisms *vis-à-vis* a horror-riddled twentieth century. The most influential such theory is, of course, the Freudian one, and its most eloquent recent interpretation has been that of Cathy Caruth's *Unclaimed Experience* (1996). For all the glaring disparities between Freud's primary preoccupations and methods – a focus on individuals and upon sexual and infantile traumata, as opposed to the generational wartime ones that pervade the Polish School – his work is strikingly, surprisingly relevant. Perhaps this is only to be expected; after all, Caruth's subtitle is 'Trauma, Narrative and History'. Freud's theory will only be the starting point, however, for an effort to grasp the main thrust both of the Polish school and of the work of Wajda in particular.

Central to Freud's work, as described by Caruth, is the disparity between two models of traumatic experience:

> the model of castration trauma, which is associated with the theory of repression and return of the repressed, as well as with a system of unconscious symbolic meanings (the basis of the dream theory in its usual interpretation); and the model of traumatic neurosis (or, let us say, accident trauma), which is associated with accident victims and war veterans. (1996: 135 n.18)

These might be termed, respectively, an 'eros' and a 'thanatos' model. If, as Caruth notes, Freud is unable to integrate them, their combination – I will argue – is the prerequisite for understanding the co-presence within Wajda's work in particular of images of wartime experience, surrealism, a practice of literary adaptation, and repeated declarations of dissatisfaction with his own works. That co-presence is most electric in *Ashes and Diamonds*, most tantalising in *Lotna* (1959), where the separate elements seem to cancel one another out, yielding a wooden blandness. Although the model of wartime trauma has primacy with regard to Polish cinema, the general model of repression and symbolisation Freud developed to describe 'castration trauma' is also relevant: one may even be tempted to say that the contents of the former should merely be inserted into the form of the latter (the account of the mechanisms of symbolisation), which should be emptied of its specifically Freudian content of infantile sexuality. It cannot be voided of sexuality entirely, however, as the symbolic castration of male experience of wartime trauma generates an anxiety that also affects the sexual.

Throughout Wajda's works, for instance, one finds both symbolisation and the delay characteristic of expressions of traumatic experience. The symbolisation occurs at two levels, as another artist's experience is utilised to symbolise one's own, while – as art – that experience itself is a metaphorical and symbolic act. The delay that characterises trauma is also present; indeed, it is continual delay, for no work ever seems satisfactorily to embody one's experience, a failing that becomes palpable only after the fact, since no image is available to consciousness to provide a pre-existent template against which to measure which of the works one might wish to adapt or corresponds most closely to one's own experience. This combination is paradigmatic of Polish post-war experience, rendering Wajda the key Polish director of the period. It may even be argued that he becomes the key (not necessarily the best) Polish artist *tout court,* and that the most serious generational national rendition of wartime experience emerges in 'the Polish School' precisely because of film's capacity to reproduce shock, of which it becomes the homeopathic, therapeutic repetition. For although Wajda saw the late-1940s paintings of his Craców art school colleague Andrzej Wróblewski – particularly the series entitled *Executions (Rozstrzelania)* – as invalidating his own aspirations to paint, the films can be seen as continuing Wróblewski's project by other means, transplanting it to a medium that not only allowed Wajda to stake a claim of his own, but was arguably even better-suited to the evocation of shock, allowing it to resonate most palpably across an arrested temporal flow. In film, art loses all semblance of the 'disinterested contemplation' of traditional – particularly Kantian – aesthetics. The reports of the first audiences' flight before the feared impact of the oncoming train isolate the shock element of film subsequently theorised and gleefully pursued by Eisenstein and the surrealists; even if legendary, they retain value as representations of cultural perceptions of the new medium. Film, a repetition of the shocks of modernity, imprints itself as something *not* understood at all levels on first viewing; and this is why Hollywood had to invest such diligent efforts in ensuring both its universal comprehensibility and the invisibility of those potential shocks known as 'cuts'. If a trauma may be defined – is, in a sense, *always* defined – retrospectively, as that to which response can only be belated, the same is true of a medium whose production and viewing conditions require its experience only after its occurrence (after 'the pro-filmic event'): it becomes nameable only after its *re-experiencing.* The shock of film, like that of war, is that of encounter with a superior technology: the meeting of human (or animal) and machine (of horse and tank, of eye and camera, for instance). The new technology itself becomes overwhelming, inconceivable, oneirically Other. This encounter lies at the heart of Wajda's *Lotna,* of course, which revolves around a Polish cavalry unit's legendary charge against German tanks, a scene of emblematic centrality to Wajda's oeuvre. It disempowers the historical subject through what might be described as a 'feminisation' corresponding to the reduction of soldiers to objects of spectacle, and hence toy soldiers, in *Lotna,* and to the soldier's own grimacing and snapping of his sabre in the moment of defeat.

The war films of the Polish School may be described in the terms Freud employed to describe the dreams of trauma sufferers: 'these dreams are endeavouring to master the stimulus retrospectively, by developing the anxiety whose omission was the cause of the traumatic neurosis' (1967: 60). This lack of anxiety entailed unpreparedness, which for Wajda's generation was both national unreadiness to counter the technological shock of modern warfare (Wajda describes the nineteenth century in Poland as ending in 1939) and the result of the widespread youthful belief in one's own immortality. For purposes of comparison, one might note Mary Gordon's evocation of the reaction of Joan of Arc, a young girl, even to a wounding she had foreseen:

> She fell back, in shock and in great pain. She wept, despite her foreknowledge of the nature of her wound. It is as though she were surprised, not that she had been struck by an arrow, but that it hurt. This is a particularly adolescent brand of surprise: the shock at the vulnerability of a body imagined invulnerable. (2000: 53)

The homeopathic functions of film for Wajda's generation include that of arming the psyche for a new war, the Cold War equivalent of what Adorno speculated surrealism may have achieved for inter-war Paris, whose real preservation depended upon its destruction in the imagination (1975: 158). It is thus unsurprising that Wajda should identify and mobilise surrealism as the strongest source of – and hence most powerful homeopathic remedy for – anxiety. It is therefore hardly surprising also that Freud's declaration that 'what appears to be a reality is in fact a reflection of a forgotten past' (1967: 40) nicely characterises film's combination of the apparent phenomenal immediacy and irreversibility of reality with an actual, metaphorical indirection and preterition, though of course his words were not intended as descriptive of film. In the case of art, Freud's worries over how the compulsion to repeat may be related to the pleasure principle are in fact probably misplaced, as art fuses the two, with the retelling of the story a source of growing pleasure as the waves of new versions either erode the contours of the emotion attached to the original event or veil it with the ripples it has generated.

In a sense it may be possible to argue that the film's repetitions are fed by a will not only to comprehend the overwhelming moment of trauma but to rediscover the self that absented itself (donning a protective carapace of numbness) during its experience: blown up in the trenches, one awakes only afterwards, or wakes up still dazed, like Tancred in the important incident from *Gerusalemme Liberata* (1547) by Freud:

Its hero, Tancred, unwittingly kills his beloved Clorinda in a duel while she is disguised in the armour of an enemy knight. After her burial he makes his way into a strange magic forest which strikes the Crusaders' army with terror. He slashes with his sword at a tall tree; but blood streams from the cut and the voice of Clorinda, whose soul is imprisoned in the tree, is heard complaining that he has wounded his beloved once again. (1967: 45)

Tancred's unconscious slaying of Clorinda in a duel is reiterated in his wounding of a tree that encloses her soul. The lack of awareness of the true meaning of one's first action triggers its inevitable repetition. Particularly intriguing is the inscription of unconsciousness in the metaphorical disguising of the army as a forest, a link made explicit in *Macbeth* and in the theories of Elias Canetti for whom the significance of the forest in German culture resides in its cryptic symbolisation of armies (1962: 173–4). Although Freud does not analyse it in these terms, Tancred's second 'war' experience is steeped in 'unconscious symbolic meanings' and is, indeed, a waking dream. In this context, Michael Herr's despatches from the Vietnam war, cited by Caruth (1996: 10), are particularly telling evocations of a Tancredian simultaneous consciousness and unconsciousness of experience: 'The problem was that you didn't always know what you were seeing until later, maybe years later, that a lot of it never made it in at all, it just stayed stored there in your eyes.' (One may note the importance of film as work of the eye to Wajda, the one-time art student.) Thus the eyes may well not have been 'yours' but those of the camera, or a human dehumanised into a viewing machine, seeing without seeing because forbidden or unable to interpret: the I as a camera rolling even after the cameraman's fall to the ground. The imagery of falling Caruth discerns in a variety of works of trauma has its correlative in the filmic image of wartime death, the distantly-viewed and appallingly sudden collapse of someone striding or running in the fullness of life, so that calling the dead 'the fallen' is not merely euphemistic but registers the eerie incomprehensibility of watching them die. Repetition becomes necessary, among other things, to discover the meaning of *killing* when performed at the distance made possible by modern technology.

Dreams of Another('s) Life: Literary Adaptation and Surrealism

Observation of the traumatic experience of others – often that of the Jews – is central to, and frequently thematised by, Wajda's work. The person who tells their story is by definition a survivor. The absenting of the self in the moment of trauma is strangely doubled, reinforced and undermined by the self's actual physical absence from the battlefield. Thus Wajda has described his own experience of September 1939 – the period covered by *Lotna* – as one of the imagination:

> We spent the first days of September in the cellar. The gas masks distributed to all members of officer families were terrifying. When a dust-cloud arose on our street, a gas alarm was started at once. None of us either recognised the sound of planes or could gauge the distance of the bombing. The whole war was played out in our heads, in the imagination... (2000a: 20)

Wajda has spoken also of the experience of battle as something he feels he ought to have had, and sought to acquire through artistic creation:

> But these films were in a sense an extension of a lack in my biography. I made them out of a deep conviction that this ought to be part of my life, and perhaps the engagement in them, and the themes of war and occupation which flow obsessively through them, met a need to supplement my own biography. For if fate had spared me this in reality it was my duty to make up for this in my films. (1996a)

Wajda remarks that the experience was denied him because of his youth; and yet, of course, 16 – the age he was in 1942 – was also a call-up age, as he himself notes in his autobiography. A possible equivocation over whether or not he should have been a soldier may have fed both guilt and an imaginary probing of the experiences of others. What occurs in his work is thus an overflow from the experience of other, older men: *Kanal* depends on the memoirs of Jerzy Stawiński, for instance, and *Ashes and Diamonds* upon a novel – and then script – by Jerzy Andrzejewski. These scriptwriters become, as it were, substitute fathers, older brothers, alter egos and ideal egos in one: familiar compound ghosts. Wajda's literary adaptations are of the works of older men: *men who were there first*. His practice of literary adaptation is further rooted in the sense, born of his father's death at Katyń, that – as he puts it – 'our generation was a generation of sons who have to recount the fate of their fathers, for the dead cannot speak' (2000a: 54). The speech of the elders who survived stands in for that of those who did not. But because their experiences were not directly his own, only imagined, their imagination was always likely, sooner or later, to slide into daydream. The surrealism of traumatic personal experience can become kitsch. This is what happens in *Lotna* (of which more below). Wajda's repeated assertions of a wish to remake it can be seen as in part an effort to arrest this near-inevitable slackening of creative tension.

The reproduction of experience in images is a dream-like procedure of naming experience namelessly, allowing it to enter consciousness while retaining the patina of an original incomprehensibility. The translation of literary texts into images becomes, in Wajda's case, their translation back into the traumas they seek to master, whose nagging refusal to abandon the unconscious and allow the ego full access to them, gives the lie to the project of naming, and to literature also. Wajda's literary adaptations are thus far from the evasions as which they have often been stigmatised, but rather critique their originals in the name of the traumatic incomprehensibility of the experiences they gloss over with a language Wajda unpicks as scar-tissue. (The trauma's persistence in the unconscious may even be symbolised and embodied in the darkness in which film unfolds.) Lacking direct access to his own experience, Wajda grasps the texts of others as mirrors of Medusa, the precondition of whose viewing is *indirection*. It is surely significant that even *Everything For Sale* (*Wszystko na sprzedaż*, 1968) – the only work he himself scripted, and the one most thoroughly permeated by catastrophe, the repeated aftershocks of the death of Zbigniew Cybulski – remains oblique at its heart, replacing Wajda himself with a director stand-in whose substitute status becomes all the more glaring in a context in which everyone else 'plays themselves', and leaving Cybulski himself both unrepresented and unnamed. This indirection, of course, generates obsessive repetition: the story always remains largely occluded, untold, and the successive works that represent it are in fact stabs in the dark at locating it: a series of symptoms.

At various points in his career Wajda mentioned the importance of surrealism for his work. Indeed, *Wajda mówi o sobie*, a compilation of materials dealing with the middle films of Wajda's career, begins by citing Luis Buñuel (Wertenstein 2000: 2). The interaction in Wajda's work of the libertarianism of surrealism and the apparently non-surrealist, constraining practice of literary adaptation is intriguing, as the self-imposed imperative of 'fidelity' – that issue that has bedevilled both literary adaptations and their discussion – arguably diverts the director's inventiveness into possibly trivial or decorative details, such as, in *Pilate and Others* (*Pilatus und Andere*/*Piłat i inni*, 1972), the odd assortment of spectators perched high above Yeshua's interrogation by Pilate. For Wajda, surrealism serves various functions, providing an outlet for his painterliness and interest in extreme compositional contrast, an aesthetic adequate to the violence history has visited upon Poland, and a source of allegorical images to baffle the censor. These images include the famous white horse of *Ashes and Diamonds* as, among other things, the steed upon which – in mocking Communist party polemics – General Anders was expected to liberate post-war Poland, and the rubbish dump across which Maciek Chełmicki stumbles as the sign of an elimination by historical necessity that breathes more existential anguish than the Marxist triumphalism it simulates.

Wajda's multiple, mixed intentions suggest a surrealist anti-intentionality, a dreamlike fragmentation of the self, while the death-denying rapidity of his rhythm of production resembles that of automatic writing. One case of the mixed motives that flow through so many of Wajda's films may be the above-mentioned double politics of the allegorical images of *Ashes and Diamonds*. They suggest a director frequently groping in the dark both for an audience and for coherence of self, the relentless quest for an audience itself being one for a spectatorial look to unify his fragments.

A further source of non-intentionality in Wajda's works is the substitute status of so many of them, particularly the literary adaptations. Stand-ins for scripts he was unable to film, they are crosshatched with frustrated shadows of the unmade. This is the case from the very outset of his career: the experiences of the (Party-approved) People's Army have to stand in for the (forbidden, unrepresentable) ones of the majority Home Army, to which Wajda belonged. Wajda's career contains a long list of unmade films, the most sensitive being a proposed version of Stefan Żeromski's *Pre-Spring* (*Przedwiośnie*), a novel partly set in the 1920 Polish-Soviet war (Modrzejewska 1991: 43–4). Tadeusz Lubelski, meanwhile, has shown that even *Ashes and Diamonds* was made instead of a planned work – *We Are Alone in the World* (*Jesteśmy sami na świecie*) – about the despair of the young, which then seeps into the film that actually could be made (1992: 161). Wajda's adaptations can be 'automatic writing' in the sense of simply giving the director work to do; to keep his hand in, manifest continued existence, and ward off the nihilistic self-doubts of unemployment. If the adaptation is also meant to function as a Trojan Horse, in some cases the horse's belly is sealed: from the outside, by the authorities; from the inside by the artist sensitive to their vigilant breathing nearby. The inside of the horse can become a womb that fails to come to term. Alternatively, the authorities may allow only one meaning to emerge, as when they asserted that the ending of *Promised Land* (*Ziemia obiecana*, 1974) demonstrated its Marxism. The blocked intentionality of *Pilate and Others*, meanwhile, is augmented by the confluence within it of the separate non-intentionalities of surrealism and literary adaptation. No wonder Bolesław Michałek could term it incoherent, or that Wajda himself could wonder 'whether, in the midst of the allusions, free associations and fantasy, I lost the main thread' (in Wertenstein 2000: 84). His assumption that 'the story is so well-known that one can allow oneself certain "variations on the theme"' (*ibid.*) overlooks the fact that it is the Gospel story, not Bulgakov's, that has this status: variations upon Bulgakov's own variation may be less comprehensible. Surrealist fantasy becomes a parasite that overruns the text upon which it depends. Could it be that such works as this and *Lotna* failed to reach an audience because – as Adorno puts it – 'after the European catastrophe [World War Two and the Holocaust] the surrealist shocks have become impotent'? (Adorno 1975: 157–8). If this is so, the historical moment of the movement would indeed be the inter-war one, and post-war surrealism would fall easily into the kitsch with which it was always already complicit in Dali, and would be later in Wajda's own *Lotna*.

Surrealism, Kitsch and Quotation

There are of course various definitions of the phenomenon vaguely haloed by the term 'kitsch'. One of the most suggestive is that of the Austrian Jewish writer and *Kulturkritiker* Hermann Broch, who viewed it as a form of radical aesthetic evil, because concerned to work *beautifully* rather than *well* (a view that problematises the value of spectacle, to say the least) (1955a: 344). Broch's ascription of perniciousness to the will to beauty, meanwhile, endorses the widespread perception that kitsch is a late nineteenth-century *fleur du mal*. Broch's linkage of beauty and evil would of course have been accepted by the Satanists among the Aesthetes, though in rejecting a morality they deemed vulgar they claimed to uphold the morality of artistic production instead, not subvert it, as Broch would argue they did. For Broch, kitsch is art with a bad conscience, a characteristic particularly apparent when it proclaims an irrationality (the widely-required *sine qua non* of the bourgeois notion of 'Art') it actually manufactures through careful recipes (1955a: 346).

Wajda's *Lotna* can help test this thesis, while the thesis itself can aid assessment of the film's reception. *Lotna* tells the story of a group of cavalrymen unanimously admiring a horse whose name means 'the swift one', but who die successively on assuming individual ownership of her. As the first colour film of a director who trained as a painter, it engages with the idea of spectacle in a manner new for Wajda – one many critics would see as thinning out narrative in the interests of the picturesque. Its mythical narrative of mysterious, potentially trans-historical fatality is set against – perhaps pasted onto – the backdrop of the disastrous Polish campaign against the German invasion of September 1939. If the cavalrymen's fate allegorically represents that of a gentry-led pre-war Poland ill equipped for modern technologies of warfare, the significance of the horse itself is partly obscure. Splicing together allegorical readability and Symbolist obscurity, it does indeed raise the question of the degree of rationality underlying the work's signifying strategies, while that very Symbolist unreadability can generate spectacle of a paradoxical purity, beyond interpretation.

Writing in *Ekran*, one of the two key Polish film weeklies of the late 1950s, the leading Polish critic and theoretician Alicja Helman ascribes a surrealist genealogy to the film (1959: 3). Helman's title – 'A Sarmatian on a Giraffe' – itself employs surrealist dislocation and alludes to Buñuel's *L'Âge d'or* (1930), a work Wajda had gone on record as admiring (1967: 235–6). Indeed, *Lotna* was originally to have begun with the Buñuelian image of ants crawling across a hand (Mruklik 1969: 40). Nevertheless, Helman's dissatisfaction with such images as the burning of the eagle – that Polish national emblem – or the bridal veil catching on a coffin skewers a variety of symbolisation less surreally suggestive than redolent of the metaphysical conceits of the Baroque (one notes the frequency with which Wajda's works in general will be deemed 'Baroque'). 'In *Lotna*' – she argues' – 'we find a symbolisation that is cheap, blatant, univocal … The symbols do not suggest but insistently scream. What ought to be subtextual, merely touched on, becomes vulgar, unacceptable' (1959: 3).

Lotna's reviews repeatedly allege such cheapness or vulgarity of symbolisation, indicating the relevance of the category of kitsch, which applies class judgements to forms of the aesthetic that are often mass-produced and described as simplified (the issue of simplification will return later). Since such terms discount the class whose aesthetic preferences kitsch ostensibly reflects – 'the vulgar' – their persistence in the criticism of a *soi-disant* socialist society itself piquantly and symptomatically displays that society's failure to eradicate its own class distinctions. Does this make the Wajda who sees himself as a spokesman for popular discontents inevitably the purveyor of kitsch? (Irrespective of one's conclusion on this issue, it is surely only the *failed* artist, the painter of the variety of Hitler, who justifies references to 'evil' where kitsch is concerned (Broch 1955a: 348).)

For Helman, meanwhile, this work's evil lies elsewhere, in a cruelty she likens to that of Buñuel, despite the difference between its symbolising procedures and Wajda's. The forced paradoxes issue from a system. Her critique of the symbolisation matches Broch's contention that in kitsch a mechanistic rationality underlies the semblance of the irrational. Wajda's subject matter is indeed of a kind many reviewers would associate with kitsch. Reviewing Wajda's previous film, *Ashes and Diamonds*, the influential Krzysztof Teodor Toeplitz had praised its ability to tap Polish artistic traditions without succumbing to kitsch about 'hussars and a girl by a well' (1958: 7). One may almost suspect Toeplitz of tempting fate, like those sports commentators whose praise of a player magically triggers disaster, for the later film recklessly courts the danger the earlier one skirts. May the problem also involve *Lotna*'s hermetic detachment from the present that – for all its period (1945) setting – had entered *Ashes and Diamonds* through the fevered, 'existential' contemporaneity of Zbigniew Cybulski's performance?

The question is worth asking because Broch links kitsch to the historical novel, all images of the past being in a sense 'beautiful' (1955a: 345–6). One may even say that for him kitsch falls under the double curse Plato pronounces upon art, being doubly imitative because mimetic of fantasy rather than reality. Elsewhere he deems it able to imitate only the simplest of forms, the most primitive aspects of the prototypical artworks (1955a: 346). One may link this simplification (leading towards the rationalising streamlining – and hence the kitsch? – of Art Nouveau) to the pervasive leaning towards history, that homeland of spectacle, in late nineteenth-century art. Because our perceptions of historical reality lack the check of its grainy immediate presence, they slide seductively easily into projection, fantasy or wish-fulfilment. The historical novelist's or art director's assiduous archival research yields an apparent visual simulacrum really at odds with other elements of the work, such as contemporary faces, gestures or stances – to say nothing of issues. Wajda's own contention that there are no historical films is a truism (however great one's doubt whether many texts necessarily rework their present as simply allegorically as many Film Studies analyses have presumed); but it also fulfils a compensatory function, denying the bad faith perceived by onlookers sceptical of how the making of historical films demonstrates commitment to the here-and-now (significantly, *the same question* as the one posed to the literary adaptation).

For Umberto Eco, meanwhile, kitsch represents a quotation unable to forge a new context (1967: 119), the replication of a fragment of another work in complete indifference to the passage's shaping by, and transmission of, the original work's dominant themes. Kitsch's affinity with quotation may be the fact that its surface elements are not interconnected in their depths by a dialectic of development, but are all separable. The separability of the elements permits the excision and replacement of any particular one. The artist quoting thus views the original text as a potential array of fragments. This fragment-quality is projected onto it by the magpie eye's quest for the shiny and impressive, the potential fetish or talisman: the eye of the spectacular, perhaps. In Wajda's case, these fetishes are the images of late nineteenth-century painters like Kossak and Grottger, of Buñuel, and of Andrzej Wróblewski (Mruklik 1969: 41–2). Another word for such talismanic key-moments may be the one proposed by Matthew Arnold to designate the objects sought by his own form of criticism by quotation: touchstones. Arnold's practice extends beyond his own period into the Eliotic shoring of fragments against ruin in *The Waste Land* (a paradoxical enterprise, since the fragments *derive* from the text's ruination) and Syberberg's kaleidoscopic arrangements of elements of the German artistic tradition. In all cases, the fragmentation is part of the legacy of Romanticism, a movement Hermann Broch deems likely to generate kitsch through its refusal of intermediate values (1955b: 296–7): whatever fell short of the cosmic was relegated not to an acceptable middle-order but to the depths of the absurd, since to utilise the language of genius (the only one available to post-Romantics) and then deliver mediocrity was to fail. And it is worth noting, of course, how often Wajda has been described – and self-described – as the inheritor of the Polish Romantic tradition.

The longevity of the tradition of fragmentation may represent the prehistory and afterlife of surrealism, endorsing its claims to the status of the key modern movement both Wajda and Walter Benjamin perceived it to be: the surrealist scissors' ability to cut all objects (stone as well as paper) corresponds to their moribund nature, their lack of resistance. This rottenness may be explained in economic terms or existentially. Perhaps, as Wajda's film suggests, kitsch is the truth about surrealism, a revelation of the fundamental repetitiveness and uniformity of all the superficially startling dissonances. After all, in *Lotna* the surrealist dream slides with fatal ease into daydream, reverie (one reason perhaps why Irena Merz felt surrealism was a misnomer for Wajda's procedures (1960: 6)). Of course, kitsch is less 'the truth' about surrealism than its underside or temptation. For how can one control what enters the mind during automatic writing? (Notions of control, to say nothing of taste, have of course long since been discarded.) Is there any guarantee that everything that does so explodes from repressed, subversive depths? If kitsch necessarily shadows surrealism, then surrealism's gaudy patchwork of irrationalism would also display the rationality of a machine and be as deeply dependent on processes of commodification as kitsch, albeit hiding the link more effectively. If so, its widespread adoption in advertising regimes concerned above all to seduce and startle becomes all the less surprising, and Wajda's films (*Everything For Sale* in particular) may be, in the idiom of Norman Mailer, 'advertisements for myself'.

The Sublime or the Beautiful: The Return of Eros and Thanatos

Although *Lotna* is generally agreed to be a failure, its causes – and even the possible virtues of the film in question – deserve investigation. After all, it is a film that has haunted Wajda, who has repeatedly voiced a wish to re-make it, and it is worth considering why. Its frequently noted proximity to kitsch may also be read in Syberbergian fashion, as one to *myth*. After all, for Syberberg, 'In kitsch, in banality, in triviality and their popularity lie the remaining rudiments and germ cells of the vanished traditions of our myths, deteriorated but latently effective' (1982: 9). The callowness of the actors – a poor casting identified as one cause of the film's failure by Wajda himself,[1] (2000d: 30) – is an inexpressiveness that creates a sense of their being under a spell, not fully there. It is as if they are Grail Knights, more medieval – pre-individualistic – than modern, and for that very reason lacking personality. Alternatively, that inexpressiveness may resemble the bereft condition of the Grail Knights in Bresson's *Lancelot du lac* (1974), drained in the aftermath of the Grail's loss. And yet, of course, Wajda is not telling a story of Knights of the Round Table: unlike Syberberg, he does not speak of the Grail as the Ur-form of all utopian dreams, even though the mystique attributed to Lotna, and the Wheel of Fortune movement of her transfer, would indeed fit well within a medieval legend. Thus a further, deeper cause of the work's failure may lie in its inability to connect an image of the sacred to a larger myth such as the Grail one: a myth far more resonant than that of the glorious Polish cavalry, even though for Wajda himself, of course, who first viewed these men with the adoring eyes of childhood, they already had the larger-than-life quality of mythical figures (a characteristic that justified their subsequent transfer to the modern home of all such figures, the cinema whose passions are as enormous as the screen itself). *Lotna* may be the Wajda film that comes closest to acknowledging a sacrum (the heart of a wartime experience that becomes sacred because unrepresentable, and because of its linkage to family experience [2]): in which its sun begins to threaten to burn away an enveloping this-worldly existential mist. It does not succeed in so doing, however: it only becomes a blank disk, a marker of the location and existence of the sacred, not the blinding effulgence of the sacred itself. The sacred is as muted as the acting – as the cavalry horn on the soundtrack. For Wajda, thus, as the sacred becomes truly unspeakable, so does the film. It too does not quite come into focus. It falls back from the sublimity intimated in Lotna, the white horse that – as Helman points out (2001) – does not exist, and that therefore figures apocalypse and transcendence; instead, it becomes primarily beautiful – and so can be defined, in Broch's terms, as kitsch. The slippage from the transcendent to the quotidian, from the sublime to the beautiful, is marked and matched by the overflow of spectacular beauty from the horse to its male observers that has allowed Christopher J. Caes to speak, in this volume, of the work's evocation of a homosocial male brotherhood. That brotherhood is always already broken by a rivalry that dooms it. It also dooms the film, sanctioning a reading of the spectacular beauty of Lotna herself as a repression and displacement of the spectacular beauty of the men: the film would thus accord primacy to male beauty, not the sublime Otherness of the horse. Her femininity, meanwhile, would insinuate into sublimity the beauty that is so often coded as 'feminine', and that here subverts the Sublime. The two become confused – and the movement from the one to the other is enabled – in the long moment of the charge, described by Wajda as his main motive for making the film. That being the case, it is hardly surprising that spectators should have become as fixated upon it (both positively and negatively) as the film-maker himself. They may ignore the rest of the film in the same way as in a sense he has, treating it perfunctorily, not really *making* it (investing himself in it fully) but merely tracing its outline: that of the band of the ring holding the fetishised sequence, where man and horse flow together, only to separate thereafter, as he who has charged upon Lotna has become one with his beautiful death and hangs limp, spent, in the saddle in the end. The charge thus becomes an ecstatic *Liebestod*, itself the Grail of the film, a death sought again and again through the succession of riders, and then through re-imagining the film itself again and again, locating it in the mythical realm of the endless, cyclical repetition of its failure to come into being. The repetitions of the death, of course, indicate its imbrications with the sexual. The failure to make this explicit is that of the film as a whole, which replicates Freud's inability to fuse *his* two models of trauma. The making and reception of *Lotna* (including the little-publicised death on set of the first candidate for the horse) may be counted among Andrzej Wajda's most genuinely traumatic experiences.

Notes

1   It is possible that the speed of the work's realisation, and the sketchiness of its script, also played a part. The screenplay was passed on 14 August 1958 for shooting that autumn, during the September period it deals with. Some members of the Script Assessment Commission worried about the haste and the script's thinness, but decided that Wajda's reputation was sufficient guarantee. (Asked if there had to be such a rush, Wajda replied 'haste always pays off'.) The closing statement by Żukrowski – the author of the novella on which the film is based – stating that 'one will have to avoid views à la Kossak', becomes unintentionally ironic in retrospect (Anon. 1958: 4).

2   In his autobiography, Wajda poignantly describes one of his projects for the reworking of Lotna as incorporating memories of his father and mother (2000a: 306).

CHAPTER THREE

'He Speaks To Us': The Author in Everything For Sale, Man of Marble and Pan Tadeusz

Tadeusz Lubelski

The intuitive conviction that Andrzej Wajda was the first Polish film-maker who – still in the times of *A Generation* (*Pokolenie*, 1954) and *Kanal* (*Kanał*, 1957) – made the category of the author dramatically meaningful has led me to concentrate on the figure of the author in Wajda's films. Wajda was the first Polish film-maker who challenged his viewers by introducing this category into his cinema. His films problematise the following questions of representation. Who really speaks through the picture on the screen? What tools would they have at their disposal in formulating utterances? How can we, as viewers, recognise this authorial presence? In search of verifiable answers to these questions, contained in Wajda's films themselves, I have concentrated in particular on these titles which thematise the problem of the author/film director, and which thus transform it into one of the structural axes of the work.

Wajda himself appeared as an author in his films twice: in *Pilate and Others* (*Pilatus und Andere*, 1972) and in *Rough Treatment* (*Bez znieczulenia*, 1978). Yet the figure of the author does not become a key structuring element in either one of them. Neither one of these appearances organises the work in a significant way. Two other titles present themselves as obvious choices for my analysis. In *Everything For Sale* (*Wszystko na sprzedaż*, 1968) and in *Man of Marble* (*Człowiek z marmuru*, 1976) the protagonists who are film directors play crucial roles in the story. This does not mean, however, that one should automatically assume that they merely iterate the opinions of the author. The directors within the films enter into an array of relationships with other characters. We can interpret their function only in the context of each of the films as a whole. The third film I have decided to include in my analysis is less of an obvious choice. In *Pan Tadeusz* (1999) the way in which the narrative agency is presented endows it with the generalised characteristics of the image of an author. In earlier Wajda films the authors themselves personified this agency – Jarosław Iwaszkiewicz in *The Young Ladies of Wilko* (*Panny z Wilka*, 1979) and Tadeusz Konwicki in *A Chronicle of Amorous Incidents* (*Kronika wypadków miłosnych*, 1986). In those films the two authors' unique personal qualities led the viewers to think about these particular, individual instances of creative lives. The case of *Pan Tadeusz* is different not only because an actor plays Mickiewicz, but also because the narrative situation that is created around his character bears the characteristics of an effective generalisation that makes one think about the role of the author. The way in which Wajda presents the author in *Everything For Sale* bespeaks his attitude to the problem of the author in all of his earlier works. *Man of Marble* takes this reflection to the peak of Wajda's multifaceted activity as an author, producer and a socially involved person. Finally, *Pan Tadeusz* carries Wajda's self-reflexive deliberations into his most recent film. Thus, an analysis of the author's constructions in these three films captures the evolution of this category throughout Wajda's creative career.

Everything For Sale

The text itself provides an indication of the scandalous aspect of this film. The centre of gravity shifts very clearly from the figure of the actor who perished tragically to the person of the director. Bogumił Kobiela gives the reasons behind his own withdrawal from the project and he expresses his distaste: 'This is going to be a film about you, about the way you are making a movie.' The most insightful reviewers took note of the change of subject that had been announced by the legend that preceded it. 'It seems that when Andrzej Wajda for the first time picked his topic and wrote a script, he wanted to include in the film certain elements of the trade that he's been involved with, to scrutinise them, to evaluate them from a distance', remarked Bolesław Michałek (1970:

112). Michałek's observation indicates that the author of the film spins his reflection over and above or rather through the character of the film director who is present in the story. Thus, this is not just a film about the particular film that is being made. Most commentators who spoke about reflexivity in *Everything For Sale* tended to overlook that.

It is a noteworthy fact that whenever Wajda has commented on the film from the distance of time, he has maintained that he regretted the decision not to play the role of the director himself. Initially, when the film was still being edited, Wajda was thinking of including Jerzy Ziarnik's entire documentary *On the Set* (*Na planie*, 1968) in the film (Wertenstein 2000: 57–8). The documentary was shot on the set of *Everything For Sale*, and it presented the film-maker's actual frustrations. Just a trace of this idea remained in the film's soundtrack. At the end of *Everything For Sale*, when the crew is working on the scene at the fateful railroad crossing we can simultaneously hear the real voice of Wajda, giving directions to people who were working with him on the real set of the film. Had he incorporated the document into his film, he would have further strengthened the self-reflexive aspect of *Everything For Sale*, but in his interviews Wajda never goes back to this idea. He does, however, express his regrets about something else: if he had played the director himself, he could have introduced the theme of the real Zbigniew Cybulski's spiritual legacy in the second part of the movie. He would have accomplished this by including the biographical testimony of people who were near to Cybulski or by incorporating some footage of Cybulski himself. Had Wajda followed through with these ideas, he would have succeeded in making a film that would have met the demands of New Wave cinema by blurring the border between feature film and account taken from reality. But this type of cinema did not really correspond to Wajda's artistic sensibility and thus it is not surprising that the film-maker rejected it. Similarly, it is understandable that he did not bring another of his then current ideas to fruition: he did not cast Jerzy Skolimowski in the role of the film director. Skolimowski had been, in the second half of the 1960s, the only Polish film-maker involved in realising the New Wave model of cinema. Wajda concluded that he himself should be represented onscreen by someone of his own generation, and he decided to cast Andrzej Łapicki in the role of the film director. It has to be said that until the last moment he pursued the idea of casting Skolimowski in the role of one of his assistants, the one whose part was in the end played by Witold Holtz (see Wajda 1996: 185). It is a pity that Wajda did not succeed in implementing that casting decision. Had he done so, Jerzy Skolimowski and Andrzej Kostenko would have played the two assistant directors. The two were real-life friends who, moreover, complemented each other in their work. They co-wrote a truly European new wave film, *Start*, just a year before the filming of *Everything For Sale*. Such casting would have reinforced these elements of the film that the following analysis uncovers.

If we accept a 'cinemacentric' point of view, the crucial issues of the film have something to do with choosing a cinematic model permitting its authors to re-establish their link to reality. A sufficient number of motifs in the film clearly indicate that, according to the author, contemporary Polish culture in general and cinema in particular have entirely lost their ability to communicate anything truthful about surrounding reality. This realisation becomes especially poignant when put in the shameful context of the events following March 1968, and in particular the outbursts of anti-semitism that immediately preceded the making of the film. Let us recall the scene of the '*beau monde*' reception, and the subsequent one with the merry-go-round, or the sequence of the director's visit to the set of a historical super-production, a film that is not named, yet easily recognisable as *Colonel Wolodyjowski* (*Pan Wołodyjowski*, Jerzy Hoffman, 1968), in production at the time. The first of the scenes is a travesty directed against the art circles of the 'Duchy of Warsaw' (Daniel Olbrychski uses this ironic name in the film); the second one mocks the intellectual and artistic horizons of Polish cinema of the time. Then again, the director played by Andrzej Łapicki, along with his entire crew, is also implicated in the rules of the game that has come to dominate contemporary culture. They participate in the rituals of this superficial reality.

At the same time, the film-maker does not have any doubts concerning one issue: cinema has to be reinvented, refreshed and transformed. Only one model suggesting a realistic route towards this type of transformation appears on the cultural horizon of the time. It is the New Wave model. As a result of the tragic circumstances that precipitated the film project, the author has his film director instinctively select this option. It becomes clear that any film director in this vein has to introduce his own personal issues into the film and to pose the questions to which he himself seeks answers. He has to violate the rules of traditional scriptwriting, follow reality, improvise and show people in the way he knows them, people who function and act as they do in their every day lives.

In all these crucial points Wajda's *Everything For Sale* did indeed adhere to the New Wave model of authorship. It has to be pointed out that at the time of the film's making this model had already began to age and show signs of deterioration in the flood of imitations that followed it. We may assume that there were two options for the model's prolonged vitality. Each of the assistant directors is trying to talk the director into choosing one of them. The one whose role was supposed to be given to Skolimowski but eventually was played by Holtz encourages him to continue along the lines of *cinéma vérité*: he advocates the use of a hidden camera in order to tape real people. He is also the one who, following in the footsteps of the authors of *Le joli Mai* (Chris Marker, 1963) and *Chronique d'un été* (Jean Rouch, Edgar Morin, 1961) hides himself in a closet with a recording device, and who interviews people during the actor's funeral. Kostenko, in turn, wants to convince the director to imitate the fashionable aesthetics of the most talented – as it then seemed – pupil of the New Wavers, namely Claude Lelouche: 'One should film that' – tempts Kostenko – 'with the long lens, with the foreground blurry, without any pastels; a bit of a fair and at the same time such sadness caused by the absence of a guy who is not there any more … That's what I believe in.'

At first glance, the director, used to a different mode of work, rejects both of his assistants' suggestions. 'What! Have you lost it?' says the director following Holtz's suggestion that they tape authentic dialogues of crew members with a hidden camera. 'That's enough, that is enough, Kostek' – with these words the director interrupts the monologue of the other assistant director during a discussion that takes place after they review some footage. But the construction of the film as a whole convinces one that the contrary is the case. Wajda accepted both of the sets of suggestions concerning the film's aesthetics put forth by the fictional assistant directors. The film was photographed in the way suggested by Kostenko. No wonder some of the shots from *Everything For Sale* were referred to as 'Lelouches'. It was not difficult for the character of the assistant director and the film's actual cinematographer to arrive at a mutual understanding. Not long before the realisation of *Everything For Sale* Andrzej Kostenko and Witold Sobociński collaborated on the photography for Skolimowski's *Hands Up* (*Ręce do góry*, 1967), a film that had just been shelved. Holtz's suggestion, to open up to the stream of life, is at the film's end introduced into the plot. It is Holtz who, fascinated with the sight of the young actor Daniel's spontaneous race after the horses, advises the director to abandon the usual routine of work and to direct the camera towards this manifestation of youthful vigour. 'This is wonderful', exclaims Holtz. 'All right, all right, why don't you carry on yourself', responds the film director, with a noticeable tone of scepticism in his voice. And this is the last line we hear in the film.

In her review of *Everything For Sale* for *Young Cinema*, Alicja Lisiecka, a prominent figure of the Warsaw salons in those days, made the following comment about the film's final scene: 'At this point Wajda gives up the film, having come to understand that the problem is not how to reconstruct the myth, but how to free oneself from that myth.' And she added, casually, 'The old shop of the Polish School has been closed down for good – the bloody dummy abandoned on the side of the road'. The Polish periodical *Kwartalnik Filmowy* (*The Film Quarterly*) cited her opinion (see Curi 1996/97: 253–4). In reality, the meaning of the film is the exact opposite. The problem is that in order to return to a myth, in order to gain access to it, it is not enough to apply the poetics of New Wave cinema superficially, in the way suggested by the young assistant directors. The truth that the film director is after is not revealed as soon as the tape recorder is turned on, or when the fashionable lenses are installed. It is indeed worth listening to the younger generation. Their daring attitude inspires the author to make himself into the film's protagonist when he realises that this is going to work best for his project. It is also worthwhile to encourage them in their efforts to tell their own stories, in their own ways. As the student riots in March of that year had proven, these stories of the younger generation might indeed inspire rebelliousness. That, ultimately, is the advice the film director gives to the younger assistant director. He himself has already found his own way towards recapturing the myth.

What, exactly, is this way? The answer lies concealed in the subtle messaging of *Everything For Sale*, underneath the surface of the self-referential story of the film's making. It is possible to discern three layers of meaning in *Everything For Sale*. On one level, this is a film about a film; the actor who was to play the main role dies, the producers are considering a departure from the original idea, the director hesitates. The following layer is truly self-referential: the film becomes a treatise on the expressive possibilities of contemporary cinema. Finally the third, most profound level presents the story of the director's spiritual transformation. The experience of loneliness enables the film-maker to reach his myth of initiation. This myth encompasses issues such as the meaning of creative activity and the film-maker's obligations *vis-à-vis* his viewers.

The third level of meaning becomes accessible to viewers when we place the film and in particular its main protagonist in the context of the author's biography. This context suggests that Wajda picked two spiritual patrons for his director's spiritual transformation. Two of Wajda's peers and friends, two artists who had a decisive influence on his own work share this crucial role. The painter Andrzej Wróblewski was able, already at the beginning of his creative activity, to reach a level that – to Wajda – seemed beyond his own grasp. Consequently, Wajda decided to abandon painting, the first field of his artistic activity. The acquaintance with Zbigniew Cybulski with whom he shared the experience of an artistic fulfilment convinced the director to concentrate his efforts in the area of film-making. Wajda's interaction with both of them had at some point strengthened his own conviction that artistic endeavour is a mission. They suggested the meaning of this mission. As the result of a series of unfortunate incidents, just at the time of the film's making, after the events of March 1968, both these men appeared along his path. Cybulski had just died, and so he imposed himself on Wajda both as a subject and as a problem. Wróblewski became present again, ten years after his tragic death, when a commemorative exhibit of his work opened first in Poznań and then in Warsaw. In May of 1968, Stanisław Grochowiak published a review of this exhibit entitled 'He Speaks To Us' in the Warsaw periodical *Kultura*.

When the film's protagonist, the film director, begins to trace the steps of the two patrons of his spiritual transformation, he first experiences loneliness. It would appear that all the members of the crew are searching for the missing actor. But it does not take long to realise that they are all looking for him in order to satisfy their own desires. Initially, the same is true of the film's director. An actress who starred in the theatre opposite Cybulski brings this aspect of the entire situation to the director's attention: 'Don't you get this? It's only your own actor who matters, your own film, your script...' Immediately after this scene, in his conversation with the assistant, the director for the first time formulates the key problem: 'Doesn't the question pester you? What was he really like?' And the assistant's answer is, of course, 'no'. Later the director visits the Wróblewski exhibit all by himself, left alone by his wife who is also his actress, and who does not want to look at 'these paintings so cruel'.

Loneliness is an element of the second overarching sensation that the author experiences when he remembers Wróblewski and Cybulski: these memories bring him in contact with death. Not only have both of Wajda's friends died tragically and prematurely; death was among the leading motifs of their work. Cybulski, as we know, made close encounters with death into a staple element of his acting career. It was only natural for Wajda to frame *Everything For Sale* with two different stagings of the actor's death. In the text of the film, the village club manager refers to the legendary scene of Maciek's death in his account of a meeting with the actor. Had Wajda realised his idea of including clips from Cybulski's films in *Everything For Sale*, this scene from *Ashes and Diamonds* would have surely been there as well. Quite significant, too, is the choice of Wróblewski's pictures that the director looks at when he visits the painter's exhibit in *Everything For Sale*. Death is the subject of each of the eight pictures. What's more, almost all of them, including five canvases from the well-known cycle of *Executions* (*Rozstrzelania*), come from the

Movie director lost in snow: *Everything For Sale*

years 1948–49. Wróblewski and Wajda were in those years fellow students at the Kraków Academy of Fine Arts. The one exception, the 1956 *Chauffeur* (*Szofer*), a painting that opens the series in the film, continued a series Wróblewski had begun in 1948 with *The Blue Chauffeur* (*Szofer niebieski*). Wajda considers the years 1948–49 to be the most important in his friend's creative career. He writes in his autobiography:

> After the 1996 Wróblewski exhibit in Kraków I read in the papers that his late works, the ones that came after his struggles with socialist realism, were true art. I am of the opposite opinion. In my view, Wróblewski fully expressed himself only in several pictures he painted in the years 1948–49. Those were the canvases he felt compelled to produce. He was also profoundly and continuously frustrated after having painted them. (2000a: 55)

Mariola Jankun-Dopartowa pointed to the link between 'the characteristic iconography of Wróblewski and Cybulski's constructions of a protagonist'. In her insightful essay she connected both elements with the existentialism that, following the encounter with the two totalitarianisms, provided an answer to the paradoxes of human fate (1997: 189–98). I prefer to call this phenomenon a search for re-establishing a link to the myth. The predominance of the subject of death in the 'oeuvres' of Wróblewski and Cybulski is important for the understanding of *Everything For Sale*. But equally significant is the fact that Wajda attaches unquestionable value to these 'works' and that he may have been a witness to their making. Wróblewski's and Cybulski's accomplishments provide a testimony of the life experiences of Wajda's generation. They pose important questions concerning the fate of both those who died and of those who lived but who remember that they may at any moment share the fate of their deceased peers. Both artists had to give this testimony, and both of them felt 'a profound and continuous frustration' after doing so. They refused to give in to the indifference that surrounded them. They both believed in the ethos of the intelligentsia, which meant taking responsibility for others. Agonising over the question 'who were they, really?' provides Wajda with a means of rediscovering how to become one of them, once again. *Everything For Sale* does not stand for a 'closing down of the shop of the Polish School'. Quite the contrary, the film proclaims a return to the tenets of the School. Such a return cannot, obviously, mean regression to a different time, a different stylistics, and it cannot be addressed to a different audience. The film-maker has to search for a new language, akin to contemporary sensibilities, just as the New Wave film-makers did. But at the same time, he has to follow his own path by staying true to the myth of art in which he believed in the times of his youth.

Man of Marble

In one of the first interviews with Wajda after the premiere of *Man of Marble* in 1977, interviewer Krystyna Nastulanka from the weekly *Polityka* pointed out similarities between *Everything For Sale* and *Man of Marble*. The film-maker confirmed her opinion. Both are first of all films about films. But Nastulanka's comparison went beyond the obvious affinities of subject matter. She hinted at the parallel plot structures based in each case on the reconstruction of the deceased protagonists' lives. At the same time, such retrospectives serve the purpose of introducing issues relevant for an analysis of contemporary society (see Wertenstein 2000: 110). When we look at the way Wajda constructs the image of the film-maker within the text, we notice that the two films are quite similar. The discourse of contemporary cinema and, by implication, contemporary culture emerges from the scenes that present a closer look at a film crew. Underneath this discourse, a more profound issue lies hidden; the problem of the film-maker's inner transformation. In each case, he is ready to work in a way consistent with his initial intentions only in the film's finale. A comparison of the two structures reveals certain differences that may be significant for the understanding of the discourse of the author in *Man of Marble*.

The image of the film-making community and the author's opinion of contemporary cinema that motivates this image are the first questions to consider. Years have passed since the making of *Everything For Sale* and it shows. The way of telling stories has become different, faster-paced. The young film-makers have their own, different stories to tell, as if they were following the advice the older director offered to one of them at the conclusion of *Everything For Sale*. The former assistant director, incidentally, still belongs to the crew. Towards the end of the welcoming scene at the airport terminal a very preoccupied Witold Holtz tells Burski about current production problems. Other young film-makers are establishing their voices and becoming successful, as suggested by the Venice Film Festival award they display for the journalists. Still, within the world of the story, new tendencies in the cinema are judged with scepticism. During her first conversation with the young film-maker Agnieszka, the perceptive editor who may be speaking for the author, goes over the types of projects in which the young woman may have been involved: 'Cortazar, for sure, or maybe something according to your own script.' She then adds, with a still greater dose of irony: 'Oh, I know. Life caught unawares, a camera hidden in a watchman's booth. Television likes that, the viewers less so.' The film director Burski is just as patronising in his remarks concerning her project: 'A bunch of archival clips, dialogues in front of the camera, a sort of *cinéma vérité*? But we have already seen that, you know.' What we can gather from the two experienced film-makers' ironic remarks is that New Wave inventions have already degenerated, and they have reached the level of cheap imitations. It is not a coincidence that the route of the film crew includes such propaganda landmarks of the Gierek era as Warsaw Central train station, the new Łazienkowska road, and the 'Katowice' steel works. They appear with a frequency that makes them into a nuisance. Eight years after *Everything For Sale* native culture has in fact become faster-paced and superficially glossier, but it still lacks authenticity. There is just one significant difference: someone like Agnieszka could only emerge from this culture in the decade of *Man of Marble*.

How could we describe Burski, the other protagonist of the contemporary portion of the story? And what is his relationship to the authorial agency of the film? In terms of popular opinion, this character has been seen as Andrzej Wajda's alter ego. This reading has also occurred in scholarly analysis. In her study of Wajda's political film-making, Janina Falkowska interprets the Burski character in this way (1996–97: 259). If we examine the issue more carefully, the situation proves to be more complex than that. Most certainly, the character played by Tadeusz and Jacek Łomnicki in *Man of Marble* is not a self-portrait of the director to the same degree as the protagonist created by Andrzej Łapicki in *Everything For Sale*. Already the first scene in which Burski's name appears is inconsistent with this line of interpretation. He is first mentioned as the author of an unfinished film, *Birth of a City*. 'I did not know that Burski was involved in this sort of thing', says the surprised Agnieszka when she sees the material. *Nota bene* that she is not commenting on a Stalinist propaganda film, but a film that, from the perspective of the official propaganda, would have been considered rebellious. 'Unfortunately, he did not make films like this for long', adds the editor. Were Wajda to be identified with Burski, this dialogue would have been the opposite. In real life a mature film-maker would have been in the position to enlighten a younger colleague who just saw a film such as *The Ilza Ceramic* (*Ceramika Iłżecka*, Andrzej Wajda, 1951), or has just heard the dialogues from *A Generation*.

Later on, upon hearing about Agnieszka's planned visit to the well-connected Burski, the sound technician remarks sarcastically: 'That's right, the film director Burski likes to show his support for young talent.' Agnieszka punishes him with a punch. At the airport Agnieszka watches Burski and sees how he is trying to charm the journalists. Just as was the case earlier, she does not seem to regret that she is not one of his pupils. Rather, she is hoping to find the real Burski, or the Burski that could have been, in the course of her impending conversation with the film director. The following sequence of her dialogue with Burski confirms this impression. All of this happens because, unlike Andrzej Łapicki in *Everything For Sale*, Tadeusz Łomnicki incorporates elements of parody into the way he plays the film director. This parody is aimed, first of all, at the official image of Wajda, always well mannered for the media, and always smiling. But what's more important, Łomnicki's film director was intended to embody a group portrait. Łomnicki, a great actor who at the time was a high-ranking party activist, mocks himself by playing Burski – the all-powerful dignitary.

Burski's life story coincides in some ways with the biography of the film's scriptwriter, Aleksander Ścibor-Rylski. Finally, the externals of the image created by Łomnicki make one think of another real life film-maker. Those with a primary interest in film history would probably place the name of Czesław Petelski first on the list. In the credits to the documentary *Architects of our Happiness*, Wajda listed himself as an assistant director to Burski. As Wajda himself remembered after the premiere of *Man of Marble*, in 1950 he worked in Nowa Huta as an assistant to Petelski, who was then directing a novella entitled *The Price of Concrete* (*Cena betonu*) from the socialist-realist compilation *Three Stories* (*Trzy opowieści*, 1953) (see Wertenstein 2000: 101). Perhaps the most accurate identification of Łomnicki's film director Burski with real life film directors should run along the following lines: Petelski could have become like Burski, had he had Wajda's talent. Wajda would have become like Burski, if he had had Petelski's personality. Thus, Burski the protagonist should not simply be interpreted as representing Wajda within the text of the film.

Much indicates that the image of the author has in *Man of Marble* been split in two. It is a Lacanian kind of split, in which every encounter with the other promulgates the potential of a change. Burski embodies the dark and self-mocking side of this image, within the previously indicated context. Agnieszka represents the side of light. Already the film's second sequence suggests that, according to the authorial agency, Agnieszka is the ideal film-maker. In this sequence, Agnieszka grabs the camera from Leonard Zajączkowski, she mounts the Birkut statue, and she shoots a long and precise hand-held pan of it. Mr Zajączkowski, the most experienced of all the film-makers to appear in the story, is visibly impressed by her: 'Oh, wow, that's a girl!' These words promote her to the rank of professional film-maker. What is more, thanks to the passion she has for film-making, Agnieszka is ready to take the ultimate risk, and that is something that the senior film-maker would not have been capable of even in the times of his youth.

The sequence of Agnieszka's meeting with Burski concludes with a similar act of recognition for the novice's professional abilities. Agnieszka turns out to be an improved version of Burski. She has a chance of finishing the exact same project that the now famous director once abandoned: a graduation film, an honest documentary portrait of Mateusz Birkut, a Stakhanovite who was first elevated to fame and later degraded. The source of the difference between the two film-makers becomes apparent in the course of their conversation. When Burski tells Agnieszka about his beginnings as a film-maker, their stories are very much the same: 'You see, I was once young, too. I had to get started. I had not been able to make a single film. Everything was too dark.' It is the following phrase that marks a difference: 'But I became wiser.' Burski discovers the reason why Agnieszka is not going to follow along the path of compromise in the end of the same scene, in a dialogue that is crucial for understanding the difference between the two. Łomnicki-Burski asks all of a sudden: 'Are you leaving? You have all this luggage.' Agnieszka-Janda answers: 'This is all I have.' Burski: 'That is not much.' Agnieszka: 'It makes it easier to shoot films.' Burski: 'Perhaps you are right.' Agnieszka does not have anything to lose and that determines the way she engages in film-making. Just before *Man of Marble*, in *Everything For Sale* the younger generation had only the superficial attributes of modernity to offer. Thus, for the older director, it was not worth it to follow them. In *Man of Marble* the story is different; the young film-maker is engaged in something that the author's generation was in the past not able to accomplish.

What about the profound transformation that the viewers are becoming aware of? Is it the way in which Agnieszka herself changes? Indeed, Agnieszka does change. She relaxes in her outward appearance, but she toughens up inwardly. Due to this transformation, and in spite of a temporary setback – even in the most difficult circumstances, after the producer denies her access to the tools of her work – she will still be able to bring her project to fruition. Such at least is the message the film as a whole seems to communicate. It is still going to be the same project she set out to realise, and the one she outlined in her conversation with Burski: 'My idea is to follow him every step of the way.' It is the same project state television was initially going to finance: a biographic documentary about Birkut entitled *The Stars of One Season*. We get a good idea about the contents of this film on the basis of the pertinent parts of *Man of Marble*. Once the state sponsors realise the explosive potential of the film, they withdraw their support. Thus, the document that the young film director may eventually make will be different from the film we watch. We may therefore conclude that Agnieszka does not function as a fictional alter ego of the director of *Man of Marble* himself.

Burski's experience provides a negative starting point for Agnieszka's project; she does not simply continue along the path charted by the older director. The young woman in Wajda's film brings to life the statue of a worker, whose myth had been created by Burski, and she does so by using Burski's materials. *Man of Marble* becomes possible because of another symbolic transformation: Burski becomes Agnieszka. After their last exchange – 'It's easier to make films'/'Perhaps you are right' – Burski becomes superfluous for the narrative. A composite character Agnieszka, who has been enriched by Burski's experience, represents the figure of an author in the film.

Before the transformation could occur, the film-maker had to cleanse himself of his past ideological involvement and political misjudgements, that is, give an account of his participation in Stalinism and come to terms with the silence that surrounded this issue in the period of the Polish School. Burski's character plays a central role in these cathartic processes, but one should not overlook the generational dimension of the account of past experiences Wajda provides. He considered it important to introduce as many witnesses and testimonies of film-makers into the text of the film as possible. Among the ones that can be identified one should list the shameful fragments of *New Art* (*Nowa sztuka*) by Tadeusz Makarczyński (1950), Andrzej Munk's *Direction Nowa Huta* (*Kierunek Nowa Huta*, 1951), Aleksander Ścibor-Rylski's stories published in the years of Stalinism in the series 'The Stakhanovite Library', the appearance of Leonard Zajączkowski, a pre-war professional who in 1950 worked as a director of photography for *The Masters of Fast Melting* (*Mistrzowie szybkich wytopów*) directed by Roman Banach, and finally Wajda's own assistant directorship that could remind his viewers of his later post as an assistant director to Aleksander Ford in *The Five from Barska Street* (*Piątka z ulicy Barskiej*, 1954).

The character of Agnieszka signifies the realisation that all of these past faults may be redeemed and that one can be born anew. Wajda draws upon two sources of inspiration in creating this protagonist. In the first place, she is related to actual young film-makers who served as her prototypes. Among them, Wojciech Wiszniewski was known for his fascination with Stakhanovites and the uncompromising Agnieszka Holland always strove to realise her artistic goals. Secondly, the fictional Agnieszka draws a lot from Krystyna Janda, the actress who plays her. Janda's function in the film may be compared to the role that Zbigniew Cybulski played 18 years earlier in the making of *Ashes and Diamonds*. According to Wajda's own account:

> I could not take my eyes off of her on the set. This must have convinced her that she could do as she pleased. Some among the crew claimed that her acting was overdrawn, like caricature. I did not agree with that for a moment. I wanted to put contemporary life on the screen, not only by way of photography and narration, but especially through the way in which Agnieszka behaved. (1996: 71)

As was the case with Chełmicki in *Ashes and Diamonds*, the director conceived this character in the framework of the tragic. Years after the film's making Janda remembered: 'I could have simply played a journalist. But Wajda wanted me to play Antigone, Fedra, Medea ... He wanted something ultimate' (in Bielas 2000: 8). In the making of *Man of Marble* the author finally realised what the director/protagonist of *Everything For Sale* had vowed to accomplish. He gave an account of his own generation's experience without skipping the times of Stalinism, something that had until then been forbidden.

A similar analogy between *Man of Marble* and *Pan Tadeusz*, a film made 23 years and a couple of historical epochs later, is not readily apparent. However, one should not be deceived by the author's presumed withdrawal into the shadows backstage. Statements from the author might seem to support the illusion of such a withdrawal. Wajda says, for example, that 'We strove for freedom in order to be free from having to gamble with the feelings of the audience' (in Bielas 1998: 23). Nonetheless, an authorial agency appears in *Pan Tadeusz* with great intensity. It is there as a result of the consistency and coherence of the film's structure, as well as due to the clearly outlined situation of narration. In my concluding remarks, I offer a concise analysis of this situation.

Mickiewicz's Parisian salon becomes the location of the narrative situation: the writer reads his poem to his émigré listeners. The presence of this narrative device is not limited, as is usually the conventional case, just to the filmic frame. In Wajda's film, the salon returns to the screen six times. In each case an actor made to look like Mickiewicz (Krzysztof Kolberger) reads from the text. If we add to this all of the instances of the narrator's voice-over, the number of the narrator's interventions goes up to 17. This is a considerable number, and according to some reviewers, it may even be too high. Zdzisław Pietrasik, for example, wrote: 'In my view, there could have been fewer of the writer's appearances. Some of them are redundant' (1999: 17). But Wajda is not interested in just making the writer's presence known to the audience. The frequent foregrounding of a situation in which someone tells a story becomes part of the author's strategy. It provokes an interest in the very situation of narration created in the salon – along with the presence of an obligatory, though initially rather sketchily drawn – element of the audience. The great emotive power of the scene that concludes the plot, the mythic *Polonaise*, finds its opposite in the scene that concludes the narrative. The curiosity of the film's viewers transcends the conclusion of the plot. We look attentively at the members of the diegetic audience gathered in the Parisian salon, who are now, in the final scene, presented in a way that allows us to get a closer look at them.

A more observant look at this audience reveals that all of its members have two contrasting features in common. On the one hand, they are obviously identical with the protagonists of the plot. But it is also clear that they have been severed from the myth that animated the world in which the plot was set. The vivid and radiant myth of Poland removed to the past contrasts with the painful loss of any link to that myth that characterises the group of listeners gathered in the salon.

There can be little doubt as to the purpose of the device used by Wajda. The author wants the actual cinema viewers to identify with the group of diegetic addressees of 'the writer's' narration. By implication, this strong feeling of the viewers' identification with the audience within the film leads to the association of the diegetic author – the poet who reads from his poem – with the film's author. The device of authorial narration provides a link between the two. Thus, according to Wajda: 'Today we are all émigrés' (in Bielas 1998: 27). Moreover, as was the case with the Polish School, and later in the times of *Everything For Sale* and *Man of Marble*, the role of the author has remained the same. His function is therapeutic. In the case of *Everything For Sale* Wróblewski who came from Wilno and Cybulski who was raised on a country estate serve as guardians of the Romantic myth of origins. Within this myth, the artist invites his audience to participate in a communal ritual. This ritual's goal is to recognise the community's identity. To use the words of the playwright Stanisław Wyspiański, with whom Wajda feels a special affinity, the artist invites his audience to answer the question: 'Do you know who you could have been?'

(Translated by Izabela Kalinowska)

CHAPTER FOUR

Dangerous Liaisons: Wajda's Discourse of Sex, Love and Nation

Elżbieta Ostrowska

Bride:	But where is this Poland, where? Do you know?
Poet:	You may search, dear Bride, all over the world for Poland, and never find it.
Bride:	Then searching is a waste of time.
Poet:	But there is one small cage – Jaga, place you hand on your breast.
Bride:	There's a fold in this corset, they made it too tight.
Poet:	Do you feel something beating?
Bride:	What kind of lesson is this? My heart -? -?
Poet:	Ah, now that is Poland.

– Stanisław Wyspiański, *The Wedding*, act III, sc.16 [1]

This famous quotation from Stanisław Wyspiański's acclaimed play, spoken by Ewa Ziętek and Andrzej Łapicki in Andrzej Wajda's film adaptation, contains the metaphor of the motherland so deeply rooted in Polish collective consciousness that in popular perception it seems to lose its figurative sense and becomes an almost transparent image of the Motherland. Indeed it is an image that could be called, after Dorota Siwicka, 'an intimate motherland' (1993: 7). Many artists had invoked this metaphor before Wyspiański; many will invoke it afterwards. Hardly ever though does such a distinct element of physicality, also linked to a trivial woman's garment, this 'fold in this corset … made too tight', appear in literature or iconography. In Wyspiański's play, the poetic and metaphoric vision of the motherland, conjured by the Poet, is unexpectedly integrated with the Bride's down-to-earth perception of the world, while the spiritual metaphor of Polishness suddenly acquires an almost sensual tangibility.

The metaphor of the motherland in Wyspiański's play, even though still admired for the beauty of the poetic verse is not, as already mentioned, an original figure. It has become one of numerous images of feminised Poland, popular in Polish culture since post-partition times (see Janion 2000: 35–42).[2] Those images, broadly speaking, sublimate feminine physicality into an allegorical or metaphoric presentation of the homeland and, by doing so, bring about the metamorphosis of an individual being – after all, the hair and eyes of all these women have some colour – into an ideal being, a collective vision of the motherland. Thus, all these images remain on the border that separates the private from the public. The alternation between the public and the private, or, more precisely, free movement from one to the other, seems to be an idiosyncratic feature of a great majority of Polish artworks. It is particularly discernible in specific spatial solutions, such as the Soplicowo manor houses in Adam Mickiewicz's epic poem *Pan Tadeusz* or Korczyn in Eliza Orzeszkowa's *On the Banks of the Niemen* (*Nad Niemnem*, 1887), Ślimak's hut in Bolesław Prus' *The Outpost* (*Placówka*, 1884), the manor house in Witold Gombrowicz's *Ferdydurke* (1938) or the protagonist's room in Tadeusz Różewicz's *Personal File* (*Kartoteka*, 1960). The village house which becomes a metaphor of Poland in *The Wedding* is, however, particularly poignant. Andrzej Wajda's imagination often seems to follow or draw upon these literary tropes. The Monopol hotel in *Ashes and Diamonds* (1958), the manor house in Kurów in *Promised Land* (1974), the villa in *Holy Week* (1995) are all good examples of it. The inhabitants of the worlds created by the director are often fully aware of the metaphoric nature of the space in which they have been situated. The words of Maks Baum (Andrzej Seweryn) in *Promised Land* seem to confirm this. During one of his visits to Kurów, Baum tells Anka (Anna Nehrebecka) that 'Since I started coming over here, I have come to understand Poland and Poles better'.

The interaction between the public and the private is not only a rhetorical figure employed in Polish art and iconography but also reflects a social topography typical of Poland over the last two centuries. The political history of the country – deprived of statehood for 123 years and subjected to Soviet oppression after World War Two – as well as its retarded process of economic transformation where a strict distinction between public and private accompanied the emergence of capitalism, prefigured a more enduring division between public and private spheres. As Jan Prokop states:

> The Polish home, as a 'channel' through which national identity is transferred, takes over the functions which are performed first of all by public institutions in independent countries ... Strengthening of national legacy and the formation of identity in those countries are responsibilities of school, administration and army. The nineteenth-century state took special care to differentiate between the sphere of the private, the sphere of family life and the sphere of the public and the national ... Everything is turned upside down in Poland's situation. Although, similarly to the West, family is still a unit isolated from the outside world, the meaning of this isolation is fundamentally different ... the Polish home was a fortress and national temple closed off from the partitioning powers, but not a place where an individual found retreat with other members of his family from his compatriots. (1993: 23–4)

It is difficult to imagine this 'fortress and national temple' containing a boudoir that concealed a Polish lady's intimate affairs or a drawing room similar to that in which Jane Austen's protagonists endure their marital problems. There is no space either metaphorically or literally in Polish literature for Emma Bovary's love dilemmas, while any young man seeking refuge in a lady's closet would probably be a soldier or a wounded insurgent.[3]

Wajda deplored the deficit of the Polish Madame Bovary in his presentation at the session *Pan Tadeusz – Polishness and universality in literature and film*. As he noted,

> all Polish literature, in the majority of its great oeuvres, is a literature without women. And literature without women cannot be universal. ... The protagonist of Polish literature is a young boy, between 18 and 20, sometimes 22, a cadet or an officer, fighting for Poland. Can such a hero be interesting? Hardly. On the other hand, just look – Emma Bovary, all these women in Dostoyevsky – how beautiful it all is, how profound. These women teach me more about the world than men do. (2000c: 276–7)

It is easy to see that Wajda's films also expose this feature of Polish literature and art to which the director alludes. The world in his films is an acting arena for young boys, and women usually inhabit the space on its margins. Those young boys prove their masculinity for other boys rather than in a relationship with a woman, by fighting for a 'cause'. The paradigm of a triangle typical of psychological or romance literature assumes in Polish art, as in Wajda's films, a distinctive form. The 'third one' is substituted by the abstract idea of a cause, motherland, and a moral duty toward the community to which one belongs. The distortion of the model typical of Western literature is a reflection of the altered division into the public and the private.

While sexuality falls exclusively within the private sphere in the Western bourgeois world, it does not have its own place in a world in which the taboo of intimacy barely exists; it always plays second fiddle to the 'cause.' As Michel Foucault states, in the nineteenth century, 'Sexuality was carefully confined; it moved into the home. The conjugal family took custody of it ... A single locus of sexuality was acknowledged in social space as well as at the heart of every household, but it was a utilitarian and fertile one: the parents' bedroom' (1979: 3). One can search for 'the parents' bedroom' in Wajda's films in vain. In fact, the reverse of what Foucault describes happens here, and images of eroticism are actually images of 'sexuality in exile'. The director usually situates erotic scenes in places that belong to a more or less defined public space. There is, for instance, the hotel room in *Ashes and Diamonds*, the sewers in *Kanal* (1957), the manor loft in *Lotna* (1959), the meadows in *Landscape After Battle* (1970) or *A Chronicle of Amorous Incidents* (1986), the train carriage in *Promised Land* and so on. Images of 'sexuality in exile' are in most cases a reflection of a more general existential predicament of the heroes: the situation of exile. These people are 'without a home and motherland', first of all in a spiritual sense but sometimes also in a literal sense. Erotic scenes set in accidental and erratic spaces seem transitory and incidental. The narrative accentuates the impression of incidence as those scenes usually precede either the death of one of the protagonists or some other dramatic conclusion of his/her life which once and for all obliterates the possibility of settling down, returning home or establishing it.

Even though the character of Stokrotka (Teresa Iżewska) in *Kanal*, for instance, brings from the very beginning a clearly defined femininity and sexuality, they can only be revealed when she is looking death 'in the eyes', when Korab (Tadeusz Janczar) is on 'the other side of the bars'. Their single desperate kiss is, as it were, a passage to a different dimension of reality, or fleeting witness to a finite reality they will soon have to leave. In *Ashes and*

No way out for Polish insurgents: *Kanal*

Diamonds, Maciek (Zbigniew Cybulski) kisses Krystyna (Ewa Krzyżewska) with the same desperation shortly before Szczuka's assassination and his own death. In *Lotna*, Ewa's bridal veil gets caught in the coffin with the body of the deceased captain, while the wartime honeymoon becomes a kind of 'journey towards death'. In *A Chronicle of Amorous Incidents*, Wajda, in the spirit of Tadeusz Konwicki's novel on which the film is based, presents the myth of romantic love ironically. Two young lovers, still children, decide on a love-suicide pact through which they will be wed forever. Wajda's idyllic image of the two bodies lying on a flowery meadow, 'the sacrificial altar of true love', is, however, disrupted by exploding bombs marking the beginning of World War Two. The deafening report of cannons awakens the lovers, who, it turns out, have decided to spare each other after all. Holding hands, they walk towards the horizon while the earth is ripped apart by falling bombs. It is only then that they face death, which will probably show them no mercy.[4] Thus, History once again delineates a real dimension of existence nullifying individual love tragedies, which because of their extreme theatrical form, appear here as completely detached from 'real life'.

Interestingly, Wajda often visually 'alienates' erotic scenes using key cinematographic devices. Such stylistic 'alienation' is particularly effective in the erotic scene between Maciek and Krystyna in *Ashes and Diamonds*. While deep-focus photography, which Bazin considered crucial to achieve the effect of realism, is the stylistic dominant in the film, spatial realism is done away with in this sequence. Shown almost entirely in close-ups, using diffusion, distance from reality is enhanced. There emerge in its place a series of unreal poetic icons suggestive of a world of pure emotion in which physicality and sexuality are sublimated into romantic love, that is, love in which failure to achieve fulfilment is contained *ex definitione*. Of course in Wajda's films, History is to blame for this crucial failure.

The tension between love discourse and sexual discourse is typical of many films by Wajda. As William Jankowiak points out:

> No culture is ever completely successful or satisfied in either synthesising or reconciling love and sex, although every culture is compelled to make the attempt. No matter how socially humane, politically enlightened, spiritually attuned, or technologically adapted the culture may be failure is a name of the game. Some degree of dissatisfaction exists everywhere, since we rarely, if ever, realise a comfortable balance between the two. (1997: 49).

Although the gap between love and sex may be perceived as culturally universal, it is articulated in a specific way in each culture. Wajda's films confirm this in a particularly convincing way. He allows his characters to fulfil their sexual desire more often than to satisfy their need for love. Put simply, a contented love is absent from the world of Wajda's films (*Pan Tadeusz* is the only exception). Although the reasons for this are diverse, the destructive influence of History is often to blame. As a result, the power of sexuality that threatens History may not be fully revealed. Of all Wajda's films, I can name only one that presents love as threatening sexuality in the way typical of many cultures. I have in mind, of course, *Promised Land*. This film, however, has a special place in Wajda's work as it employs the model of genre cinema. (Nurczyńska-Fidelska 1998: 118–26). In the majority of his films, sexuality appears as substitute for or prelude to a love that can never be fulfilled. This type of relationship between love and sex is, according to Jankowiak, characteristic of specific cultures:

> cultures that are not organised around dyadic bonds are based in alternative forms of solidarity, such as the lineage, the large extended family, men's houses or, in the twentieth century, a feverish involvement in national causes. In these societies, the heterosexual love bond is held

to be a potential rival to other, more important non-dyadic loyalties. It should be further understood that feelings of sexual attraction can lead to deeper forms of feeling, which in turn can develop into full-scale resistance to parental authority. In these societies romantic love is considered more dangerous than premarital sex. (1997: 54)

Indeed, in the context of all Wajda's films it is clear that heterosexual love-bonds are almost always subordinate and overshadowed by the bonds uniting individuals into a nation. Sexuality, in turn, often engenders a conflict between individual love and 'the collective cause'.

This conflict is revealed to powerful effect in *Landscape After Battle*. The film, a kind of post-script to the war trilogy, deals with the situation of former prisoners of a concentration camp liberated by the American army. The prisoners are waiting for further evacuation in a displaced persons' camp. The situation is observed from the point of view of a young Polish poet, Tadeusz (Daniel Olbrychski). On the one hand, he keeps aloof from the recurrent clashes among his compatriots. On the other hand, like everyone else he is 'contaminated by death' and tries to exorcise the trauma of his war experience through poetry. When a young Jewish woman, Nina (Stanisława Celińska), arrives from Poland, an opportunity of rebirth-through-love arises.

Nina, young, sensuous, beautiful, wearing a bright floral dress that differentiates her from the grey world of camp uniforms and the equally grey clothes donated by the American army, conveys a physical presence that Tadeusz fails to notice. Their first meeting illustrates this very well. An old violinist (Aleksander Bardini), a friend of Nina's parents we later find out, accompanies the couple. Initially only the two men speak, while Nina is sitting on the table slightly to the rear. The violinist, who is reading out loud passages from a patriotic propaganda leaflet, points to the woman and says, 'And this lady has just escaped from the "living heart of the nation". A Jew.' Only then does Tadeusz, who seemed not to have noticed the girl even though her face is opposite his, turn towards her. He takes her by the chin as if she were a little girl and asks, 'And how's Poland?' The woman remains silent for a while blowing provocative smoke rings, and looks Tadeusz straight in the eye. Tadeusz, however, does not take up this obvious sexual game: he waits patiently until the girl says something about Poland as if it was his only interest. As the girl slides off the table and stands on the floor, she touches Tadeusz with her body. He is clearly embarrassed. The old violinist unexpectedly takes advantage of this physical intimacy by adroitly slipping his hand under Nina's dress, under the table, to which she reacts by slapping Tadeusz in the face.

This scene could easily develop into a typical narrative triangle. In a way, it does: even *mise-en-scène* suggests it. The characters are presented in triangular composition. The violinist's desire is directed towards Nina, Nina's towards Tadeusz, who breaks up the pattern of the triangle, turning his desire towards absent Poland, even though what he desires is only information. The incompleteness of this triangular composition, though modified several times throughout the film, is preserved to the very end.

The imbalance of desire between Nina and Tadeusz is suspended later on, only to be re-affirmed in the film's conclusion. In a long sequence in which this 'suspension' takes place, the two take a walk outside the camp. Again it is Nina who initiates this outing, approaching Tadeusz and virtually dragging him out of his bolthole in the camp. This scene, photographed in very tight close shots, contrasts with the distant long shots at the start of the next sequence and set in open spaces, first a field and then a forest. A colourful abundance of trees in leaf stands in opposition to the grey reality of the camp, separated from the line of barbed wire that seems to run on endlessly, an image repeated throughout the film. Against the backdrop of this warm pastoral setting and freed from the horrors of the recent past, Nina again tries to get Tadeusz's attention. The couple lie on the grass; Nina faces the ground. The camera, positioned very low on the level of the couple, shows in the foreground Nina's bare legs exposed up to her thighs. Nina's physicality and sexuality sharply contrast with the figure of Tadeusz, whose gaze is directed somewhere up into the sky and whose detachment from the external world is visually reinforced by his thin-rimmed glasses. Tadeusz muses over his camp memories, 'I still haven't told you how we made soup in the camp…'. When Nina lies down on him and tries to kiss him, Tadeusz abruptly shakes her off, grabs his knapsack and walks away. In the next scene we see him curled in foetal position on a pile of dry leaves, desperately trying to hide inside. After a while, Nina sits down by his hiding-place, now reminiscent of a grave (or his mother's womb?), and starts talking to the invisible Tadeusz. She asks him to write her a poem and reminds him once again that the war is over. Tadeusz emerges out from the leaves and shows Nina the camp number tattooed on his forearm. In a close-up, we can see Nina sensuously kissing the forearm, while Tadeusz speaks from behind the camera: 'You can't kiss it off. It's a waste of time. This is good German work. It stays on until you die.' The war is not over for him and it will never be over for the survivors. The camp number tattooed on the arm proves that the past is not only a traumatic recollection, a nightmare from which memory and thoughts cannot get free, but that it actually persists in the present, embedded in human physicality until, as Tadeusz puts it, one dies.

Thus physicality, which defines the somatic limits of human subjectivity and its intimate 'I', has been appropriated by History, and the personal has been incorporated into the public. The motif of Tadeusz's 'dispossession' of his physicality is reiterated in the film: when he is driven to irrational, compulsive eating, when he rejects or ignores Nina's sexuality, or when he obsessively wants to hide in tight, murky places which take him in like the mother's womb. Nina seems to be aware of the regression Tadeusz is experiencing. At some point, she tells him, 'You have to learn how to walk again.'

Tadeusz's experience of the 'dispossession' of physicality is not connected exclusively to his own body. Later in the scene, a girl cycles past Nina and Tadeusz. A close shot foregrounds her long blond hair, wind-blown in the air. Tadeusz is struck by what he sees. Nina, somewhat disturbed, asks, 'Who is it?' and adds, 'Pretty'. 'Very pretty, and this hair. Yes, yes, I remember this hair, lying on my face', replies Tadeusz deep in his thoughts. 'Where do you know her from?' asks Nina, increasingly anxious. The reply: 'I'm not sure but I think she ... she and two others interrogated me at the Gestapo in Szucha. I didn't have my glasses on. They were beating me, I couldn't see. They must have bent over me and I remember the smell of the hair, sweet flag smell.'[5] The woman's hair, smelling of sweet flag, which an audience might expect to be a memory of sexual adventure, actually turns out to be a memory of the horrors of the war. In this short scene Wajda achieves the effect of complete surprise, if not shock. It comes from an unexpected transition, abrupt yet also smooth and for Tadeusz, a natural transition from the individual/erotic plane to the collective/political plane.

In the next scene, the heroes stage a mock-confession in a near-empty church. Tadeusz sits down in the confessional and questions the kneeling Nina. The questions, however, are not as might be expected, about past affairs or relationships with men, that is, intimate things. Tadeusz wants to know one thing only: why Nina left Poland. He actually wants her to 'confess this sin'. The situational context in which the heroes talk about why she left Poland somewhat makes the audience accept the point of view of Tadeusz, for whom first and foremost the moral and ethical dimension of the decision should be considered. The heroes continue to talk in the meadow in the next scene. Nina suggests Tadeusz leave Poland, study abroad, at Sorbonne, for instance:

Tadeusz: I don't know French.
Nina: You'll learn.
Tadeusz: I can learn all languages but I will still feel and think in Polish.[6]

Traumas of love and war: *Landscape After Battle*

Nina takes off his glasses and starts kissing him, but he is still musing about emigration:

> *Tadeusz*:   What can I write about there and for whom? Everything
> I'm made of is Polish. I can't, I don't want to obliterate
> this Polishness in me ... Do you think the motherland is
> nothing but landscapes?
>
> *Nina (sobbing)*:   What is it then, what is your motherland?
>
> *Tadeusz*:   Our motherland. I don't know but I think it's first of all
> people. Tradition ... language. The language we speak and
> understand the best.

Nina's words close the conversation: 'You're not a man, you're a Pole. Then go back to this Poland of yours.' The resentment of the disappointed and disillusioned Nina connects to a more general question: the project of supra-individual identity built into the character of Tadeusz. His behaviour, his words and his relations with others explicitly show that his identity is primarily defined by a sense of national belonging. Jan Prokop comments on this problem on a more general note:

Being Polish ... refers more to the roots of individual identity ... than to a sense of community of interests of individuals who situate their own identity not in the national sphere but in the sphere of either 'being a person' or 'being oneself'. This makes the sense of national belonging appear external, accidental, detached from the essence of 'me myself'. 'The Polish fate' usually takes a different course, Polishness is like an indelible stigma. (1993: 22)

'Polishness like an indelible stigma' also reverberates in the case of the hero in *A Love in Germany*. The film, based on Rolf Hochhuth's novel, *Eine Liebe in Deutschland*, tells the story of the tragic love between a Polish man and a German woman 'in the time of cholera'[7] and examines the conflict between the individual and the collective. However, the changes introduced by Wajda into his film seem so characteristic of our general theme that I want to examine them in greater depth. Hochhuth's story, dispassionate, supplemented by historical documents from the period, explores the phenomenon of a Nazi ideology that in practice oppressed anyone falling within its reach. This broad issue is unexpectedly transformed by Wajda, in ways viewers might see as inopportune or annoying, into a tragedy of a Pole who defends his Polishness at the expense of his own life.

The shift of emphasis in the film is already discernible on the level of narration, which focuses on Paulina (Hanna Schygulla) in the first half of the film only to give way almost exclusively to Stanisław (Piotr Łysak) in the second. Hochhuth's novel, on the contrary, presents the lives of the two protagonists symmetrically up to the end. In Wajda's film, the audience sees the 'forbidden' love between a Polish man and a German woman from the perspective of the woman, who is shown to be the active part in this relationship, from the scene in which she buys condoms to the scene in which she visits Stanisław in hospital. When the Nazi authorities are informed about this 'dangerous liaison' Stanisław takes over the privileged position in the narration while Paulina appears only occasionally, as if to keep up the appearance of symmetry.

It is also in this part of the film that the most significant deviations from the novel become apparent. The development of the 'Germanisation' plot is, in my opinion, of great importance. While Hochhuth briefly quotes documents related to the issue, Wajda constructs a separate amplified narrative around it. A German police officer, Mayer (Armin Müller-Stahl), present on the screen for a great part of the film, fights first 'for' Stanisław and then 'with' him, with a determination that is sometimes incomprehensible. Mayer's truly obsessive desire to 'Germanise' Stanisław and thus to 'spare' him, reminiscent of Liza's struggle 'for Marta' and 'with Marta' in Andrzej Munk's *The Passenger* (*Pasażerka*, 1961), is confusing and his behaviour, I would argue, quite irrational. The motivation behind his desperate attempts to turn Stanisław into a German in the film is not clear at all. However, Mayer's erotic fascination with Paulina, developed in Hochhuth's book and left out in Wajda's film, could be used to account for the police officer's behaviour. As we read in the novel:

> This thirty-six-year-old greengrocer had crept beneath the bedclothes of his imagination. So potent was her erotic aura and so strong her sexual attraction that not even the sack-like prison smock which was meant to standardise her figure, not accentuate it, could deprive her of something that Mayer, with petty bourgeois bravado, euphemistically described as 'worth a trip to the confessional'. He could never have explained why Pauline stimulated him to such an extent that indifference overcame him in the bedroom at nights. Sympathy for this 'dishonoured' woman, who has violated 'wholesome public sentiment', as the official definition ran, was sapping his conception of duty. More than that, he paradoxically extended that sympathy to the man under provisional sentence of death who had 'had', or taken, what his jailer could only dream of. (1980: 173–4)

Thus, in the book Mayer determinedly tries to 'Germanise' Stanisław as he knows that it is the only way in which he can save Paulina. No traces of this plot can be found in Wajda's film and consequently Mayer seems to be waging an utterly abstract struggle between 'Germanness' and 'Polishness'.

The national theme is expanded in the conversations between Stanisław and Victorowicz (Daniel Olbrychski) in the prison cell. Changes introduced by Wajda in the letter Victorowicz promises to write are particularly interesting and characteristic. While the letter in the book is addressed to Stanisław's parents, it is addressed to his mother in the film. In the book, the men decide

> … that Victorowicz should tell his parents that their son had been shot for falling in love with a German girl. He had died instantly, and he asked them to console themselves with the thought from which he himself had tried to draw some consolation: that unlike so many of the fellow-conscripts who accompanied him straight from the schoolroom to the front, he at least had known love – a really great love – before his death. (Hochhuth 1980: 259)

Wajda changes the situation completely. Stanisław asks Victorowicz not to mention Paulina to his mother at all. In the film, the experience of love, so important in Hochhuth's book, is reduced to an indecent sexual relationship concealed from Stanisław's mother. I find this alteration highly important. While Stanisław is a mature person capable of self-reflection in the book, he regresses in the film. Shortly before his death, he is a grown-up man brought back into the position of a son, ashamed of his relationship with Paulina and not wanting his mother to know about it. Even though Stanisław's words, 'Don't say anything about Paulina' may be interpreted as 'Don't say anything about my relationship with a German woman', they are permeated with a double fear. It is a fear of a man who becomes a boy-son at the moment of his death and is afraid to let his mother know about his sexual desire for another woman. It is also a fear of a Polish man who is anxious that his sexual relationship with a German woman may be recognised by his mother as kind of 'national betrayal'. The general nature of Stanisław's request makes it impossible to determine categorically which of the interpretations offered here underlies his motivation. At the same time, it also implies that both interpretations are interwoven, thus fusing psychosexual identity and national identity. On the one hand, shortly before his death, Stanisław, probably unaware of it, defines femininity and positions himself in relation to this femininity. To put it simply, Stanisław abruptly and unexpectedly rejects the role of the lover and declares 'loyalty' to his mother and his motherland – and, in fact, they coalesce into one. 'Don't say anything about Paulina' and 'Long live Poland' are the two phrases that Stanisław uses to define his own person. Both are articulated quite clumsily, with the infantile determination of a small boy who tries to hide from his mother that he has been up to mischief and wants to convince her that he is still a 'good boy'.

Even though some critics would be inclined to attribute Stanisław's behaviour in the film to Piotr Łysak's inept performance, the dialogue, I believe, proves that it is the way the character was already constructed in the script. His childish or even patriotic affectation in Wajda's film contrasts with the rationality, not to say scepticism through which Stanisław considers the national problem in the novel:

Nationality was no sort of criterion on the threshold of death, not to any decent person, considering the havoc it had wrought on nations and countries – on whole eras ... The Germans were going to murder him, but it was a German who had tipped him off about escaping to Switzerland, a German who had loved him ... Nationality was the most pernicious, depersonalising homogenising label that could ever be attached to the human individual. Why bother with it, now least of all? Yet it was the dementia of nationalism that had brought him, first into war, then into captivity and ultimately to this cell, so the thought of it was quite inescapable. To dismiss it as irrelevant would only accentuate the horror of his situation, for who wanted to think himself the victim of something utterly senseless? On the contrary, he would have – because he didn't believe in God – to rebuild his sense of nationality into a last supreme arbiter, into the sea-anchor which would, if only for a few hours, steady his existence as it drifted into death. To have to tell himself that he was dying for no good reason would be the bitter end, precisely because it was true! (Hochhuth 1980: 196)

In the film, on the other hand, Stanisław's debates with Victorowicz on this issue are a logical consequence of Stanisław's spontaneous resistance to Mayer's attempts to 'Germanise' him. Thus, the tragedy of an individual oppressed by the Nazi ideology as presented in the book is transformed in Wajda's film into a tragedy of a Polish man who sacrifices his life in the name of his Polishness. *A Love in Germany* shows the transition of the individual to the collective in a particularly ostentatious way.

The problem of the tension between the individual and the collective persistently reappears in Wajda's films. Among his recent works, *The Crowned-Eagle Ring* (1992) offers a demonstrative example of the uneasy relationship between the individual (sexuality) and the collective (nationality). Wajda returns here to World War Two. In one of the scenes when the outcome of the Warsaw Uprising has practically been decided, the female protagonist Wiśka (Agnieszka Wagner) takes care of her wounded beloved, Marcin (Rafał Królikowski). The *mise-en-scène* and iconography produce the effect of a Pietà. This universal religious symbol is embedded in national discourse through the narrative action. Wiśka gives her beloved the ring with a crowned eagle, the symbol of pre-war Poland and symbolic betrothal thereby acquires a double meaning. It obliges the man to remain faithful both to the woman and to the motherland, fused again into one entity. The symbolic fusion of the two is reinforced later in the film when Wiśka is raped by Soviet soldiers. The 'icon' of the motherland raped by the invader, an icon ever popular at the time of the Partitions, is revived here by Wajda in an ostentatious, even annoying way. When the heroes meet later, Wiśka discovers that the crowned eagle has lost its crown and she leaves without a word of explanation. It turns out once again that the individual has been subjected to the pressure of 'the collective' and thus, in a way, annihilated.

Uprising – Motherland – Pieta: *The Crowned-Eagle Ring*

The structure of interconnections between sexual, national and love discourse in Wajda's films analysed here, runs parallel to a key tendency noted by Frederic Jameson in the literature of the Third World. Jameson points out that political or social involvement is expressed through personal issues or in psychological terms in Western literature, whereas psychological or specifically libidinal involvement in Third World writings is conveyed in political or social categories. As he states:

> One of the determinants of capitalist culture, that is, the culture of the Western realist and modernist novel, is a radical split between the private and the public, between the poetic and the political, between what we have come to think of as the domain of sexuality and the unconscious and that of the public world of classes, of the economic, and of secular political power: in other words, Freud versus Marx ... Third-world texts, even those that are seemingly private and invested with a properly libidinal dynamic – necessarily project a political dimension in the form of national allegory: the story of the private individual destiny is always an allegory of the embattled situation of the public third-world culture and society. (1986: 69)

As already mentioned, the Polish division into public and private spheres has not only been subject to frequent alteration. It has never assumed so crude a form as in Western societies. Therefore, the distinction Jameson mentions in relation to the culture of the Western, capitalist world could not appear fully in Polish culture and thus the conflict between Freud and Marx to which he refers could never be fully articulated. It may, for instance, be assumed that in the domain of the private, the Polish collective historical experience must inevitably have influenced the universal psychoanalytical model according to which personality is formed, with the Oedipus complex central to it. As Jan Prokop points out in his analysis of the Polish home and family:

> Unlike many other independent European countries, the family home in Poland does not draw upon the macrostructure of the state. In those countries, the figure of the father – head of the family – supports the head of state through his authority, while his paternal power is validated by the authority. There, also, the son who rebels in the name of the right of an individual by this disobeys the monarch (president) and the father. Both family and state will represent in his eyes the apparatus of oppression and violence.
>
> In an invaded country, state rule is imposed from outside. The figure of the father thus does not function as a link between the private and the public. The son crushing the shackles of bondage usually does not blame his father for complicity with a foreign usurper … The conflict of the young who fight with the existing world is therefore usually directed outside the boundaries of the family home … How often the *Polish Oedipus* [my italics], swearing revenge, sharpens on his father's grave the dagger with which he will kill the tsar-usurper … Polish imagination is often haunted by the vision of killing the tsar, never of killing the father. (1993: 25–6)

Patricide, however, does appear in Wajda's imagination, in *Ashes and Diamonds*. It must be stressed, however, that Szczuka is a symbolic figure of the father who abandoned his son for an idea alien to the Polish patriotic thought. He belongs to the world of foreign ideas and traditions, highlighted by the scene of his Spanish Civil War memories that so greatly contrasts with the sequence in the bar when Maciek and Andrzej light candles for the souls of their dead friends. Therefore the symbolic act of 'patricide' perpetuated by Maciek belongs more to national discourse than to the individual, psychological one. In other films by Wajda, relationships between adult men and young boys differ drastically from that in *Ashes and Diamonds*. For example, in the final scene in *Kanal*, Lieutenant Zadra returns to the sewer to meet sure death because he wants to look for 'his boys' who have got lost somewhere on the way. The relationship between Mateusz Birkut and Maciek Tomczyk (both played by Jerzy Radziwiłłowicz) in *Man of Marble* (1976) and *Man of Iron* (1981), however, is the most characteristic example of the bond between generations and the son's loyalty to the cause for which his father fought. Metaphorically, the triumph of Solidarity's revolution in 1980 was possible because the son did not rebel against his father but remained faithful to him. In *Man of Marble*, Agnieszka's (Krystyna Janda) father is Birkut's ally. This simple railway worker makes his daughter realise her moral duty to complete her project about Birkut even on her own. Wajda himself once said, 'our generation is a generation of sons who must tell the story of their fathers because the dead cannot speak any more' (2000a: 54). In *Promised Land*, Karol Borowiecki's (Daniel Olbrychski) decision to act against his father and the tradition represented by him brings about his moral defeat and the exclusion from the national community.

Thus, if the 'son' cannot foreswear obedience to his father, then the process of becoming a man must be deferred. It may be the reason why most male protagonists in Wajda's films are 'boys' – both the director himself and the majority of critical texts employ this term. The identity of 'boys', that is 'not-yet-men' – including their sexual identity – has not been fully formed because they are still subject to their parents' rights which, in the Polish situation, were codified by the Romantic tradition with such concepts as homeland, honour, freedom, sacrifice, duty. The hero remains a boy until the end. At the moment of death, premature and somewhat absurd, he becomes a child who, like Korab in *Kanal*, finds shelter in the arms of the caring Stokrotka or, like Maciek Chełmicki in *Ashes and Diamonds*, leaves this world in a foetal position which symbolically takes him back to his mother's safe womb, or, like Stanisław in *A Love in Germany*, bids farewell to life with the word 'Mum'.

(Translated by Joanna Kazik)

Notes

1 This passage from Stanisław Wyspiański's *The Wedding* closes Norman Davies' book, *Heart of Europe: The Past in Poland's Present*. The quotation is preceded by the following commentary: 'Throughout the century ... the most moving and the most relevant of texts was the one written in exactly

1901 by the Cracovian artist and dramatist Stanisław Wyspiański' (2001: 433).

2   The persistence of this thematic topos in Polish art was illustrated by the exhibition *Polonia*, organised at the 'Zachęta' Gallery of Modern Art in Warsaw in 2000.

3   The theme of a wounded insurgent hidden at the manor house by a noblewoman is the main theme in Stefan Żeromski's novel *The Faithful River* (*Wierna rzeka*).

4   Tadeusz Konwicki ends his novel on a realistic note. Wicio wakes up at home to find out that Alina is in military hospital. At the very end of the book, the protagonist hears another alert for an air-raid. It is thus only a suggestion of the image with which Wajda concludes his film.

5   'Sweet flag, which in some parts of Poland is also called the Tartar weed, has two smells. If you rub its long green leaves between your fingers, you will release the gentle scent of "waters shadowed by willows", slightly reminiscent of Oriental nard. But when you tear open a strip of sweet flag and put your nose to the seam lined with a kind of woolly fluff, you will sense, along with the musky scent, the smell of marshy loam, of rotting fish scales, of mud.' Jarosław Iwaszkiewicz, 'Sweet Flag', in Maria Kuncewicz (ed.) (1963) *The Modern Polish Mind: An Anthology*. New York: Grosset & Dunlop, 172–9.

6   Wajda repeated this idea almost verbatim at the Academy Awards ceremony when, after the introductory 'Ladies and Gentlemen' in English, he switched to Polish, 'I will speak Polish because I want to say what I think, and I always think in Polish' (2000c: 299).

7   I borrowed this phrase from Grażyna Stachówna, who used it in her paper 'The Chronicle of Love Accidents According to Andrzej Wajda', delivered at the 'Cinema and Theatre of Andrzej Wajda' conference, Łódź, October 2001.

CHAPTER FIVE

Changing Meanings of Home and Exile: From Ashes and Diamonds to Pan Tadeusz

Izabela Kalinowska

Many east-central European societies, including Poland, bear traces of traumatic events that often separated people from their homes, and irrevocably removed them from their homelands. The psychological dimension of such dislocations often proves to be just as important as the actual physical distance that separates refugees and emigrants from their native lands. Home remains beyond the caesura of trauma, which compels the mind to remember the traumatic loss but also further complicates the prospects of a return. Such circumstances facilitate the creation of mythologised images of home. This essay traces the passage from the homeland lost to a representation of a home regained within the cinematic oeuvres of Andrzej Wajda, a film-maker whose work has rightly been characterised as that of the 'essential Pole' (Michałek 1988: 129).

World War Two provides the necessary starting point for any consideration of Polish culture of the second half of the twentieth century, and for the analysis of Wajda's work in particular. Between 1939 and 1945, the Polish lands were subjected to the most extreme forms of foreign exploitation and abuse. As Wajda records in his autobiography, right after the war 'Poland started tallying war-related losses, and the truth of this matter turned out to be more horrifying than the worst expectations had been' (2000a: 35). The immensity of wartime destruction would be for many years a constant reminder of the disappearance of the world as it once had existed. The trauma of the war coupled with the political realities of post-war Poland created a situation where a condition similar to exile affected not only those who settled outside of Poland but also those who remained in Poland.[1] These circumstances have found their reflection in post-war Polish culture, including Polish cinematography. The compulsion to relive the wounding experience of the war underlies all of the most remarkable films of the Polish school of cinematography, including *Ashes and Diamonds* (*Popiół i diament*, 1958). Moreover, a tension between the sacred, mythical space of a lost home and various places of transit and impermanence characterises later Wajda films as well.

Tadeusz Lubelski identifies the pain that results from an individual's severance from myth ('utrata mitu') as the most significant theme of *Ashes and Diamonds*. 'It's the abandonment of myth that makes the real world into a place of eternal exile, where an individual has no chance of regaining the lost values' (2000: 174). Lubelski's insight invites further interrogation of the relationship between the myths and the losses that underlie both the story itself and the way in which it is told in *Ashes and Diamonds*. What, more specifically, are the film's protagonists longing for? Does this longing itself represent a constituent element of the myths born as a result of sustained losses? Does the disappearance of either a physical home or the rituals and traditions connected with it give rise to myths of original wholeness that subsequently adorn once real and existing places with the aura of the sacred? Wajda fills the empty space of a former home with his characters' and ultimately his own longing for that home. Amidst rising pressure exerted by the outside world to forget whatever lies in the past, the film-maker makes sure that the myth of the lost home lives on in this and his other films.

The opening sequence of *Ashes and Diamonds* establishes a tension between spaces sacred (and inaccessible) and profane. On the one hand, we see the chapel located at the top of the hill, and, on the other, we see the lower part of the grassy knoll where Maciek (Zbigniew Cybulski) and Andrzej (Adam Pawlikowski) await the arrival of Szczuka's car. The film opens with a shot of the cross-bearing chapel roof. Within the same shot the camera begins to tilt down gradually to include the two assassins, stretched on the grass. While the roof of the chapel rises vertically towards the skies, by the time we get to the two male figures we cannot see much of the horizon. The spatial arrangement evokes medieval iconography, with its clear vertical delineation between heaven, earth and hell. The fate of the young men appears to be tragically predetermined. The ants that invade Maciek and walk all over his gun in one of the following shots provide another earthbound element, an unwanted link to the grassy plot of land where he has been resting, to a profane space. The space of the chapel opens up in the assassination sequence, when the door gives way to the banging of the worker searching for a place to escape the assassins' bullets. Pierced by a series from Maciek's machine gun, the worker falls down into the chapel. Maciek's close-range gunfire sets his victim's clothing ablaze. This fire stands between the Home Army fighters and the inner space of the chapel. Just as the fiery revolving sword placed by the God of the Old Testament at the entrance to Eden, the fire here may be taken to signify banishment. Lubelski notes that in *Ashes and Diamonds* Wajda used relatively few point-of-view shots and thereby privileged an authorial perspective (2000: 161). The following shot from within the chapel may illustrate the point. It does not belong to any of the characters: the film-maker usurps this kind of perspective to situate Andrzej and Maciek outside the space of the sacred. The young men's confinement to a space profane that was already suggested to the viewer in the first shot is thus confirmed. The shot of the ploughed land with the farmer emerging left of centre injects still another spatial dimension into the film's symbolic geography. Without a path in sight, timelessness and purity infuse this picture of the tilled soil. The shot privileges the texture of the soil over the visually insignificant figure of the worker. This is not just any stretch of land. If this diegetically unmotivated rustic landscape contains the symbol of sacred national soil, then the field as national space emerges parallel to the chapel. As a result, national space becomes coterminous with sacred space. Like the sacred space of the chapel, the field remains off limits for the fighters. In the film's conclusion, the barren wasteland of the dump and not the plowed field provides the final resting-place for Maciek. In a broader cultural sense, Maciek and Andrzej represent post-war Poland in general. The war has rendered them homeless, and Soviet domination will prevent them from rebuilding their home. The only place left for them to inhabit is the hotel.

In 'Traveling Cultures', James Clifford defines the hotel as a metaphor of his own discipline, contemporary cultural analysis. He cites other texts that rely on the same metaphor to describe modernity, quoting Joseph Conrad. The first passage of *Victory* refers to 'the age in which we are encamped like bewildered travelers in a garish, unrestful hotel'. He then continues:

In *Tristes Tropiques*, Levi-Strauss evokes an out-of-scale concrete cube sitting in the midst of the new Brazilian city of Goiania in 1937. It's his symbol of civilisation's barbarity, 'a place of transit, not of residence'. The hotel as station, airport terminal, hospital: a place you pass through, where the encounters are fleeting, arbitrary. (Clifford 1997: 17)

In Wajda's film the hotel provides a fitting metaphor for the all-embracing homelessness of post-war Poland.

People who, in one sense or another, have been exiled populate the landscape of *Ashes and Diamonds*. The events presented in the film take place in a provincial Polish town, but most of the characters Wajda introduces into the plot have either arrived at the town from elsewhere, or are about to leave it. Significantly, most of the film's action does take place in a hotel, the epitome of transience. Maciek and Andrzej come from Warsaw. They were forced to flee the city after the defeat of the Warsaw uprising. Similar displacements have affected most of the people whom they encounter. Maciek is able to befriend the hotel's porter (Jan Ciecierski) thanks to his Warsaw background: both of them come from that city, they share the experience of having lived through the war there, and of having to abandon it. The tranquil beauty of the barmaid Krystyna (Ewa Krzyżewska) conceals memories of painful war experiences and losses that may never be compensated. She tells Maciek of her background: born and raised on a country estate in Western Poland, she lost her parents during the war. Given what she has been through, we understand why Krystyna fears new commitments. Even though she is able to overcome this fear, all-embracing uprootedness tragically dooms her relationship with Maciek. The communist Szczuka (Wacław Zastrzeżynski) also joins the gallery of Wajda's 'homeless' protagonists. The ideological 'home' of his youth, the time of the Spanish civil war, is now just a distant memory. The central position of the hotel in Wajda's film predetermines the character of human relationships in the world of *Ashes and Diamonds* – to the extent that such relationships are at all possible. It is here, at the hotel, that we witness the mingling of representatives of different social groups and adherents of various political orientations. But people do not get a chance to get to know one another. They meet, they engage in small talk, and they part.

Only one home has been left standing in the world of *Ashes and Diamonds*. The remnants of the town's pre-war high society gather in the apartment of Mrs Staniewicz (Halina Kwiatkowska). A medium close-up of Mrs Staniewicz introduces this social milieu to the viewers. In the background we see a huge uniformed portrait of a cavalry officer and, at the side of Mrs Staniewicz, a servant polishing a saber. The 'patriotic kitsch' (Lubelski 2000: 163) of the *mise-en-scène* in this sequence presents the cultivation of a lifestyle at odds with the surrounding. The old elite still drinks tea from fine china and uses titles to address one another. At the same time, aware of their status of unwelcome remnants of a time past, these people are just waiting for the summons from Mrs. Staniewicz's husband, who is already in the West, to leave Poland. Aural effects, the tremor of the china and the screeching of the wardrobe doors that will not stay closed, suggest that the stability of this home is a mere illusion. Thus, even this place, 'the only respite from the world out there', as one of the visitors puts it, is not only grotesquely out of step with the surrounding reality. It is also about to be abandoned. For most of the film's protagonists, home is consistently marked as absent in *Ashes and Diamonds*. Moreover, Maciek's death on the city dump eradicates any hope of a return.

Occasionally, the film-maker does scrutinise some of the myths of a lost homeland that he himself reasserts or creates. One of the films that interrogate a worldview determined by the ostensible nationalism of the dispossessed, *Landscape After Battle* (*Krajobraz po bitwie*, 1970) deserves mention in the context of Wajda's symbolic geography. The film continues the theme of an individual's homelessness in a world devastated by war. At the same time, Wajda appears to be skeptical of any efforts to provide simple solutions to the dilemma of the lost home. This skepticism speaks at first through the film's main protagonist, Tadeusz (Daniel Olbrychski). Once liberated from a German concentration camp and confined to an American-operated Displaced Persons camp, he resists participation in the 'national mystery'. He will not march to the nationalist tune. Unlike a fellow inmate who simply rejects the 'national cause' in order to help build a communist Poland, Tadeusz does not readily embrace this option either. Even though he is not bound by party politics, he is still a captive of an 'in-between'. 'This is still quarantine. This is neither a concentration camp nor freedom', says Tadeusz to Nina (Stanisława Celińska), a young woman who ran away from Poland and who becomes his main interlocutor in the film. Like much of post-war Polish culture, Tadeusz is caught up in the circle of reliving the traumatic experience of the war. Moreover, in Tadeusz, the realms of individual experience and of textual culture clearly intersect. Wajda's viewers easily recognised those of Tadeusz's monologues that were drawn from the most poignant and memorable fragments of Tadeusz Borowski's concentration camp stories. Ultimately, Tadeusz turns out to be fettered by his identification with national traditions. When encouraged by Nina to leave everything behind and to begin a new life, he chooses to define himself through the relationship to his place of origin and its culture: 'People, the language, we cannot have that individually. Not even as a couple.'

Nina, who, as a fellow traveller describes her, 'escaped from the living body of the nation', feels no allegiance either to her Polish or her Jewish heritage. She looks forward to a life free from the burden of past traumas and liberated from the constraints of a group identity determined either by religion or by nationalism. In *Ashes and Diamonds*, Maciek had expressed hope for finding such freedom when talking to Krystyna among the ruins of the church. But, in the end he decided to stay true to vaguely defined loyalties. This decision resulted in his death. In *Landscape After Battle*, Tadeusz's choice spells a death sentence for Nina who, just like the protagonist of *Ashes and Diamonds*, perishes from a senselessly fired bullet. This fatalistic commentary on the young woman's search for a third way leads to the conclusion that no such option exists: once you have lost your homeland, you will forever be consumed by the loss. The one-dimensional presentation of the American officers and soldiers further undermines the more nuanced consideration of the complexities of an individual's relationship to the lost homeland. Wajda relies on a negative stereotype of the Americans to communicate the uniqueness and complexity of the East Central European experience and its inaccessibility to outsiders. But, as often happens with the simple divisions of people into 'us' and 'them', this contrast is too strong.

Unlike both *Ashes and Diamonds* and *Landscape After Battle*, in *Promised Land* (*Ziemia obiecana*, 1974) the main protagonist's place of origin, the home of his father and his forefathers, does enter the picture. In the film's original version, the first ten minutes devoted to the Kurów sequence raise the question of the status of that home. In the world of the film, the manor house exists and it still belongs to the Borowieckis. The intricately structured opening sequence is subdivided into two parts: the morning/mid-day part and the evening tea and return to the manor house. The latter ends with a conversation between the older Borowiecki (Tadeusz Białoszczyński) and his son Karol (Daniel Olbrychski). The passage from day to night within the sequence signals that the sun over Kurów is setting. An ominous fog begins to envelop the house and its environs. As the priest (Aleksander Dzwonkowski), a friend of the family, boards his carriage at the end of the day he promises to come to Łódź to bless the factory, to marry Borowiecki and Anka, and to baptise their child. Even though we hear his voice, his figure is shrouded in darkness. The old way of life is subsiding. The priest will look strangely out of place when blessing Karol's new factory. And that will be the last occasion for the two to interact. Karol has no desire to remain true to the centuries-old family traditions. He is very open about this in the conversation with his father; 'I have to be free from the past, from the gentry traditions ... Only the man who himself incorporates the past, the present and the future can succeed.'

Paradoxically, the allure of Polish gentry's traditions as well as his business acumen attracts Maks (Andrzej Seweryn), Moryc (Wojciech Pszoniak) and even the old Müller (Franciszek Pieczka) to Karol Borowiecki. As Maks, infatuated with Anka (Anna Nehrebecka), Karol's fiancée, states in his conversation with her: 'Since I started coming to Kurów, I can understand the Poles better. Your life is so quiet, so simple, somehow superior.' The *mise-en-scène* here is reminiscent of the Staniewicz apartment in *Ashes and Diamonds*. Yet similar elements of the interior (a portrait of Kościuszko, a saber) carry different connotations. Gone is the negative coloring of a space filled with patriotic props that we saw in the earlier film. The gentry home in *Promised Land* is no longer a domain of strangers. Rather, it emerges as a repository of family and national traditions. It is a sacred place, presided over by the virginal Anka. Thanks to this interesting shift, Wajda transforms the Polish manor house into *our home*, that is, the lost home of the post-war Polish intelligentsia. The sequence that presents the world of the manor house and the following morning in the city is stylistically very different. In the Kurów sequence, the camera moves in smooth panoramic shots, beginning with the opening pan of the birch forest that gradually includes the three friends riding their bicycles. The camera moves from left to right, suggesting a movement backwards. Karol returns home, to his family. At the same time, the diachronic dimension of the camera's movement takes the viewers beyond the film's diegesis. Wajda presents a nostalgic recreation of the Polish manor house; a mythical world of original wholeness which, from the perspective of the 1960s and 1970s Poland – the time of the project's inception and of the film's making – had long since ceased to exist (Lubelski 1997: 18). Within the world of the film neither Anka nor the older Borowiecki will be able to defend the old world against the encroachments of the world 'out there'. Łódź soon overwhelms the manor house. As Paul Coates has pointed out: 'The shifting of the idyllic opening of volume two [of the novel] to the film's beginning makes the subsequent passage to Łódź seem like an expulsion from Eden' (1997: 224).

Partha Chatterjee argues that anticolonial nationalism creates its own domain of sovereignty within colonial society:

It does this by dividing the world of social institutions and practices into two domains – the material and the spiritual. The material is the domain of the 'outside', of the economy and of statecraft, of science and technology (a domain where the West had proved its superiority and the East had succumbed) ... The spiritual, on the other hand, is an 'inner' domain bearing the 'essential' marks of cultural identity. (1993: 6)

She claims that the greater one's success in mastering the material domain, 'the greater the need to preserve the distinctness of one's spiritual culture' (*ibid.*). In *Promised Land*, the young Borowiecki cuts himself off from the 'inner' domain. He refuses to integrate the national/family past into the present, which is determined by the 'outside'. Contrary to his character, Wajda demonstrates a need to emphasise the distinctness of the manor house because of the pressures exerted by the 'outside'. It is quite ironic that communist decision-makers considered the film to be consistent with their own ideological dictates (Lubelski 1997: 18). In *Cinema and the Rest of the World* (*Kino i reszta świata*, 2000a), Wajda discusses an alternative ending of *Promised Land*, and one which he would not have been able to film – according to his own testimony – because of political censorship. In this ending that never was, Borowiecki travels by train to Moscow (2000a: 161); clearly, according to the director's intentions, by betraying the traditions represented by his family home, Borowiecki becomes a traitor to the national cause.

Ewelina Nurczyńska-Fidelska rightly points out that in *Promised Land*,

in the realist space of the city, a mythical reality is born – a myth of the city and the people who are obsessed with the city. The inhabitants of the 'promised land' live in the space of material reality, but the story of their lives transcends the realism of the description and assumes the form of a myth, a parable. (1998: 143)

Indeed, Kurów engenders pure myth. In contrast, the film's Łódź sequences portray a reality that is easily translated into a parable. If Kurów stands for paradise lost, Łódź represents the domain of spiritual estrangement. The notorious impermanence of industrial Łódź finds its fitting centre in the theatre, which here takes the place of the hotel from *Ashes and Diamonds*. Actors appear and disappear from the stage; nothing is permanent. The familiar life-as-a-stage metaphor gains a new lease of life in Wajda's picture. The film-maker complicates the usual pattern of theatre/cinema gazing: in addition to the gaze directed from the audience to the stage, the film-maker has the diegetic theatre spectators ogle other members of the audience. Moreover, the actress who is swinging on the stage 'appropriates' two point-of-view shots. The unstable, nearly nauseating 'looks' she casts from the moving swing add to the general feeling of instability. Interestingly, characters derive knowledge and power not only from looking but also from their role as the object of the gaze. To be looked at in Łódź means to exist. In place of the permanence of home, Łódź offers an illusory, theatre-like setting, and an existence whose fleeting character can best be compared to a stage appearance.

In *The Young Ladies of Wilko* (*Panny z Wilka*, 1979), Wajda remains true to the theme of the lost home, but he also demonstrates that his musings on the subject do indeed have a supra-national, existential dimension. In this instance 'home' also remains beyond the caesura of a trauma, that is, Wiktor Ruben's (Daniel Olbrychski) war experience. Like its literary source, the film deals more generally with questions of human relationships, the passing of time, and of memory. The narrated thoughts of the story's protagonist sum up the subject of both the story and the film: 'He was engulfed by a simple and dazzling feeling of nostalgic pity. Pity for everything that passes and floats away. For everything that one can only see from a certain perspective, like a boat disappearing behind a river bend' (Iwaszkiewicz 2001: 85). As presented in the film, the visualised, multilayered process of remembering has very familiar characteristics. Both the opening shots of Iwaszkiewicz himself, pausing over the graves seen by candle light on All Saints' Day, and Wiktor Ruben's revisitation of the manor house in Wilko create a specifically and nostalgically Polish landscape. Ruben's attempt to resurrect the immediacy of his Wilko experience fails. And, again, unlike his protagonist, the film-maker does not abandon his own effort to recreate and re-inhabit the lost home. In *The Young Ladies of Wilko* the careful reconstruction of an authentic setting attests to this effort. As Wajda remembers:

> Allan Starski [set designer] had taken me for a drive to a small place far away from Warsaw where I saw a dilapidated and not particularly pretty house which, according to Allan, was a dream location ideally suited to fulfil every hope I cherished in connection with the film … His chief argument was that the house was still inhabited, the traces of bygone times still lingered there, waiting for us to bring them back to life. And he was right. (2000d: 144).

The 1999 adaptation of Adam Mickiewicz's *Pan Tadeusz* forms the next stage of Wajda's cinematic quest for the lost home. More precisely, this film marks the journey's point of arrival. Superficially so seamless and 'glossy' that it could rival any Hollywood production, *Pan Tadeusz* continues the author's dialogue with Poland's past and present. Wajda does not merely tell the story

My old country home: *The Young Ladies of Wilko*

of Tadeusz's return home. The film-maker invites his audience to revisit a text central to modern Polish culture and thereby to return to the place of that culture's origin. According to Wajda's own account: 'I felt now that after nearly ten years of freedom the moment had arrived to try and answer the following questions. Where have we come from? Who are we? Where are we headed?' (2000a: 314). Mickiewicz, who spent most of his life in exile, wrote *Pan Tadeusz* in order to resurrect, in the lines of the poem, his long-lost Lithuanian home. Wajda recreates this home visually in order to appropriate it for himself and – by extension – also for his viewers. He ponders this aspect of his relationship to Mickiewicz in his autobiography:

> If one wants to understand the poet, one has to visit the poet's homeland. But is the place where the action of *Pan Tadeusz* takes place the homeland of just Mickiewicz? The debates concerning this issue are never going to cease because the place is the land of one's childhood. … I can say about myself that I was born in the land of Mickiewicz. Suwałki belongs de facto to Lithuania. (2000a: 315)

Wajda frames *Pan Tadeusz* with scenes in which a character representing Mickiewicz (Krzysztof Kolberger) reads fragments of the poem. The dominant colors of these exilic scenes are black, different shades of gray and brown. In the 'hired' Parisian apartment, we see the weary profiles of the protagonists of the story proper. In another one of the exilic incursions the camera focuses on the 'author's' shoes. The shoes communicate displacement. They connote the distance traveled, as well as a whole range of mostly negative phenomena commonly associated with displacement (as opposed to travel for pleasure). In the film's opening sequence, the exiles close the windows and the doors to their apartment in order to separate themselves from the hustle and bustle of the Parisian street. They close themselves off from the foreign surroundings of the present in order to remember the familiar environment of the past. 'Mickiewicz's' voice provides a bridge to the past for both the diegetic audience and for Wajda's viewers. The dark hues of the scenes of exile subside to make room for the amazing spectacle of colour and light displayed in the recreation of the lost home in the film's story proper.

The position occupied by home as opposed to a temporary residence, a place where impermanence dominates, becomes in *Pan Tadeusz* the reverse of what we have seen in *Promised Land*. In the case of *Pan Tadeusz*, home is not pushed out of the picture by exile but the other way round. Exile exists as a necessary point of reference but the spectacle of the revisited home visually overpowers exile. Wajda celebrates his *home*land in a number of ways. The display of the simple beauty of the rolling hills and the fields Tadeusz passes on his way home, the charm of the luscious green of the forest in the sequence following the hunt, to cite just a couple of examples, transcend diegesis and valorise native landscape. The dialogue between Tadeusz (Michał Żebrowski) and the Count (Marek Kondrat) in which the former defends the value of the native birch forest against the Count's assertions about the superiority of Italian landscapes provides another type of such valorisation. Wajda transforms the story of Tadeusz's return home into a celebration of the place to which he returns. The clearly marked exilic perspective explains the preeminence of idealised images of home in the picture. No wonder Wajda communicated so well with Polish audiences outside of Poland. One of the most interesting cases of an audience's reaction to a film I have ever observed was at a screening of *Pan Tadeusz* for a predominantly Polish audience in New Haven, Connecticut, soon after the film's American premiere. At times the film resonated so well with the feelings of the audience – socially diverse yet, on this occasion, united by its Polishness – that one could sense the tidal waves of emotion sweeping the auditorium. For many of the viewers, no doubt, the film provided a way of reestablishing a link to the lost home. These reactions left a group of American college students who were in the audience somewhat baffled.

Postcolonial theorists have frequently voiced concerns about the potentially reactionary character of the postcolonial subject's efforts to recuperate the pre-colonial past. 'Does revisiting the repositories of memory and cultural survivals in the cause of postcolonial refashioning have a fixed retrograde valency?' asks Benita Parry (1997: 86). The same question obtains relevance in the context of Central and East European societies' attempts to recover their 'lost' homelands. Such tales of origin are characteristic of the period following the political transformations of the early 1990s. Before we judge them to be retrograde, we should consider the status and content of these retrospective projects. *Pan Tadeusz* does not advocate the restoration of archaic social structures. Wajda's return home is curative rather than retaliatory in character: the visual reconstruction of home cures nostalgia. In *Promised Land*, 'others' were implicated in the disappearance of 'our' world. The two peasants-turned-entrepreneurs, Wilczek (Wojciech Siemion) and Karczmarek (Zdzisław Kuźniar), descend upon defenseless Kurów like vultures. Borowiecki's Jewish mistress contrasts with the 'native' ideal of femininity embodied by Anka (see Ostrowska 2000). In contrast, in *Pan Tadeusz*, the Polish gentry's world is both, colorful and desirable but, at the same time, quite ugly in its details. From the perspective of someone who is slightly on the outside, such as the innkeeper Jankiel (Władysław Kowalski) or the exiled 'author', the nobles' quarrels and the often-violent squabbles make no sense, and they bring disastrous results. By incorporating an exilic frame into the film, Wajda follows in Mickiewicz's footsteps and positions himself as an author at a distance. This attitude enables the film-maker both to appreciate native difference and to evaluate critically the world that bears the seeds of its own eradication. In *Pan Tadeusz*, the 'inbetweenness' that hangs like a curse over the main protagonists of *Ashes and Diamonds*, *Landscape After Battle*, and, to some extent, *Promised Land* and *The Young Ladies of Wilko* becomes a much appreciated home for the present. The past no longer casts a shadow. Instead, it becomes a wellspring for a positive redefinition of identity. The myth of a home regained replaces the myth of a home lost.

Notes

1   I analyse the dependencies between modern Polish cinema and exile at greater length in 'Exile and Polish Cinema: From Mickiewicz and Slowacki to Kieślowski', in Dominika Radulescu (ed.) (2002) *Realms of Exile, Nomadism, Diasporas, and Eastern European Voices*. Lexington Books: New York, 107–24.

CHAPTER SIX

Wajda's Filmic Representation of Polish-Jewish Relations

Michael Stevenson

The primary task of this essay is to discuss the ways in which Andrzej Wajda undertook, as one of his major tasks, the representation of Polish-Jewish relations. This was not a unique undertaking but was, and remains, rare in Polish cinema both before 1989 and since, and Wajda was often at the controversial heart of these matters. From the beginning of his work, there is an evident concern to trace a range of ways of understanding Polish-Jewish relations drawing upon either familiar pre-Holocaust narratives from Polish Literature (for example, in his reworkings of *The Wedding* (*Wesele*, 1972), *Promised Land* (*Ziemia obiecana*, 1974) and *Pan Tadeusz*, 1999) or which directly represent Holocaust experience (*A Generation* (*Pokolenie*, 1954), *Samson* (1961), *Landscape After Battle* (*Krajobraz po bitwie*, 1970), *Korczak* (1990) and *Holy Week* (*Wielki Tydzień*, 1995)). These films include some of Wajda's most significant work but have also often been seen, both in Poland and abroad, as amongst Wajda's most problematic, because of their particular concern to open up the ethical problems of national memory and loss. Scenes of such anxieties in these films range from the most intimate (sexual relations between Nina, the Jewish girl, and Tadeusz, the Polish poet, in *Landscape*

After Battle) to the most public (Polish, Jewish and German economic relations in *Promised Land*). Sometimes, particularly in the case of *Korczak*, such representation has raised a fury of dissent and has, perhaps inevitably given the context, never been less than contentious. Wajda's serious intentions in this field of representation ensured that his films insisted upon a continuing attention to these problems that yet remain unresolved. In this essay I wish to show that Wajda was concerned from the very beginning, in his first film, *A Generation*, and in subsequent work, to insist on the centrality of these issues for the Nation. I will concentrate mainly on Wajda's use of these systems of meaning in his first film and then refer to other texts as they further exemplify the problems in the undertaking of this task.

A Generation begins this complex engagement with representations of Polish-Jewish relationships. Critically it is a rather neglected work in Poland, not seen favourably in relation to later, more sophisticated, material. However, I believe it lays out the key elements of his concerns. Polish critics seem to find it odd that there should be any extended interest in this first directorial task. Perhaps rightly, they see it as much too caught up in the politics of the mid-1950s – far too trapped by the strictures of the State film apparatus that was deeply engaged in attempting to control the film especially at its release stage (see Fogler 1996a: 30–7). It is worth remembering that the film very nearly did not get exhibited at all because it so offended the State censors, and that several scenes had to be either re-shot or were excised altogether. Something of the vehement, frantic and apparently nihilistic brutality of some of the scenes and the film's constant intersection with issues of Love and Polishness certainly offended (Michałek 1973: 128–30). A first line of defence of the film would be that Wajda was already a thorn in the side of the authorities, already occupying a negotiating space between the demands of the new State apparatus and Polish history and the still continuing struggles for real independence. This supposedly socialist realist work, with its task of servicing propagandistic needs, clearly contained something at odds with the prescriptive intentions of the State. But it is more important at this point to discuss those scenes, albeit few in number, that are crucial in setting up Polish-Jewish systems of representation to be explored in some detail in later work. In fact these particular scenes were also those that were one of the elements of the film that state censorship found most problematic. For example, one of the scenes finally cut made direct reference to the Holocaust and Polish relations to it. In it Stach, the young working-class hero of *A Generation*, meets a scavenger outside a cemetery with an oddly bulging sack containing the hacked-off heads of corpses. They have been grave-robbed for their gold fillings (Michałek

1973: 21). Wajda's scene would have insisted on contemplating the possibility that a Pole could do such a thing – much too negative a scene of recent history to be allowed in the new certainties of a Stalinist Poland.

But other scenes that have the task of initiating descriptions of Polish-Jewish relationships were allowed to remain in the film. Even in this first film there is already a template of meaning in them allowing a complex debate to emerge. There are four of these scenes, part of an extended segment in the middle of the film. The segment as a whole is also strongly book-ended by two of them that become key moments in the film. The four scenes are those italicised below:

1. *Stach's ride to the woodyard and his humiliation.*
2. Return to the factory. The hidden guns.
3. The killing of the Werkschutz guard.
4. Jasio's home.
5. The bicycle ride to Dorota's flat. Stach and Dorota spend the evening together.
6. *The Ghetto Uprising 1. Sekuła and the 'Fighting Youth Group'.*
7. *Uprising 2. At the factory. Stach versus Ziarno and Jasio.*
8. *Uprising 3. Abram at Jasio's home.*

These scenes mark a sharp descent into a more serious engagement with the difficulties of resistance from the problems of personal commitment, to the more general task of organisation. The first of the four key scenes is a rite of passage for Stach. As yet he has not been faced with, is not as yet fully aware of the crushing and relentless pressure of, the Occupation. A key scene then follows in which Jasio, another young man, witnesses exemplary street hangings. Here Wajda adopts a Brechtian use of the double in the figures of Stach and Jasio that allows a stress on the contradictions of resistance to emerge through character polarities: innocent/aware; impetuous/dubious; cheerful/morose etc. Jasio's pessimism, subsequent on this terror, produces his refusal to join the group of Fighting Youth and immediately precedes the exhilaratingly optimistic ride to the woodyard. Now we hear, for the last time in the film, Andrzej Markowski's musical theme that has been a marker of Stach's optimism. We are with Stach on his cart looking over the backs of the two horses. He calls out to them, encourages them. It is a superb moment of release, of excitement, of youthfulness untrammelled by threat. Then, in six shots, there is the sharpest descent possible into darkness. This is Wajda's very first direct representation of the Holocaust. Stach brakes the cart and swings under a viaduct as he sees a group of Jews with the Star of David on their arms, marching left, being whipped, heads down with spades over their shoulders. Stach's cart brakes even more sharply, and he looks back at the Jews as they disappear. A flock of doves flies up between the two groups, marking the planes of action with both a physical and moral separation.

In this way *A Generation* is a very direct film. This gestic lucidity becomes one of the central organising principles of the film. The ride to the woodyard expresses a boundless exuberance and a naïveté that is abruptly deflated in the face of relentless pressure. The scene continues at some length to underline this fall into a brutal reality and we are able to perceive the complex interaction of the subjective with the historical moment, and its implication for all Poles, both Jew and Gentile. These sharp contrasts in method have been noted before in Wajda's work, and have been wrongly described as baroque or expressionistic (Michałek 1973: 21). I would rather see this strategy as an attempt to demonstrate visually the acute and immediate nature of the contradictions to be faced, as they are to be later, in *Samson*, *Korczak* and elsewhere in Wajda's work. Stach's initial attitude is thus very like the naïve attempts of characters to do the good and right thing that we find in Brecht (*The Good Person of Szechwan* for example) and in Buñuel (*Viridiana*, 1961, is probably the most well-known example but it is a central Buñuelian pattern in many of his films). Do something to change things, to resist, but this will never be equal to the magnitude, the seeming impossibility of the task. For Buñuel this was a pattern to be represented and related to the epic time of a class, the bourgeoisie, within the general Western experience. The balance for Wajda is rather more (as in Brecht) rooted in the historical, in the travail of Poland. Indeed it is in this way that the affinity between Buñuel and Wajda, as Buñuel indicates in his biography, must be understood.[1]

Two scenes follow that are intended to contrast with the ride. Both dwell on an idea of 'home' and its potential security. Firstly Jasio's home with his father's story of a violent past as a soldier in the service of the Tsar, followed by Stach and Dorota's ride on a bicycle back to her flat where there is a hint at a possible future for them together. There are, in general, few references to home in the course of the film. Home remains distant, a Polish dream almost mythically unattainable. Indeed it is difficult to find any examples of a settled home life in Wajda's films or in Polish cinema in general. As well as Dorota's flat and Jasio's life with his father there are only brief references to Stach's own home and his repressive mother and, at the end of the film, an ironic reference to an impossible ordinariness, when Stach visits a blasé young mother's shop after staying the night with Dorota and just as she is arrested by the Gestapo. In general, however, these references to home do not accumulate the iconic weight of a reference to the Polish mythos of a home that may be found in Wajda's *The Wedding*, for example, with its developed descriptions and struggle over issues of inclusiveness and exclusiveness. Yet, even so, it is striking that the scenes in *A Generation* that represent Polish-Jewish relations, at the time of greatest stress, are firmly interspersed with such potent images of home.

Now three key characters proclaim the beginning of the Ghetto Uprising of 1943, each giving a radically different tone to the announcement and requiring a different response. Firstly Sekuła meets Stach's small resistance group with Dorota as leader: 'The Jews rose today. I've come to say goodbye, to you, Dorota, and to my boys. Our Jewish comrades need help.' Here we are given a rather solemn but moving sense of solidarity, no doubt, fully acceptable in the politics of 1955, slightly redolent of a romantic and martyred optimism, still failing to represent the enormity of the task to be faced. The camera is close to the group and they listen to one of the few Good Fathers (as rare as stable images of home) in Wajda's work. Made 'good', of course, partly by the political exigencies of the political conjuncture of the 1950s. But, still, to be usefully contrasted with the considerable range of other, much more complicitly cynical male figures in the film.

The rather pious solemnity of the group of Fighting Youth is followed by an announcement of the uprising in complete opposition, as 'Bloody Ziarno' enters the factory next morning. He announces, 'Have you heard? The Jews have declared war on Jerry', concluding with a contemptuous anti-semitic gesture. His fellow workers immediately rebuff him: 'What's so funny, we'll be next.' At this point Stach, yet again, exhorts Jasio to help the group to support the Ghetto Rising. Jasio pathetically excuses himself – 'I'm a civilian', he says, as he sharpens one of his wood-working tools. These scenes are very short and could be seen as driven merely by narrative concerns. Yet their placement in the narrative structure directly up against each other, and inserted into a relation to an ideological notion of the fragility of the Polish Home, adds to a growing understanding of a historical relationship to Jews as quite distinctive and special yet with constant pressure on this affiliation.

The segment as a whole ends with the most difficult scene, the culmination and synthesis of these exchanges. The difficulty is not in the overt meaning of the scene, which is straightforwardly and directly Jasio's betrayal of a childhood friend who has once shared his home. Rather the importance is in its structural position at the end of these four isolated moments of Polish-Jewish representation in the film. Here we are given a key character, Abram, who only

Fine young partisans: *A Generation*

appears in this scene and nowhere else. This separation makes it a weighted and purposeful scene in itself, a kind of narrative break. The interruptive force of Abram is only 'for itself', even if the spectator experiences a disruption, a disorientation in the narrative flow. And, of course, it is crucial to the narrative purpose that he returns to Jasio, the wavering and uncertain young Pole, with his terrified sensitivity to and awareness of the weight of present difficulty.

It is evening at Jasio's house. Once again he is working at his 'career' as a carpenter, apparently practising his fretwork. At this opening of the scene he breaks his blade, a tiny actorly gesture suggesting a failure in his desperation to prove to himself that he must be a journeyman at all costs, 'just a civilian'. Abram approaches to make the third simple announcement, 'the Ghetto has risen'. He approaches the house in creeping evening shadows, accompanied by the singing of a traditional hymn by a group of Polish women, enacting a familiar Catholic Easter ritual. There is a faint knock on the door and Jasio opens it slowly. The creak of the door, the pace of the scene, has something of an agonised inevitability. There is a sense that we already know that a desperate rejection, a distancing and a refusal will occur. This is done through a series of close ups of the two young Poles, presumably brought up together, staring intently at each other. Abram explains why he has come in his desperation: 'I've come home, to our home, to you.' Jasio replies, 'I can't help', and Abram walks directly away. Jasio's father again insists that his son has done the right thing, 'You are right, keep out of it. You're a carpenter, not a hero', and instantly Jasio reverses his decision, goes to look for Abram, but too late. These morally decisive moments cannot bear such hesitation. Jasio will soon act in an entirely opposite way as he finally joins the Fighting Youth to go to his own martyrdom.

It is only as we consider these four moments together and see them as the beginnings of a complex moral response across the whole of Wajda's work to the histories of Polish-Jewish relations, that the final scene with Abram finally gains a crucial importance. Wajda is attempting even here at the earliest point to come to grips with one of the major themes to be tackled on many occasions in his later work. Few other films can be claimed as so determined in this task. Krzysztof Kieślowski's *Decalogue 8* (*Dekalog 8*, 1988) is one of the rare texts that join in this task of representation, in this case with an unsparingly fierce analysis of the 'ethical hell' of the dilemmas of Polish responsibility to Jews during the Holocaust first seen in this moment between Jasio and Abram.

This episode in Kieślowski returns to the debate opened up so sharply in *A Generation*. A woman professor of ethics at Warsaw University takes a class on ethical dilemmas. A visiting Jewish-American academic relates a story that has a strong analogy with Abram's visit to Jasio. A young Jewish girl is brought by a young Polish couple for protection and hiding. They renege on their promise to help, but for religious reasons. The child must have a christening certificate and a priest is waiting to provide one. The couple cannot now agree to go against their religious principles. They cannot bear false witness. The child (the visiting academic) and her guardian (the professor) leave. As in the Abram episode of *A Generation* a combination of religion, of the personal and of the terrors of the moment combine. Whether the couple are making the decision on strict moral grounds or as an excuse is not clear. The episode concludes with another link to Wajda's film. The two academics visit the childless husband of the wartime couple, now a widower. A tailor in Warsaw, he is played by Tadeusz Łomnicki, who is still recognisably like an older version of his role as Stach in *A Generation*. He refuses to discuss the events of 1943 with the American and she leaves. As he gazes out at the pair, who stand talking outside, the events of 1943 and the present (1987) conjoin. This gaze is one combining shame, regret, loss and all in a complex relation to specific Polish histories.[2]

By the completion of his trilogy (*A Generation*, *Kanal* (*Kanał*, 1957) and *Ashes and Diamonds* (*Popiół i diament*, 1958)) Wajda had become a key figure in the contemporary representation of an idea of Poland. He was a new leader in the task of describing and analysing the difficulties of achieving the many-generationed goal of a free Poland, in the immediate post-war period still not realised and still far off. Yet as an innovative guide in post-war thinking about the life of the nation, in his often-contentious address as to how to be a Pole, his project was by no means one of an idealised certainty. This task was then, and since the 1950s, a complex, varied and troubled engagement with national ideologies. In his 'Strip-tease Polonais' and in his 'scraping at the scabs of the Nation' (Michałek 1973: 133) he worked an interrogative and enquiring practice that engaged his deeply felt awareness of Polish contradictions. Nowhere is this more so than in his frequent return to the representation of Polish-Jewish relations. This was an unusual and contrary tendency in the face of Polish cultural production that frequently foregrounded and privileged those heroic processes that had protected the purity of the nation against insurmountable pressure. Wajda certainly joined in this tradition but also pointed to problems of exclusivity and inwardness that this sense of a martyred nation could potentially produce. Thus it is not surprising that Wajda has often seemed a contentious figure, at the same time as being lauded for his refined and complex attention to definitions of Nation.

For centuries, one component of debates about the nature of Polishness had been to do with the position in Poland of those Poles who were also Jews, whether assimilated, integrated or living ethnically and religiously, with a considerable degree of separation from the national mainstream.[3] It became clear that here was something of pressing importance in Wajda's work that was searching for an attention to this. His films were troubled by a kind of nagging sense of guilt over something not quite definable. Thus across his work he engaged with a notion of the 'Other', in a very Polish account of this process, and, in so doing, described a complex spectrum of problems of assimilation, integration and separation. I should add that I do not mean that this theme is being underplayed but rather that it exists as a highly problematic discourse, often seemingly disjunctive, even at odds with dominant themes. What is clear is that Wajda had become a leader in the Nation's representation of itself to itself, and that he was deeply concerned with one of its potentially most tendentious debates. This understanding of Wajda's work was paralleled and enhanced by work on Holocaust history and representation that necessarily interlocked with a critical commitment to Polish issues. The rising volume of such material post-1989 and its deepening complexity created a sense of a troubling intersection of concerns. Throughout, the forbidden and forbidding task of Polish-Jewish representation continued to be of importance to Wajda. In his attempts to negotiate the contradictions of these obdurate issues of responsibility and associated loss, no claim for success can be made in some attempt at a finality of explanation. Rather this thematic in a range of his films is a troubled and gnawing undercurrent filled with an anxious and uneasy doubt, yet always with a deepening sense of the need to continue this task.

This growing complexity in the representation of the Polish-Jewish nexus came from the changing nature of the films themselves. It was embodied particularly in a middle-period film, *Landscape After Battle*, in which there is the strong sense of the growing centrality of Wajda's concern to represent a detailed debate on Polish-Jewish issues and representations both historical and contemporary. Nonetheless, these concerns were complemented over the last ten years or so by an awareness of debates begun by Jan Błoński in January 1987 and made available in English by Antony Polonsky in his compilation *My Brother's Keeper* in 1990.[4]

As it is the central contention of this essay that Wajda demonstrated from the beginning of his work a need to open up the issues later so complexly articulated by Błoński and others, it would be useful at this point to briefly indicate the main contours of these arguments. The first point to be repeated is the problem that existed prior to Błoński's intervention, that there had been at a 'peculiar silence' up to this point since the end of the war thus disabling a national discussion of the Holocaust and thus any possibility of a reconciliation of these matters (Polonsky 1990: 54). There were a number of reasons for the silence, well recognised in Polonsky's introduction to *My Brother's Keeper*. The first and historically the most consciously understood is the attempt to suppress these issues on the part of a communist government of Poland for the purpose of ensuring the purity of the regime by ascribing anti-semitism to its enemies. Anti-semitism was merely a remnant of a capitalist past, now defeated. It was a symptom both of a pre-war Poland and of those groupings that had led the resistance during the War and in the 'Civil War' up to 1947. The enemy was Catholicism, Capitalism and falsified memories of the main resistance to Fascism, the Home Army. On the other hand, and linked with this process, was the perception on the part of the Polish people that the post-war regime had been imposed by Communist intellectuals many of whom were also Jewish. Elements of this complexity of forces conjoined in an ideological ferment that precluded any recognition of the importance of a Holocaust discussion for the future health and political plurality of the Nation. And despite the repudiation by the Catholic Church, in the encyclical *Nostra Aetate*, of its past anti-semitism, the notion of a need to give voice to the losses of the Holocaust did not emerge.[5]

But more significantly, the Błońskian proposition was formulated in relation to what he and others see as 'national psychological' problems resultant on the Holocaust. Błoński broadly contends, to put it most directly, that Poles bear some guilt for the Holocaust. Such a position is not at all obvious to many, especially as Christian Poles suffered so much during the Occupation and many resisted in the most dramatically heroic way. The incensed and contending responses to this, as well as those supportive of Błoński's position, although often with modification, is evident in the 15 essays included in the invaluable *My Brother's Keeper*. However, it should be said, that Błoński rather proposes a more indirect process of guilt and shame, one of inaction rather than commission. This must especially be so in that very few Poles collaborated directly, and then only at the lowest levels, with the perpetrators of the Holocaust in contradistinction to other occupied European countries with histories of anti-semitism. Błoński uses a poem by Czesław Miłosz, *A Poor Christian Looks at the Ghetto*, written in 1943. The poem is a direct response by the poet to his watching of the burning of the Ghetto at the end of the Jewish resistance in the Uprising, and it becomes the centrepiece of his argument about guilt and shame. For the title of his article Błoński changes, pluralises and generalises this into the national problem – *The Poor Poles Look at the Ghetto*. Błoński also uses another Miłosz poem, *Campo di Fiori*, to develop his argument. Both poems outline a Polish response of some neglect and indifference to those who should have been part of the Polish 'universe of obligation' (Polonsky 1990: 15). These poems enter into the long Christian tradition of images of indifference to suffering and to momentous events happening just beyond our consciousness in a kind of protective forgetting and blindness. From Biblical parables on this (the Good Samaritan) to Breughel's representation of the *Fall of Icarus* these images mark a familiar hesitation, fear and a turning away from our knowledge of responsibilities.[6] Wajda, in his Holocaust films, used such images and narrative patterns from the beginning. Two striking images from *Campo di Fiori* illustrate this, also directly linked to the 1943 Ghetto Uprising. In *A Generation*, a young Polish group come to the Ghetto to help. They meet at a fairground outside the Ghetto wall, as in the Miłosz poem:

a merry-go-round,
on a fair night in the spring
by the sound of vivacious music.
The salvoes behind the ghetto walls
Were drowned in lively tunes,
And vapours freely rose
Into the tranquil sky.

And later lines contain imagery very similar in intention and realisation to the scene in Wajda's *Holy Week* where ashes from the ghetto stain newly laundered sheets on a Polish mother's washing line.

> Sometimes the wind from burning houses
> would bring the kites along,
> and people on the merry-go-round
> caught the flying charred bits... (Miłosz 1996: 28–9)

Even more powerful connections are made in relation to *The Poor Christian Looks at the Ghetto* and, at an even more disturbing level, that of the Polish national consciousness. The poem centres on a returning Jewish 'guardian mole' hidden but always there in the back of the consciousness and coming back to judge Poles in the light of his 'Reading of the great book of the species'. Wajda's images of Jews waiting, watching, knowing and suspicious yet expectant of their Polish compatriots parallel this in all of his Holocaust films: Abram in *A Generation*, Jakub in *Samson*, Nina in *Landscape After Battle*, the little girl constantly wary of the Polish-Jewish love story in *Korczak*, Jankiel in *Pan Tadeusz*, Irena in *Holy Week*, and though not a Holocaust film, a key image of the ghostly emergence of Rachela into *The Wedding* which is itself a narrative microcosm of Poland. In all cases the implications of these images relate to the paradigm of the possibility of a shared and protected Polish life, in the Nation, the Home and even in (perhaps most especially) the chronicles of inter communal love stories which can never quite end in a full joining of a Pole and a Jew in marriage.[7]

Many others entered into these debates initiated consciously in Poland by Błoński and prefigured in Wajda's visual and narrative systems. Indeed, post-Lanzmann's *Shoah* (1985), with all of his strictures on responsibility in Holocaust representation, a similar debate about guilt was developing more generally across Europe with a developing intensity. Błoński's intervention into this fraught arena is no coincidence coming as it did as the Nation began to perceive new possibilities of freedom. Such a moment, if it were to be a mature new beginning for Poles (and it is striking how mature the processes of the Solidarity period were in contrast to earlier uprisings) would need to encompass much in redefinitions and reappraisals of the old, as well as accommodations with the new. One component of this was a coming to terms with Polish relations to the Holocaust and to Polish-Jewish relations in general. Thus, latterly, Wajda's films needed to be critically rethought in order to consider how a number of them contained elements of these debates in a long-lasting intertextual narrative process from 1954 to the present. If in his work Polish history is at stake, if the role of the Polish hero is at stake, if Polish gender roles are to be considered, then also central is the neglected problem of the Holocaust and associated issues of Memory and Loss. This representational process twists and turns throughout Wajda's extensive body of work developing into what can be called a long Holocaust narrative – a prolonged engagement with the centuries-old Polish-Jewish relationship and also with the finalities of the Holocaust. This narrative process across many texts is by no means certain and secure. It wavers; it trembles with uncertainty and anxiety, yet with passion in its moral commitments.

The ethical dilemmas faced by Wajda in addressing Polish-Jewish relations surfaced most strongly in *Promised Land* and *Korczak*. The problems of addressing otherness in *Promised Land* have been extensively addressed elsewhere but the film clearly represents, to the most intense degree, a split in Wajda's thinking about these issues, so much so that in 2000 Wajda felt the need to re-edit the film into a new version that attempted to avoid some of the problems that had been noted by critics as a latent anti-semitism. It is a film with a most extraordinary contradictory project. In mid-nineteenth century Łódź at the heart of Poland, a multicultural project is part of the development of a textile industry being invented from the ground up. Despite the continuing absence of a Polish State at that time, Germans, Jews and Poles began the task of constructing a kind of modernity in which all would participate. The central narrative contradiction is the contrast of this with the exploitative nature of this nascent capitalist enterprise in relation to the growing Polish urban working class. But even so there is an element of potential hope in the project of the film that a jointly shared 'Promised Land' would emerge. The film also, however, includes an extraordinarily disturbing representation of the 'Other' in the representation of the rich Jewish lady, Lucy Zucker, who is in love with and exploited by the Polish hero of the narrative (see Ostrowska 2000: 120–30).[8] These are precisely the elements revised by Wajda in the new version. In my opinion, to take such a drastic step, to respond so openly, albeit many years later, to the criticism of this representation is a mark of an especial need to make clear to a local Polish audience that every utterance in this field of meaning carries the greatest responsibility.[9] In this way Wajda demonstrates his continuing attempt to grapple with Polish-Jewish and Holocaust representation, that he understands he faces the same difficulties of choice of form and content evident from such disparate films as *Night and Fog* (Alain Resnais, 1956) to *Shoah* and *Schindler's List* (Steven Spielberg, 1993). Such attempts to work in this area of filmic representation have been amongst the most critically contested in the post-war history of cinema and *Korczak* was, for Wajda, the most problematic moment in his entire work in relation to his continuing attention as to how to continue this unforgiving task.

If his earlier films had proved controversial at times in these matters, either with the censor, with Polish critics or indeed in relation to his own conscience, this was nothing compared to the storm that broke over *Korczak*. This time the controversy was on an international stage and not confined to Poland. Wajda scripted the film during 1989 with Agnieszka Holland, at the very time that, 'Before our eyes the steel bastion of Communism is collapsing' and Wajda himself, recently elected as a senator was attempting to, 'lay down the law' as a member of the first post-Communist Sejm (Fogler 1996, vol. 2: 235). Thus he was divided between two peremptory tasks both of which represent a new beginning, for which Wajda had striven along with many others. The immediate political task of constructing a new Poland was no more important to him than his need in *Korczak* to work over once again events in the Warsaw Ghetto. Indeed, the film returns in a number of other ways to the issues, themes and even the style of *A Generation*: in the naïveté of young innocents caught up in unimaginable events, yet still striving for love; in a focused attention to thinking about issues of responsibility and guilt; and to a visual style, calm, dark and controlled contrasted with the feverish and desperate process to annihilation.

Korczak premiered internationally at Cannes in May 1990 where it received a standing ovation. Yet almost immediately a group of critics headed by Daniele Heymann launched a fierce attack on the film. Inspired by Heymann, Claude Lanzmann joined this critical group and determined to construct a small conspiracy, 'My opinion of Wajda was prepared ... I was prejudiced against the film by the article by Daniele Heymann ... I coldly undertook the decision to create a scandal' (in Fogler 1996, vol. 2: 246). Lanzmann's brutal intervention took place at a special screening of the film (intended to defend it, and Polish-French relations, and given by the then wife of the Prime Minister, Michel Rocard). At the end of the screening Lanzmann turned to Mme Rocard and said, 'You do not know how evil this is', and left the room (see Fogler 1996, vol. 2: 246). Lanzmann had already attacked other films that deviated in any way from his own conceptions of Holocaust representation and as recently as 11 April 1990, at a Yale seminar, had personally attacked Dr Louis Micheels for his film of his personal memories as a doctor in Auschwitz, *Doctor 117641: A Holocaust Survivor* (see Rosenbaum 1998: 267–76). This assault on *Korczak* certainly helped to ensure that it would get no distribution outside Poland.

There were many specific complaints against the film by its infuriated opponents but three can be usefully generalised. Firstly, the film was seen as a general attempt to absolve Poles of being in any way implicated in the Holocaust, either through action or inaction: in Heymann's phrases about the film,

> 'Poles – none. The Warsaw Ghetto? A matter between the Germans and the Jews. This is what a Pole is telling us'. Secondly, in terms of narrative elements, the prologue is seen as irrelevant and the epilogue 'almost causes faintness … [it is] a sleepy disgusting dream'. Thirdly, that the depiction of events in the ghetto such as the Ghetto Cabaret with its clientele of Jewish criminals was an attempt to show Jews as 'responsible for their own misfortune'. (Fogler 1996, vol. 2: 242).

Most of these accusations have been adequately answered elsewhere and I will dwell only briefly on one of them, the film's prologue which has been rather ignored in relation to its function within Wajda's overall project. In fact, it is a key episode in that it demonstrates his developing need to open up the Błońskian stricture to describe how Poles lived with Jews in the past in ways that allowed acquiescence with the Holocaust. One Polish critic, who one might have expected to see its centrality to the film's intention, saw it as 'unnecessary' and 'overly explanatory', dismissing its importance (Rafał Jabłoński in Fogler 1996, vol. 2: 247). Yet its precise explanatory value resides specifically in its depictions of Polish anti-semitism, a subject hardly touched upon in cinema prior to 1989. Another Polish critic, however, perceptively indicates this was already directly relevant to the mixed processes of renewal in 1990, which needed to bear the weight of past moral failures as well as proposing new ways for the nation: 'Wajda's film strikes also at the current political situation in Poland, where on a wave of general freedom, the phantoms of anti-semitism are awakening. Here Wajda throws all his name and authority into the ring' (Fogler 1996, vol. 2: 246).

The prologue contains a range of elements describing pre-war Polish anti-semitism. Wajda is at pains to describe its multiple levels and pervasive nature. It begins very boldly with the dismissal of Dr Korczak from the radio station that had been broadcasting his series entitled, 'The Little Review', made for and by Polish children, both Jew and Gentile. The politics of this censorship of the programme are explicit and describe an institutional anti-semitism. Korczak is dismissed in the clinically modern office of the station's Director, who is clearly a member of the intelligentsia with distinct 'noble

Polish' traits. The Director attempts to cover his petty anti-semitism with a guilt-ridden bonhomie, as he tries to justify his action by reminding Korczak of the problems of the current political situation. Korczak will have none of this obfuscation and leaves. The sequence then cuts to the Doctor's school in a summer scene by a river in which his orphans are playing. This idyll and a subsequent thunderstorm distinctly presage the rapture of the much-criticised ending. Into this sequence come four further elements that mark Wajda's desire to give a sharp indication, yet as familiar as possible, of the pressures of everyday anti-semitism. A washerwoman refuses to wash a Jewish child's clothes, a visiting group of Korczak's graduates remonstrate with him over the uselessness of the liberal education they received from Korczak when they are daily subject to attack from fellow Poles in their lives in the wider community (incidentally this group is shot in a very similar way to the group of Polish youth at the end of *A Generation*). Most powerfully, we see the first shots of another Polish-Jewish love story, played out in this film between Józek, a Jewish boy, and Ewka, a Polish girl. This is watched with calm yet troubled insight by another Jewish girl, Natka, who seems to see the dangerous inevitability of the progress of this relationship into another Polish betrayal. All of these elements conjoin powerfully to suggest to the film's primary audience a degree of Polish historical complicity in anti-semitism during the 1930s from minor to major acts of omission and commission.

In these essentially filmic ways, using visual and performance detail often ignored by critics too busy sharpening knives in the constant battle for the banner of Holocaust veracity, Wajda continues to maintain his position at the heart of these conflicts. He is not balanced, not always sure. How can anyone be as they peer into these darkest of matters? But in his work, variously and often contradictorily accused of being either anti-Polish or anti-Semitic, his representations of Polish-Jewish relations demonstrate his continuing need and concern for this issue to be addressed for the nation in the present. In many ways his work in this area has always been a sounding board of the kind also proposed by Miłosz and Błoński. In his most recent film of *Pan Tadeusz*, the national epic by Adam Mickiewicz, there is a moving return once again to the issues of Polish-Jewish relations. Wajda's task here is to seek for that affinity he must have always felt towards Mickiewicz's narrative purpose especially in the key figure of Jankiel, the most celebrated Jewish figure in Polish literature, idealised innkeeper and courageous Polish patriot, the calm centre of the greatest Polish national epic. Jankiel represents for both Mickiewicz and Wajda what might have been, in this failed brotherhood between, 'the two saddest nations on earth'. Perhaps this is too romantically pessimistic a view. Better to see the task of Wajda and Mickiewicz as attending much more progressively to the needs of combating prejudice through their art, in the hope that a Polish nation would emerge that would be true to its long held and best ideals. Even so, this purpose is often couched in the most moving and rapturous imagery of loss as at the end of both *Korczak* and *Pan Tadeusz*. In *Korczak*, a release from the Holocaust into the fields of a Polish summer; in *Pan Tadeusz*, Zosia, the Polish heart of the poem, greets Jankiel, the Jewish 'elder brother', whose wisdom speaks to the Polish conscience.[10] She draws him once again into the Polish comity as a national wedding of reconciliation again takes place: 'Jankiel, play for me … won't you play? You said you would play upon my wedding day.'

Here Wajda conjoins with Mickiewicz. The moment is no mere example of a Polish heritage culture, supposedly irrelevant in the new time after 1989, but rather, a quiet and joyous representation by Wajda of this broken brotherhood, of elements of the nation lost forever but always necessary to remember. Wajda's finally fulfilled and long desired task to make a film of *Pan Tadeusz* speaks directly to a Polish audience of the continuing and necessary affinities to their past, to Polish history and, in Jankiel, directly to a shared Polish-Jewish history.

Notes

1 This affinity is mentioned by Buñuel in his autobiography, *My Last Breath*: 'Wajda too delights me' (1994: 225). Also noted are Wajda's comments on how Buñuel's films had an influence on his own work. See also comments on this in Paul Coates, 'Forms of the Polish Intellectual's Self-Criticism' (1996: 294–5).

2 As might be expected, Western reviews of this extraordinary episode, sharply focused on ethical issues so often addressed by Wajda, tend to miss these essential Polish elements in the episode that would be all too apparent to a Polish audience. See, for example, the review of *Decalogue 8* by Damian Cannon at www.film.u-net.com.

3 The most developed discussion of this is to be found in Eva Hoffman (1999) *Shtetl: The History of a Small Town and an Extinguished World*. London: Vintage.

4 Błoński's article first appeared in *Tygodnik Powszechny*, 11 January 1987.

5 This encyclical was given on 28 October 1965 and specifically requires reconciliation between Jew and Gentile.

6 The best-known modern expression of these contradictions in relation to the plight of others and the dilemmas of helping is W. H. Auden's poem, *Musee des Beaux Arts*: 'In Breughel's Icarus for instance/How everything turns away/Quite leisurely from the disaster...'

7 In a review of *Poles and Jews: A Failed Brotherhood* by Magdalena Opalski and Israel Bartal, the reviewer writes, 'Somewhat surprisingly, nineteenth-century writing, in Polish, as well as Hebrew and Yiddish, features a great many inter-faith love stories. Very significantly, in Polish and Jewish works alike, the romances never end in intermarriage' (Hundert 1997: 388–91). Opalski and Bartal could not find a single exception.

8 See also Rostworowski (1993) for a full collection of Jewish stereotypes in Polish art as well as the detailed review of this invaluable book by Ezra Mendelsohn (in Hundert 1997: 398–402).

9 Possibly Wajda was influenced by Claude Lanzmann's remarks on *Promised Land*: 'In that film the Jews of Łódź are pictured in a manner worthy of *Sturmer*, the anti-semitic publication of Julius Streicher, the basest of criminals' (in Fogler 1996, vol. 2: 246). Suffice to say that Wajda decided to include these remarks in his biography and I must conclude that whilst he did not agree with Lanzmann he became aware that something of a tradition of Jewish stereotyping (again, see Rostworowski, 1993) had entered into his imagery and that, even though he had had little criticism of this at home, he decided to re-edit the film.

10 Abraham Peck both paraphrases and quotes Mickiewicz's remarks on Polish-Jewish relations as follows, 'The Jew in Poland was seen as the elder brother of the Poles. It was a belief that only in alliance with its older brother could Poland, the new chosen nation, fulfil its divine mission to free the European nations from the yoke of authoritarianism. "For your freedom and ours" became the cry of the Polish insurrectionists ... I believe that a union of Poland and Israel would be a source of spiritual and material strength to us. We would most efficiently prepare Poland's rebirth by removing the causes of its eclipse and reviving the union and brotherhood of all races and religions that regard our mother land as their home' (1999).

CHAPTER SEVEN

Remembering and Deconstructing: The Historical Flashback in Man of Marble and Man of Iron

Maureen Turim

A statue of marble, a cross of iron: these are the markers of a worker's life and death in Andrzej Wajda's pair of historical flashback films scripted by Aleksander Ścibor-Rylski. Taken together these films respond to momentous events in twentieth-century Polish history by asking some questions prompted by symbolic monuments and religious grave markers. Yet here symbolism is ironically inscribed, and if you will permit the pun, all that was iron melts into irony. Here ironic symbolism becomes all the more potent as it comes from a director whose early post-war career was marked by its use of symbolism. Irony extends in this film to the interrogation of objects as acts of representation.

'What is a monument?' The films ask, as it adds, 'What is a worker?' How has twentieth-century history been twisted by monumentalisations, followed by the destruction of these very monuments? How has the concept of the worker as motor force in history been subject to monumental distortions?

A statue of marble gives the first film its name. We first encounter this statue forgotten, assigned to the dustbin of history, to a mass project of forgetting, locked in the closed archive of the state museum. A young student film-maker picks the lock of the enclosure that would contain this statue, and by illegally filming it allows it to speak once again. To emphasise this moment, the spaces of the warehoused statues echo with the ghostly voices of the masses that once cheered them on.

What secrets are locked in archives, and how do we intrude into them to release images that will take on new meanings? In his book-length essay *Mal d'archives* (*Archive Fever*, 1996), Jacques Derrida deconstructs the archive as a repository of history, by looking at a specific case, the Freud archives read from the perspective of psychoanalytically informed biographical history in the work of Yosef Hayim Yerushalmi, *Freud's Moses: Analysis Terminable and Interminable* (1991). Much in Derrida's examination of the personal and the public as they traverse records that may be gathered and stored is relevant to our discussion of Wajda's films. Let me emphasise Derrida's opening remarks on the word archive: 'the politics of the archive' constitutes his 'permanent orientation', as 'there is no political power without control of the archive, if not of memory. Effective democratisation can always be measured by this essential criterion: the participation in and the access to the archive, its constitution, and its interpretation' (1996: 4). Derrida cites French historian Sonia Combe's work on the archive in contemporary France as forbidden or repressed. If Western states lock their archives mostly surreptitiously, those of central Europe in the communist era locked their archives boldly, making the forbidden archive one of the very emblems of state power.

Wajda, in showing a young woman picking the lock of a state archive with a hairpin to steal an image of a marble statue offers us an image that attempts to propel Poland towards a future democratisation. This key image of unlocking links to acts of investigation, discovery and retrospection through the structural device of the filmic flashback. It is my purpose here to explore how flashback structuration functions in Wajda's pair of films.

In my book *Flashbacks in Film: Memory and History* (1989) I explore the functioning of the flashback device over the course of film history. In Chapter Five, I examine the development in US sound films of what I call 'historical flashback films'. Innovative and accomplished examples of these films marked Hollywood production from 1933 through the early 1940s. These films often use biography, particularly that of a 'great man', to focalise their narratives and render individual subjectivity as our access point to historical experience. The most famous of them, *Citizen Kane* directed by Orson Welles in 1941, has often been mentioned as the prototype of Wajda's films. Let me also mention an earlier film, *The Power and the Glory* (William K. Howard, 1933), screenplay by Preston Sturges, and one made a year after *Citizen Kane*, *The*

Great Man's Lady (William Wellman, 1942) as similar structures are used for like purposes in each film. Coupling investigation with revelations from the past, the flashback structure brings a dual purpose to solving enigmas, as it allows the life story to encapsulate a commentary on political and economic history. Often the fictional protagonist is presented as a famous figure whose biography is the subject of an internal inquiry, by a journalist or biographer whose investigation spurs the flashbacks. In the US in the 1930s and 1940s the problem is how power-driven men can use capitalism to build empires, but only by betraying their beliefs, their loved ones, and finally themselves.

The structural borrowings by Ścibor-Rylski from Mankiewicz's screenplay for Welles' *Citizen Kane* tempt us to see the Polish collaboration as homage to the American precedent. *Man of Marble* (*Człowiek z marmuru*, 1976) sometimes displays similar composition of shots as in the shots of the drunken Susan Alexander and the drunken Hanka in their respective interviews, and the disgruntled Jed Leland and the disgruntled Michałak in theirs. The inhuman corridors and offices of a state bureaucracy receive a stylised minimalist treatment that in its underlining of the isolation of those in power bears traces of the more saturated expressionism that marks *Citizen Kane*'s treatment of the forbidding Thatcher library. What Wajda gains through this visual and structural citation extends beyond homage, if we see it as his invitation to read the three films intertextually, each informing the meaning of the other.

To this end, let me make a few remarks about *Citizen Kane* aimed at clarifying its relationship to Wajda's films. Consider the device of the newsreel reporter, Thompson, whose search for an angle on his story introduces suspense and an ideological frame for the narration. Ścibor-Rylski and Wajda reshape the investigative character device. Both of Wajda's films afford great significance to the investigative characters, granting each traits that contrast sharply with the other. In *Man of Marble*, the young woman film-maker plays out generational and feminist questions as well as the role of Polish filmmakers in circumventing state restrictions. The audience wants Agnieszka to uncover Birkut's story. In *Man of Iron* (*Człowiek z żelaza*, 1981) the investigator is a wholly different type of character. The compromised and collaborating reporter turns state investigator due to the debt he owes the regime for covering up past indiscretions. The audience still wants to know the story of Birkut and his son, but other narrative positioning contradicts this basic hermeneutic desire, as anyone with sympathy toward the labour movement would not want naïve interlocutors to give this reporter information he can use against Solidarity. The sharp contrast between the two investigators increases the intertextual play between the two films; rather than creating a sequel that simply continues, here the second film inverts the circumstances of the narration. This renews the structure, and allows the two films to work as a pair, so that *Man of Marble*'s structure and its ideological arguments become if anything more interesting after *Man of Iron* is made as inverted mirror image of its protocols.

In *Citizen Kane* Thompson's investigation is a quest for testimony, for narration, that provides structural detours and delays – such as narration blocked by the initial refusal of Susan Alexander to speak, or delayed by such circumstances as Jed Leland's cantankerous personality and Raymond's mercenary demand for a bribe. Both of Wajda's films use similar delays and suspended narration, but these tend to be more quickly resolved to facilitate a more complex exposition of historical events. Wajda's films dissect events in history and deconstruct representations even more complexly than does *Citizen Kane*. Granted, the reminiscences of the narrators in *Citizen Kane* are drawn in contrast to the initial presentation of Kane's life in the newsreel, screened immediately following Kane's death at the film's opening, opening the film to a critical reading of forms of filmic representation. The newsreel provides a schematic overview of all the narrations to follow. It provides a version of Kane's life in the style of popular 'yellow' journalism, a style that his own newspaper promulgated. The style and structure of the newsreel segment is a clever pastiche that satirises actual newsreels, while providing an index of reality within the fiction presenting Kane as a 'real' historical figure. The newsreel is also a form of flashback. Since Kane is a constructed character within the fiction, presenting us with a pseudo-documentary report on his life is simply a means of depicting events occurring before Kane's death, before the present moment of the narration. But as a film screened within the film, the newsreel has a different heuristic status than the other flashback narrations. It is a document displaying a certain style of ideological argumentation. It mimics the style of the 'March of Time' newsreels produced by *Time* magazine, interspersing political events and sensationalist scandals such as Kane's divorce and his attempts to legitimise his mistress as an opera singer. Everything is presented as human interest and entertainment, so that the net result of the alternating structure is to juxtapose critiques from the right and left continually. This both neutralises and trivialises the political events of Kane's life, rendering the personal much more spectacular than the major events of the day.

'Found footage', including representations of historical newsreels, propaganda films and outtakes, punctuate Wajda's pair of films as far more numerous instances of projection. These clips have functions parallel to those of the newsreel in *Citizen Kane*, yet they greatly enlarge upon the project of the earlier film. Their function as pastiche skewers not only the official discourse of the Communist system of representation, but the compliance of film-makers seeking to conform due to careerist motivations. If the 'March of Time' obscures the ideological tenets of its presentation under a veneer of balanced, opposing points of view and a gloss of entertainment, *Polska Kronika Filmowa* trumpets the Stakhanovite ideal worker. 1950s propaganda monumentalised exemplary worker productivity. It generated the heroic out of the everyday, devising schemes of scenic design, camera placement and montage meant at securing consensus. Reception is inscribed within the film, our ideal hero shown applauded by an appreciative local crowd fitted with the trappings of traditional peasantry, and accompanied by folk music and Communist anthems. The various types of 'found footage' help deconstruct each other, so that the outtakes from *Birth of a City*, for example, expose the principles of shaped and censored representation found in the finished film, *Architects of our Happiness* whose projection occurs sequentially in the initial screening for Agnieszka in the archives screening room. The outtakes, and the fragments of the newsreel which follows *Architects of our Happiness* reveal quite different events and attitudes captured by a camera or sound record-ings, destined to be censored, but nonetheless archived. What Wajda has done is create a circumstance of montage in which outtakes and fragments can be juxtaposed to an official style of film-making, revealing its sutured monothe-matic discourse to be constructed out of the effacement of other stories less politically acceptable to the State. Simultaneously, the montage operates as a chronological revelation of Birkut's narrative, linked as it is to the growth of the 'New City', whose construction is a planner's dream not of urban renewal, but of the entirely planned utopic space afforded by new technologies and new concepts of architectonic design. How ironic then that this 1950s ideal of the new rests on a foundation of rather archaic hand bricklaying, in which all that has been transformed is the pace demanded of the workers in assembly line production.

My analysis of Wajda's montage strategy here, of this juxtaposition of fragments, can be usefully compared to that of Gilles Deleuze in *Cinema 2: The Time-Image* on what he calls the recollection-image. Deleuze names the function of such images 'forking', analysing how they evoke a given moment of the past as a choice against other choices that remain virtual (1989: 47–51). He associates the recollection-image with the flashbacks in Mankiewicz's films, and sees Mankiewicz creating forking temporalities, instances of time in which the key question becomes 'What happened?' Here he contrasts the

Mankiewicz flashback to the fatality and destiny that Marcel Carné assigns to the trope in *Le Jour se leve* (1939), of which he makes a negative judgment. In later discussion of *Citizen Kane*, he reiterates this emphasis: 'each witness jumps into the past in general and at once installs himself in one or other coexisting region, before embodying certain points of the region in a recollection-image' (1989: 106). Deleuze's great philosophical gains in explaining the virtual nature of events in this analysis come, however, at a price: he is unable to address the psychoanalytical and ideological functioning of the films in question, dismissing as a result much of the vital significance of Carné's film (see Turim 1990). For *Citizen Kane* and Wajda's films, especially, I would argue that the virtuality of the event and its representation is articulated with a strong sense of the ideological dynamics of history.

If we return to Wajda's montage, we can see that Agnieszka's long interview with the film-maker Burski, coinciding with extensive flashback sequences of the building of Nowa Huta, are coloured by Burski's contention that he, the film-maker, invented Birkut as heroic figure. 'My best creation', Burski says with pride as Wajda portrays film-makers in Communist Poland as not just submissive to State discourse, but so invested in the apparatus that they themselves take pride in creating the pro-filmic reality they might otherwise be seen as coerced to document.

The cynical bodyguard turned strip-joint operator, Michałak, frames the flashbacks depicting Witek's act of sabotage in which he as brick-brigade worker passes a hot brick to Birkut. A burning message is delivered as an indictment of the State and of its production of images. Witek's act exceeds industrial sabotage; it is also the betrayal of a friendship and thus throws the solidarity of workers into question, for as Birkut asks, how could one worker do this to another? He answers by realising his own complicity earlier in conforming to an image that was being used against other workers. The Stakhanovite worker betrays by embodying an oppressive State's image of what the self-sacrificing worker should be. Michałak's duty is to add another layer of betrayal to the events, to identify Witek for the State as the saboteur. His cynicism then cloaks all sequences of Birkut's coming to knowledge, as the enormous heroic banners of him are torn down, and he is fired and evicted for questioning the disappearance of Witek. Left disenfranchised and furious, all that is left for Birkut is to pass the brick one more time, through the glass doors of the Warsaw Security Offices. The bricks become discourses, message blocks for those who have no right to deliver their messages, as the State controls all legitimation of messages. In a final cynical gesture to close this segment, Michałak demands that Agnieszka's body-miked sound recording and the film taken surreptitiously by her cameraman be handed back to him to be destroyed. The strip-joint owner is still enforcing the closed archive, still operating as an enforcer for an official, namely the producer, who will in the next sequence chastise Agnieszka for investigative reporting.

Witek, whose rehabilitation has led to an upwardly-mobile trajectory, offers his narration from his position of authority in building a larger city of progress, the steelworks at Huta Katowice. The flashbacks unfurled by his narration are brief, telling of Birkut's 1956 homecoming, at which he rejects a band greeting him as an act of reconciliation in favour of his pressing quest to return to his girlfriend Hanka. Instead Witek follows him to annotate his discovery of an empty apartment, setting up the final flashback series in which Hanka's interview narrates Birkut's sad visit to her, now resettled in a villa, a new marriage and a waitressing job.

These flashbacks are followed by another screening of 'found footage'. The first is footage Agnieszka shot as an account of 1950s Polish architecture, which she critiques as cold and inhuman. This is followed by a final archival screening of footage showing Birkut's participation in the national election, which constitutes his symbolic rehabilitation. Given that Wajda was not allowed to use the ending he wished for the film, the closing sequences beg to be read as preparation for *Man of Iron*, for only in that film will we hear of how Agnieszka attempts again to finish her Birkut project. Word of the project first comes as a dossier given to the State's investigator at the film's opening, but the final explanation will be withheld until that investigator interviews Agnieszka at the very end of the film. Agnieszka, and Birkut's son Maciek, a worker in the Gdańsk shipyards, take up the rebellion that Witek and Birkut both seemingly abandoned.

The iconicity of hero worship under socialist realism is taken to task by *Man of Marble*, with the 'found footage' playing a large role in this critique. Monumental socialist realism is a form of thought that might be seen as creating its own symbolic imagery, ripe for deconstruction. By figuring the ideal worker as larger than any actual worker could ever be, magnification becomes not only a distortion, but also a negation of human existence in the functioning of a system. Monumental socialist realism disguises as the super-heroic worker what is actually a system of production increases, a technology that drains life from human beings to siphon that energy into the production of goods, that is, into objects. In capitalist economies this systemically rationalised production is known as Taylorism, now sometimes called 'Fordism', giving to a system the name of an industrial mass production of the assembly line timed by the clock of ever more demanding efficiency experts. In *Man of Marble* scenes of increased production quotas in bricklaying are retrieved from the archived newsreels, but the focus of these found documentaries is less on the group than on the one worker enlarged by the spotlight of official attention. Birkut ceases to be himself the moment he is seen by the eye of official cameras. He becomes an image of The Worker.

What happens in the psyche of a person who becomes the image of 'The Worker?' The film uses the statue and monumentally sized banners of Birkut as means of highlighting its psychoanalytical and political *parti-pris*. These oversize representations draw our attention to the character Birkut, as a 'Statue man' in the psychoanalytical sense of the term that theorist Mikkel Borch-Jacobsen develops. He poetically underscores a Lacanian notion of the world inhabited by the self as 'so strangely petrified and static, a sort of immense museum peopled with immobile statues, images of stone and hieratic forms' (1991: 59). The ego itself here 'takes a pose for eternity', its stasis of being likened to a statue, but also a snapshot. Lacan himself likens this petrification to the 'strangeness to the faces of actors when a film is suddenly stopped in mid action' (in Borch-Jacobsen 1991: 59). Seemingly this filmic example rests on how the frozen image seems all the more strange when it becomes magnified in close-up, contorted by emotion, yet made to pose statically in the midst of action. This line of thought recalls Freud's own description of the tomb statue of Moses by Michelangelo in his famous essay of 1914. Freud analyses through a series of very complicated strategies, the meaning of sculpturally frozen action and expression. Michelangelo 'has added something new and more than to the figure of Moses: so that the giant frame with its tremendous physical power becomes only a concrete expression of the highest mental achievement that is possible in a man, that of struggling successfully against an inward passion for the sake of a cause to which he has devoted himself' (1973: 277). Freud's interpretation of a specific and glorious statue takes quite a different view of the self than Lacan's trope of the statue as representing a stasis of being cast into stone surrounded by other immobile images of stone. Let me suggest that Birkut, the *Man of Marble*, mostly embodies the alienated self that Lacan describes, and that while Maciek too has his moments of immobility, he moves closer to struggling 'for the sake of a cause to which he has devoted himself'. Maciek is struggling to remember his father, and with his partner Agnieszka, to produce a film that will revive memory and memorialise. Their passion is depicted in the film as a struggle to move beyond their own alienation to act in concert with others.

If the complex symbolism of a statue is placed in comparison with the found film footage as organising principle of *Man of Marble, Man of Iron* rests more completely on the photograph in its relationship to the spontane-ous memorial. This memorial takes the form of a makeshift iron cross that serves to designate a worker's death in struggle against the State that claims to rule in his name. The State denies him a grave marker, and consigns his life to being forgotten. The task of remembrance then rests on his son, Maciek. Yet the histories of son and father told in flashback reveal developments always out of sync; the history of student protests seem always temporally at odds with worker's protests, until the present moment of the film's narrative. For the son, Maciek has joined the working class.

The State in *Man of Iron* sets out on another task of image manufacture, in this case to sully Maciek whose image is becoming legend to a new generation of workers. Thus the first instance of 'found footage' in this film is a French television interview with Maciek, identified only retrospectively as a tape that the authority Badecki has shown to Winkiel to explain who he is being ordered to investigate. Then he gives Winkiel a dossier on Maciek, including photos. Video and photos will supplement 'found' film footage throughout as historical documents alongside the flashbacks. *Man of Iron* has fewer films shown within the film, and sometimes integrates documentary material so well into the present action that it is hard to distinguish whether it is historical footage or reenactment.

In documentary footage of worker's opinions presented as Winkiel wit-nesses it being recorded at the gates of strike headquarters, several workers, including women, offer their political analysis of the situation. This footage is blended into the fictional present as workers raise a large wooden cross memorial to those who died in the 1970s massacre. Its close-up testimony offers an earnest view of workers expressing themselves freely, in sharp con-trast to official stagings presented in *Man of Marble*, as well as to the rehearsed interviews with housewives that Winkiel is preparing to broadcast to offer governmental alibis to break the strike.

Later, a similar montage segment unfurls under Maciek's reading of the workers' demands, to be replaced on the soundtrack by a strike song sung in a contemporary folk tradition, in which a father voices his wish that his young son remember these events. Central to many of the flashbacks is the conflict between Birkut as worker father and Maciek as student son, so that the generational split of political opposition is symbolised by these figures, each propelled to be larger than life by historical circumstances. This scene is followed shortly by the lone film within the film, one that Dzidek, a friend of Maciek, shows Winkiel of the 1970 repression of an earlier strike. It too is a different type of film artifact, a contestatory, clandestinely shot chronicle, offered in contrast to official films. Dzidek says: 'This ought to be shown over and over to every worker in Poland, to rid them of any lingering illusions.' But how can images rid workers of illusions, when their history is governed by images creating illusions? Can the pair of films focus their deconstructive energies on the work of images as illusions, and still hold to the cleansing value of new image production and reception?

Expression of the difficulty of forging new imagery against a propagandistic tradition takes the form of Maciek's striking out and venting his anger at the students' communal television set as those assembled watch Communist Party First Secretary Gierek's post-1970 speech. As with an earlier speech left playing as voice-over, while Winkiel desperately attempts to salvage his spilled alcoholic drink, these inserted television broadcasts slice the official discourse into the ongoing fiction. If Winkiel reacts by even greater dependency on drink to ease him into forgetfulness, Maciek acts out his anger as hysterical symptom.

Photos will finally prove to be their last effort at political documentation. Wrenched from the official government dossiers to which they might otherwise be consigned, Maciek and Agnieszka attempt to mount a photo exhibit of scenes from Birkut's life as an exhibition to be hung in their apartment. Even this is stopped by threats from Maciek's personnel manager.

Only the successful recognition of Solidarity reunites Maciek and Agnieszka to end the film on a vision of success of the worker's free union movement. The film never gets made except through its traces across these two films as a series of bound fragments, speaking through their imagery of a link between Polish generations in protest. The man of marble, the ideal worker alienated from himself by State usurpation of his likeness, gives way in Wajda's imagery to the men and women of iron, forged through a contestatory reading of the archives. Not forgetting becomes that which the film hopes to represent.

CHAPTER EIGHT

'Visual Eloquence' and Documentary Form: Meeting Man of Marble in Nowa Huta

Bjørn Sørenssen

In the autumn of 1977 I was in Poland for three weeks on what was called a 'cultural exchange' visit. This was a great opportunity for a Norwegian with very limited experience in the field of Polish cinema to get better acquainted with the impressive output of Polish films in the 1950s, 1960s and 1970s and I was also given the opportunity to get better acquainted with Polish history and culture. That the version presented to me by my official hosts necessarily was a slanted one was a fact acknowledged by both host and visitor, but I was fully able to gain access to other and more reliable sources.

However, as open and liberal my hosts appeared, there were some areas that soon would appear taboo-ridden. At 'Film Polski' I was assured that I might have access to whichever of the newer Polish films I wanted to see – with one significant exception: whenever I would raise the question about seeing Andrzej Wajda's *Man of Marble* (*Człowiek z marmuru*, 1976), I would be showered with alternative offers: What about Zanussi's *Camouflage* (*Barwy ochronne*, 1977) and *The Structure of Crystal* (*Struktura kryształu*, 1969). Or Kawalerowicz's *Death of a President* (*Śmierć prezydenta*, 1977). Fine with me – I watched these and many other interesting new Polish films, but whenever I would come back to my initial request for *Man of Marble*, I would be met by the ubiquitous Polish phrase of that time, combined with a shrug of the shoulders: *nie ma*.

Imagine then, the thrill I felt on a Friday afternoon when I ran into a Norwegian colleague on a street corner in Cracòw and he informed me that *Man of Marble* was playing in Nowa Huta. I knew enough about the film to know about the significance of this coincidence, so I assured my official interpreter that she could take the weekend off and that I would be fine on my own and soon found myself on the bus on the road to Nowa Huta.

The cinema where the film was showing in Nowa Huta seemed to date, like most of the surrounding buildings, to the early post-war years, to the building of the steelworks of Nowa Huta as described in Wajda's movie, with its Stalin-Baroque columns and old-fashioned interior. For an outsider the audience had an interesting and intriguing appearance, as there seemed to be an enormous generation gap: I was among the Nowa Huta veterans and their children. As the film progressed through the flashbacks to the early 1950s, the two audience groups seemed to have opposite reactions to the events on the screen.

As the images of old newsreels, the reconstruction of the Stakhanovite-style competitions in bricklaying, the brass band music and the red flags fluttering appeared on the screen, the older part of the audience acknowledged their past with nods of recognition, while the younger generation reacted with derisive and sometimes incredulous laughter accompanied by irritated hushing from the elders.

For me it became a fascinating viewing experience and a useful excursion into newer Polish history, where I had to fend for myself in terms of coming to an understanding with the film and its reception. In spite of the fact that my fluency in Polish was restricted to the *nie ma* expression and the ability to order beer and chicken in a restaurant, I nevertheless felt immersed in the story about the champion bricklayer Birkut and his fate and felt less of my linguistic handicap than could be expected.

Wajda's 'Visual Eloquence': The Attic of Repressed Memories

This fact came back to me several years later, when I was able to see *Man of Marble* with Norwegian subtitles on television. What then struck me was how much of the action – and dialogue – I had somehow managed to understand that evening in Nowa Huta, without really understanding Polish. This again set me reflecting on what I have chosen to call Wajda's *visual eloquence*, since I have had similar experiences with other Wajda films. This concept, which perhaps rather should be widened to the term *audiovisual eloquence*, manifests itself in highly compressed 'capsules' of audiovisual information.

In *Man of Marble* one of the main manifestations of this kind occurs in the title sequence, when Krystyna Janda in the role of the young film school student Agnieszka enters the art museum in search of the marble statue of Birkut. It is an emblematic Wajda sequence with extensive use of a tracking and panning camera. In this case the combination of tracking and panning shots becomes a journey through the 'official' visual remembrance of the Polish nation in 1977. While the camera follows the aggressive young woman in pursuit of her goal, as it tracks or pans through gallery after gallery, it also takes in the various paintings and other art objects on display in the museum. This is the representative Polish art, the images that manifest tradition and history.

And let me at this point interject an observation that I made in 1977 during my stay that shattered my preconceptions of Poland as just one more of the 'Soviet satellite nations': the prevalence of modernistic art in the visual arts, theatre, music and literature. It was quite clear to me that avant-garde modernism was more firmly entrenched here than at home and furthermore, that the Polish modernists seemed to have something our modernists back home lacked – a real and enthusiastic audience. Some years later, reading Czesław Miłosz's *The Captive Mind* (1980) this struck me as being an example of what he defined as *artistic ketman*: seeking refuge in the area of officially sanctioned and presumably 'unpolitical' art. In the wake of the events of 1956 and 1968 this area of officially sanctioned art seemed to have been considerably enlarged in comparison with other countries behind the Iron Curtain and had made Poland a Mecca for many Scandinavian artists in terms of painting, graphics and design.

In the museum sequence of *Man of Marble* we are mainly confronted with the art of earlier days, while modernism, although introduced by a couple of abstract sculptures in the foyer of the museum, is implicated mainly through Agnieszka and her tendency to break with the given rules of classic cinematography. The tour of the museum underlines the continuity of Polish art history through the turbulent times of the Polish nation. Only when the camera comes to a stop, does one realise that there is a significant (or, if you would like – insignificant) gap in the cavalcade of Polish art presented during the protagonist's journey through Polish art history: stowed away in the attic, locked inside cages of chicken fence wire is the heritage of Stalinist socialist realism. From their cages, steel-jawed heroes and buxom worker-peasant heroines stare from their oblivion – a visual reminder of the repressed past in the modernised 'people's democracy' of the 1970s.

For a Norwegian, this 'attic of repressed memory' instinctively calls up an analogy with Ibsen's attic in *The Wild Duck* – the symbol of a repressed shameful past that the author is intent on revealing in order to deal with the 'life lies' of his characters. For the Norwegian spectator among Birkut's contemporaries and their children in 1977 Wajda seemed to be on a similar Ibsenesque mission, a fact underlined by similar 'capsules' of audiovisual eloquence in *Man of Marble*. A recurring formal trait in the film is the use of long tracking shots, the first of which actually shows up in the second sequence of the movie where the female protagonist pleads for her movie project with an unsympathetic advisor while they walk through seemingly endless corridors. Wajda leaves the viewer in no doubt about the fact that his film is about history and that the course of history is a dynamic one – with no final stops.

Of course, this hardly is news for anyone even vaguely familiar with Wajda's cinematic oeuvre. The history of Poland runs like a constant thread through his work, from the War Trilogy in the 1950s to *Pan Tadeusz* in 1999 and is the very focus of *Man of Marble*, a fact that could be strongly felt by the foreigner in the Nowa Huta cinema. This poses, of course, a problem for the viewer without an intimate knowledge of themes and symbols pertaining to Polish history, but in hindsight it may be stated that Wajda's frequent use of these visually encapsulated historical references is of a kind that draws attention to these also for the non-initiated. You do not have to be in the possession of total knowledge of Polish history to appreciate the importance (and the beauty) of the historical symbolism in *Ashes and Diamonds* (*Popiół i diament*, 1958) – the ploughman and his horse in the second sequence of the film (a reference to the painter Ferdynand Ruszczyc, who also turns up in the gallery sequence in *Man of Marble*), the crucifix over the murdered men in the chapel, the white horse galloping through the streets, Maciek's blood mingling with the white sheets to create a perverse version of Polish national flag and finally the drunken Polonaise performed by the highly unheroic guests at the banquet.

In the same way, the significance and chilling beauty of the shot in *Kanal* (*Kanał*, 1957) where Mądry hauls himself out of the sewers of Warsaw and into the blinding sunlight to taste freedom for a couple of seconds before he is able to recognise the jackboots of a German officers near his head is hardly lost upon one for whom the intricate background of the Warsaw uprising is unknown. Neither does it require intimate knowledge of Wyspiański's play to appreciate the dynamics of the title sequence in *The Wedding* (*Wesele*, 1972) which literally sets the stage for the action. In this sequence Wajda excels in combining audiovisual elements into a tour-de-force. Within a couple of minutes the class alliance and antagonism of the wedding couple and their guests is established, the collision between tradition and modernity, the historical fate of tri-partite Poland at the beginning of the twentieth century is whirled before the spectators' eyes and ears. And again the driving force of history is recognised as *movement* as the wedded couple rolls from the streets of Craców into the countryside.

Rhetorics: 'a man of marble without quotation marks'

Man of Marble and its sequel *Man of Iron* (*Człowiek z żelaza*, 1981) are both highly *rhetorical* films, in the sense that they advance an argument about the topics and values of a defined historical period. (The period in question in *Man of Iron* reflects, of course, the contemporary events surrounding the production of the film.) Thus, one might argue that eloquence becomes a natural part of the filmic discourse and, accordingly, that this also might explain the frequent occurrence of rhetorical tropes like metaphor and metonymy in these films.

I have already cited the museum sequence as an example of Wajda's visual eloquence in *Man of Marble*. In this case the art museum functions as a metaphor for the Polish historical consciousness, with the Stalinist past placed behind lock and fence in the subconscious of the attic. Another metaphor is the Man of Marble himself. In Mateusz Birkut, Wajda has created more than an ideal worker – he has created an ideal man. Wajda himself has said of his protagonist:

> Birkut is in reality a man of marble without quotation marks. Independent of the play of Fate – whether he is popular and hailed or has fallen out of favour – he acts according to his moral convictions, according to his understanding of honesty and seriousness ... I defend the man who remains true to himself and his ideas of justice through all situations ... Birkut's biography is unusual and atypical. (in Eder *et al.* 1980: 84)

If the Birkut character in all its uniqueness thus comes close to representing the super-human, the characters that surround him are only all too human in their weaknesses and opportunism, the kind of flawed character that we find represented in literature from classical Greek tragedy onwards. Wajda's rhetorical device here is metonymic rather than metaphoric – that of the *synecdoche*. These characters have become a part of the past that has been projected into the contemporary Polish society of the audience. Unlike Birkut, the characters of Witek, Hanka, Burski and Michałak change and adapt to the demands of time and changes in society and in this way they forge a link between the historical past and the contemporary audience. In the light of Birkut's stubborn refusal to change his ideals over time they become reduced to recognisable types in a contemporary setting.

These characters, who help Agnieszka reconstruct the fate of Mateusz Birkut, all represent various ways to conform and adapt to the dramatic changes in Polish political and social life between 1950 and 1977. His friend and co-model worker Witek who, like Mateusz, gets caught up in the purges of the early 1950s, has become a pragmatic leader of modern socialist planned economy and Burski, the young eager director of the documentary portraying the triumphs and heroics of Birkut's bricklaying team, has become a glamorous internationally successful jet-setting director. (Burski is described here by Wajda with more than a little hint of sarcastic self-portraiture.) We also witness how the beautiful Hanka, who deserts him after his arrest and later opts for a life in material security, has been reduced to a pathetic alcoholic.

Perhaps the most interesting portrayal of these 'witnesses' is that of Michałak, the secret police agent who plays an important but ambiguous role in Birkut's downfall. In the original version of Aleksander Ścibor-Rylski's screenplay from 1962 Michałak is in jail when he is being interviewed by Agnieszka. When Wajda finally managed to make the film, in 1977, he felt that he needed to update Michałak's fate. For a 1962 audience the events between 1950 and 1956 were so near in time as to warrant a 'jail sentence' for a member of the secret police. For the 1977 audience these events had become history and Wajda makes another choice (see Wajda 2000d: 130). So Michałak, the informer of the 1950s becomes the shady strip-tease joint manager of the 1970s with a double allusion to his status – 'pimp' – and his activities – voyeurism – linking the unsavoury character of the 1950s with an equally unsavoury character of the 1970s.

The means through which this transformation is made is simple, almost crude. It is mainly achieved by simple pro-filmic markers like the costume and make-up of the Michałak character – the sunshades, the leather jacket and the sparse beard – in addition to the scenography and the lighting of the set. When Agnieszka enters the locale where Michałak oversees the audition of prospective strippers, Wajda creates an overall feeling of having descended into a shadow world. The lighting is so subdued and sparse that it makes a mockery out of her film team's attempt to do a 'hidden camera' interview. Furthermore, Michałak is filmed in a way that leaves his face in a permanent shadow. The allusion is clearly one that implies that Michałak has stayed behind in the world of shadows and deceit, activities that cannot endure daylight. The rhetorical figure is again that of the *synecdoche* – Michałak the overseer of the shady strip-joint is a direct link to the henchmen of Bierut's secret police of the 1950s and – most important to the 1977 audience – to their heirs in Gierek's secret police of the 1970s.

The difference between Mateusz Birkut and the other persons who help Agnieszka in reconstructing his story is also connected to a difference in *ethos* – according to Aristotle's *Rhetoric* the most important factor in convincing an audience about the validity of one's argument (1991: 38). Of the characters of the past Agnieszka comes across, only Birkut passes the test of trustworthiness so crucial to the *ethos* of the classics. In one way or another the others have failed the ideals they might have shared with Birkut, with the exception of Michałak who obviously has had no ideals at all.

This rhetorical element in *Man of Marble* is above all present in the contemporary setting of the film, in the story sequence related to Agnieszka's hunt for Birkut, and is conspicuously conveyed by visual means. The visual metaphors and metonymical links described above stand out clear and loud, but, exactly because of the ambiguity customarily ascribed to the image, they offer an excuse in the face of official censorship. The criticism of contemporary society is implicit, not explicit.

The image Wajda wanted to end his movie with was, however, too strong for the liberalised Polish censorship in the 1970s: that of a dead shipyard worker carried on a door through the streets of Gdynia after the suppression of the 1970 strike. Wajda knew that, and did not even attempt to include it. His second choice, which he actually filmed, also proved to be too strong for the censorship board in 1977: Agnieszka leaving flowers for at the gates of a cemetery in Gdańsk in memory of the murdered worker-hero, Mateusz Birkut. This scene was later used, under more favourable circumstances, in *Man of Iron* (see Wajda 2000d: 132). In order to get past a censorship that would block any direct reference to the massacres of December 1970 in Gdańsk and Gdynia, Wajda again opted for the symbolic. Agnieszka's quest for Mateusz Birkut ends at a pedestrian overpass near the Lenin shipyard in Gdańsk, an indirect reference to a similar overpass in neighbouring Gdynia, a place where a large number of workers were killed by the security forces on 20 December 1970. This event, repressed and unmentionable in official discourse, nevertheless lived on in popular memory and the visiting Norwegian in Poland in 1977 was quickly informed about the importance of this image and its connotations.

Man of Marble and the Expository Documentary

The film genre most closely related to traditional rhetorics is, of course, the documentary. In the words of Bill Nichols, documentary is 'telling stories with evidence and arguments' (1991: 107). Consequently documentary form has been developed with the explicit aim to convince the viewer about the validity of its arguments. *Man of Marble* and *Man of Iron* both offer a frame narrative (a 'narrative within a narrative') based on documentary form. In both films this frame narrative has the function of a retrospective narrative agent, presenting the viewer with the *fabula* of the film.

Man of Marble presents this frame narrative as a series of nested narratives. A common denominator for these nested narratives is the frequent allusion to the documentary, the most obvious one being the fact that the protagonist of the outer narrative is a documentary film-maker. At the very beginning of the film, before this protagonist is introduced, the audience is presented with a 'mini-documentary', covering the rise and fall of the exemplary worker, Mateusz Birkut. This 'mini-documentary' leads directly into the next frame narrative, where we meet Agnieszka pursuing her editor through the corridors of the television house in order to get support for her own documentary on Birkut.

Wajda also offers his own examples of the documentary style of the 1950s. In a chilling reminder of the propagandistic use of the medium he presents a fictionalised issue of the Polish official newsreel in 1952, where Witek and other victims of the purges of these days appear in court accused of sabotaging socialism. More important for the film as a whole is, however, the complete 1950s-style 'mock documentary' *Architects of our Happiness* shown to Agnieszka in the screening room – complete with credits naming a certain 'Andrzej Wajda' as assistant director. Apart from functioning as an introduction to Burski's narrative, this 'documentary-within-a-documentary-within-a-fiction-film' further enhances the feeling of opening a narrative Chinese box, as it is constructed using the same retrospective narrative technique that dominates the overall structure of *Man of Marble*.

This structure has a strong resemblance with what documentary theorists describe as *expository form*, usually connected with the strongly didactic films of the British documentary movement and with the classic newsreel tradition. According to Nichols, 'the expository text addresses the viewer directly with titles or voices that advance an argument about the historical world' (1991: 34) and the viewer will have no problem in placing the carefully reconstructed 1950s-style 'documentary' within this concept. The rhetoric of this kind

Uplifting hero uplifting bricks: *Man of Marble*

of documentary is characterised by a strong authorial presence, usually manifested in the soundtrack narration and the vocal delivery style of the narrator. The authority emanating from the narrator again lends credibility to the images, but the didactic qualities of the expository documentary are not confined to the soundtrack alone. Ever since the two 'model films' of this tradition – Robert Flaherty's *Nanook of the North* (1922) and John Grierson's *Drifters* (1929) – the expository documentary has relied on a didactic visual dramaturgy reinforcing the arguments put forth in inter-titles or on the soundtrack. Furthermore, the classic Griersonian documentary was unabashedly 'propagandistic', its explicit aim being to explain and propagate a better insight into societal affairs, placing the documentarist on a pulpit, to use Paul Rotha's phrase (1935: 114).

As mentioned above, this expository mode of documentary is parodied in an excellent way in the alleged 1950 'documentary' *Architects of our Happiness* made by the fictional character Burski. All the classic elements of expository form are there: the authoritative commentator with his newsreel delivery style, the up-beat music based on marches and enthusiastic choir music, the emphasis on smiling faces and jubilant crowds in addition to images of the building of industries and homes. The feel of authenticity is enhanced by Wajda's clever inter-cutting of fictional scenes with genuine film material from the period. In one such sequence we see original footage of party leader Bierut visiting a factory and talking to workers. We see a shot of Krystyna Zachwatowicz (in the role of Hanka) wearing a bandana talking to someone off-screen. Wajda then inserts, as a reverse shot, archival footage of Bierut talking to a female worker with a similar bandana and her back to the camera, creating the illusion of a direct conversation between the historical Bierut and the fictional Hanka. This mixture of archival material and fictional material lends a sense of authenticity to the fictional account, functioning as a guarantee for the validity of the portrait of the historical period in question.

The symbols of the 1950s original documentaries, the giant portraits of Bierut and Stalin, the mass manifestations and parades are now reused with their symbolic value reversed in a film dedicated to expose the corruption and cruelty of the Stalinist policies in Poland up to the 'October thaw' of 1956. The expository character of Burski's documentary is repeated in the overall structure of *Man of Marble* in that it still centres on Mateusz Birkut, but the insistence is now that it purports to portray the *real* Birkut, as opposed to the glorified version of the past. In the tradition of the classic documentary, there is an invisible omniscient narrator piecing together the puzzle that Agnieszka is busy collecting material for through her research until, at the end, the images from the overpass in Gdańsk leave the Polish audience in no doubt about Birkut's fate.

Man of Iron and Observational Documentary Form

Interestingly, *Man of Marble* is also hinting at an alternative way of 'telling stories with evidence and argument' through the activities of the young film-maker Agnieszka. Whereas the story of Mateusz Birkut is presented very much in an expository manner, Agnieszka represents another tradition in documentary film-making, the *observational* and *intersubjective* documentary method developed from the mid-1960s and onwards.[1] This documentary form arose partly in response to the perceived artificiality of the expository documentary and was facilitated by the development of lighter camera and sound recording equipment. The American *direct cinema* and the French *cinéma vérité* tradition claimed to be able to record life 'as it was' and insisted on doing without the trappings of commentary, direction and reconstruction of the classical expository documentary. In this the 'new' documentary also hoped to lay claim to a greater credibility than its forerunner due to its direct 'fly-on-the-wall' approach to events and persons.

We find several references to this way of documentary film-making in *Man of Marble*. The contrast between the 'old' and the 'new' documentary is frequently alluded to in the relationship between Agnieszka and her older cameraman Leonard, who was also the cameraman for Burski during the making of the documentary on Birkut in the 1950s. He is of the old school, insisting on the use of a tripod, while Agnieszka demands that her film should be shot 'in the American way', that is, with a hand-held camera. In the museum sequence this difference in attitude becomes apparent when the team is going to film the marble statue. Leonard complains that there is neither place nor time to set up a tripod shot, while Agnieszka snatches the camera from him, getting her shots hand-held.

Agnieszka's *direct cinema* approach is also underlined in her attempts to use a hidden camera in the meeting with Michałak. This attempt is thwarted and on a later occasion, while interviewing Hanka in Zakopane, Agnieszka is confronted with the problematic ethics of this kind of filming when she discovers that her sound recordist is recording her private conversation with Hanka without her permission. On this background it might be argued that the kind of documentary Agnieszka wants to make in *Man of Marble* in many ways is realised in *Man of Iron*. While the former is rooted in the traditional expository documentary of the 1930s, 1940s and 1950s, *Man of Iron* is clearly influenced by the observational style pioneered by television reportage in the 1960s and 1970s. The omniscient and invisible narrator of the expository documentary is now replaced by an omnipresent, but equally invisible camera/narrator.

At first glance, the narrative structure of *Man of Iron* resembles that of *Man of Marble* in its use of a frame narrative introducing a series of retrospective narratives. The protagonist of the frame narrative of *Man of Iron* is, fittingly enough, a broadcasting reporter, Winkiel. But unlike the heroic Agnieszka, Winkiel is a negative protagonist. An alcoholised and weak character pressured into the service of the secret police in order to compromise Birkut's son Maciek, Winkiel becomes an unwilling narrator of Maciek's fate during the days of the Gdańsk strike in 1980. Like Agnieszka, he even makes use of hidden recording equipment, but in the case of Winkiel he does it on behalf of the secret police. Whereas the narrative emphasis in *Man of Marble* is solidly planted in the retrospective flashbacks initiated by the frame narrative, the main narrative interest in *Man of Iron* is concentrated on the contemporary events. Here the retrospective is offered as a relevant background to the events unfolding during the time of narration, with the emphasis on the contemporary events. The *ethos* of this narration is based on that of the observational and intersubjective documentary in that it assigns a status of witness to the camera by virtue of its mere presence. With Winkiel as its medium, the audience is confronted with the people, the discussions and the personal narratives behind the events of 1980 in Poland, ending in the short-lived triumph of the Solidarity movement.

The documentary quality of *Man of Iron* is, like in its predecessor, achieved with the help of mixing fictional and factual footage. But while this technique was based on archival footage and used to support retrospective narrative in *Man of Marble*, the events of 1980 and 1981 are being used in order to support the contemporary narrative. The Polish Association of Film-makers had been granted permission to film in the Gdańsk shipyards by the striking workers, and a good deal of this material eventually also found its way into the fiction film. The prominent scene, being, of course, that of Lech Wałęsa signing the agreement with his oversize 'Pope Paul' ballpoint pen, a scene that had already taken on iconic qualities.

As a natural consequence of the conditions under which the film was made, *Man of Iron* goes a step further, and integrates fact and fiction on the contemporary story level. By enlisting Lech Wałęsa as an 'extra' in the role of best man at Agnieszka's and Maciek's wedding, Wajda blurs the boundary between fact and fiction and lends further strength to the argument of the contemporary frame narrative in *Man of Iron*. The leading question in *Man of Iron* is not so much 'what has happened' but 'what is happening now?' There is an overall feeling of *urgency* in the film, a feeling that would eventually become justified with the declaration of martial law and the suppression of Solidarity later in 1981.

This urgency is reflected in the rhetorics of *Man of Iron* and contrasts with the visual subtleties in the rhetoric of *Man of Marble* that the argumentative burden to a much larger extent is placed on the dialogue – speaking to the contemporary Polish audience. Typical of these are the reading of a poem by Czesław Miłosz and Krystyna Janda performing the ballad about Janek Wiśniewski who was killed in the 1970 uprising. In this context one should remember that, in spite of the show of force by the Solidarity movement, the repressive apparatus was still in place and both the examples mentioned above were on the list of suggested cuts by Polish censorship in 1981 (see Wajda 2000d: 164–5). That these and other 'objectionable' scenes made it to the final version bears witness to the perceived strength of the Solidarity movement by its official adversaries in the spring of 1981.

True, there are also moments in *Man of Iron* where we find Wajda's visual eloquence put to use, but in two of these cases – the procession of workers carrying a killed worker on a door and the scene of Agnieszka leaving flowers on the cemetery gate in Gdańsk – they are images that originally were written for *Man of Marble* and as such they belong stylistically to this film rather than to *Man of Iron*. Interestingly enough the one scene definitively cut from the released version of *Man of Iron* by the board of censors is a scene containing the kind of visual eloquence so characteristic of Wajda's work in his historical films. The scene in question is one where Maciek comes down to the harbour to identify a KOR (The Citizens' Self-Defence Committee) member murdered by the security forces and it is included in the DVD version of *Man of Iron* issued in 2000 (Vision Film Distribution).

But first and foremost *Man of Iron* is a topical film, a film that speaks to its contemporary audience in a sense of urgency and in a situation where direct address to this audience has become possible. In a situation like this, the communicator has to rely on the most effective means of communication available and Wajda finds that mainly in the use of the spoken word and the technique of observational documentary cinema. *Man of Iron* thus is a film of and for its time in the same way as the *Man of Marble* I was confronted with in the cinema theatre of Nowa Huta in 1977 was a film for its time. Here Wajda had cleverly used the rhetoric means available in that historical situation to make a film that in many ways drew a map of the events in post-war Polish history that led up to the events of 1980 and beyond. Through almost a quarter of a century of representing Polish history and contemporary society on film he had developed a rhetorical style utilising a rich imagery allowing a meaningful communication in a situation where the use of plain words were more or less impossible. Three years later, the possibility of direct address was there, and he seized it. In this way the two films also reflect different uses of the documentary medium, uses that do not conflict or contradict each other, but rather function in a complementary way in two films that ought to be viewed as one, and as one of the most influential documents on Polish society in the twentieth century.

Notes

1   Nichols (1991, 1994) operates with five different documentary *modes of expression*. In addition to the expository and observational mode, he also proposes the expressions *interactive*, *reflexive* and *performative* to designate modes of expression that in different ways directly implicates the film-maker. Since these modes descriptively tend to overlap, I have chosen to use the expression *intersubjective* to cover this area (see Sørenssen 2001).

CHAPTER NINE

Catastrophic Spectacles: Historical Trauma and the Masculine Subject in Lotna

Christopher J. Caes

Andrzej Wajda has been referred to as 'the essential Pole' (Michałek & Turaj 1988: 129). This essay, while making the common qualification that there are other rich models of Polish culture aside from the romantic tradition of which Wajda is a part, will have no quarrel with this characterisation. Indeed, it will continue to insist on its validity. At the same time it will suggest this assertion is not as self-evident as it appears and that the romantic strand of Polish national identity in the twentieth century, particularly in the films of its main current representative, deserves to be more rigorously theorised. To this end I will bring together the tools of the psychoanalytic tradition with a historicised reading of the romantic tradition by focusing first on the culture, unique and volatile, of Poland in the late 1930s, then weaving these two methodologies together through a reading of Wajda's early biography, artistic and personal.

I want to begin by revisiting Wajda's 1959 film, *Lotna*, focusing in particular on the (in)famous scene of the cavalry charge on German tanks in order to generate a trio of themes – vision, modernity, and masculine subjectivity – that might be fashioned into a framework for examining his cinema as a whole. Wajda's cinema relentlessly thematises vision. It constructs and highlights positions of spectatorship and spectacle. Naturally, this can be ascribed to his reflexive inscription of the cinematic medium into the texture of his films (for instance, *Man of Marble*, 1976), but a source can also be found in the unique role played by vision in Polish romantic culture. In a suggestive passage, Polish literary critic Jan Prokop writes: 'The knightly-cavalry model calls for recognition and fame, demands *teatrum* – we exist in the eyes of others, their praise or contempt inspires our behavior ... The individual is, then, other-oriented, he chooses *paraître* rather than *être...*' (1985: 29). In other words, the exhibitionist quality of many of the heroes of Wajda's cinema can be linked to the necessity of producing spectacle in order to become a (national) subject. Wajda's unique inflection of the model of national subject with regard to spectacle will be dealt with later. For the moment I want to return to the cavalry charge. Here too, we see a twinning of the reflexive impulse of film with the national impulse: the cavalry, in Polish, often referred to as *jazda*,[1] is filmed as it thunders across the plain in a long tracking shot, which is also known as *jazda*. The captain, earlier that morning, prior to setting off for battle, recommended to the nobleman's widow that she secure her carriage at a fine vantage point near the forest, to insure herself, as it were, a front row seat, informing her, 'You'll see a beautiful cavalry charge this morning.'

Aside from underlining the spectacular nature of the charge, his comment discloses that he and the cavalrymen are not only the executors of a military manouvre, but also actors in a performance. Moreover, the cavalrymen stage this production not only to intimidate the enemy and dazzle the Polish nation, but for themselves as well. They are spectators of their own performance, a fact that introduces a unique inner doubling into the visual structure of the charge. In other words – and this is implicit in Prokop's notion of 'existing in the eyes of others' – the cavalrymen must not only see and be seen by the other cavalrymen, but they must *see themselves being seen*. The bodies of the other cavalrymen become for each of them a mirror, which functions not only as a source of pleasure that sends back to them the knowledge of their own performance, but also as a challenge, further, an injunction to produce at all costs in one's own body the 'spectacle of the masculine.'[2] Finally, this unique dialectic between spectator and spectacle may be seen here as an attempt to overcome the inherently voyeuristic position of cinema spectatorship, for in addition to tracking the cavalrymen, the camera further highlights the spectacle of individual riders through a series of cuts to close-ups of the bodies and faces of Captain Chodakiewicz (Mieczysław Łoza), Corporal Jerzy Grabowski (Jerzy Moes) and Lieutenant Wodnicki (Adam Pawlikowski), inserting the spectator, as it were, into the reciprocal visual relations at the heart of the charge.

Naturally, the cavalry is most associated not with modern mechanised warfare, but with pre-modern warfare and this scene, particularly Corporal Grabowski's infamous strike at the tank barrel with his saber, is frequently seen as a critique of interwar Poland's unpreparedness for World War Two, in contrast to the hypermodernity of the German war machine. However, the opposition between the modern and the pre-modern can be located a bit differently, not only between the Germans and the Poles, but on the side of Polish culture itself. Though World War Two sealed the fate of the cavalry, the fact remains that in the late 1930s when the cult of the cavalry, of which Wajda was an ardent follower as a child, was in full swing, this pre-modern military formation was seen not as some relic of bygone times, or even as the conservative preservation of a tradition for patriotic purposes, but as a modern military force *par excellence*. And we can point out that Wajda, too, to call forth once again the term *jazda*, is modernising the cavalry by implicitly construing it as a visual practice analogous to cinema. (In interview, he has associated the spectacle of cavalry drills with the experience of being at the movies.) Crucial for the purpose of reconnaissance, the cavalry was literally also a way of seeing and Wajda draws out those elements of it, such as swiftness and mobility of vision, that have a modern 'feel'. Indeed, one of the sources of superiority the cavalrymen feel they have over the ungainly tanks is that the latter possess not vision, but are blind – 'czołgi idą na ślepo', says one rider: 'tanks can't see where they're going.'

The final aspect of the scene I want to discuss is its function as a staging for male beauty. As so often the case in battle scenes, the charge becomes a study of the male body, not only of its physical subjection to the dictates and rhythms of the military performance, but also of its transformation into a material sign of the political and socio-cultural order that stands behind it. The order of the late 1930s, through the cult of the cavalry, put prime importance not only on the aesthetic spectacle of the male body. Enjoining men to enter into a sort of system of 'cross-censorship' (Bryson 1994: 231) – each rider must not only 'live up' to the model himself, but also insure that others are doing so – it had the effect of redirecting masculine desire to the bodies of other men. This is not to say that those who fell under the sway of the cult of the cavalry had conscious homoerotic intentions. Indeed, such a possibility would have been very difficult to enunciate. At the same time as masculine desire was being redirected towards the bodies of other men, symbolic substitutes for the masculine body were being simultaneously produced so that male desire never strayed beyond fierce competition.

This is quite clearly illustrated in the opening sequences of *Lotna*, where women are explicitly absented from the home, the context in which they are traditionally active. When the riders arrive at the manor house, Jerzy is hungry and Wodnicki tells him that if he can find a woman, he might be able to get her to make him something to eat. But none are to be found. Jerzy finds an overflowing bathtub and muses as to who could have been bathing there. Wodnicki tells him that if he can find her, 'she might let you wash her back'. Male desire is represented, but women are always already absent. Another object of desire will, in any case, soon insert itself between the two men. Throughout these initial scenes in the manor house, they have had difficulty concentrating because the sound of horse hooves has been echoing inexplicably throughout the house. When the source of the sound is revealed to be the white horse, *Lotna*, who literally moves about inside the house as if she were its true lady, all thoughts of women leave their minds. As the men enter the room of the old nobleman who is lying in bed, they discover the horse, which, as if literally wanting to get in bed with the old man, is rubbing its head against his pillow. The bequeathing of the white horse by the old nobleman to the cavalry captain is an Oedipal passing on of the mantle of authority and sexual prerogative from symbolic father to son that occurs in the absence of the mother, without whom this process is generally unthinkable. But here the horse rather than the mother's body acts as mediator for negotiating the passage. The only woman, whom the old man, after several unsuccessful summonses, is able to call, is a servant whose class and age disqualify her as erotic object in the eyes of the cavalrymen.

Meanwhile, that evening as the captain snores and Jerzy drowses, Wodnicki sits swiftly sketching a graceful image of the white horse at full gallop. Jerzy wakes up and catches him at this activity, and Wodnicki, inexplicably ashamed, quickly turns over the drawing, as if to hide something very private and illicit. But Jerzy encourages Wodnicki to show him the drawing, saying to him, 'You and I have the same taste.' Wodnicki gives in and reveals the sketch to Jerzy, saying, 'No girl is equal to her.' At that moment, the captain stirs in his sleep and is suddenly wakened by a dream that he has been shot in the heart. Somewhat compromised in this moment of weakness in the eyes of Jerzy and Wodnicki, he immediately guesses that the thought of his death has brought to the minds of the two of them the possibility of ownership of the white horse he has just received from the nobleman. He restores his authority and at the same time contains their desire for the horse by involving them in a wager.

Jerzy pulls the short match and wins next right of ownership in the event of the captain's death. And it is well over a half hour into the film, following the captain's death in the charge and his assumption of possession of the horse, that he can now even begin to think about women, and he becomes engaged to the school-teacher, Ewa. However, even then, he cannot fully direct his desire towards his bride. At one point, standing in the horse stable (where Jerzy and Ewa sleep together!), he gazes lovingly at his newlywed wife and his horse, saying 'A woman and a horse are the only things a man needs'. The film leads us to doubt the strength of his desire for the former, however, since it is the white horse that Jerzy will die trying to save.

These scenes and images show the disengaging of masculine desire from women and its firm relocation within the homosocial group of the cavalry riders.[3] More important to them than how they 'exist in the eyes' of women, is how they *will* 'exist in the eyes' of one other, if only given the opportunity to ride Lotna. At the same time, the horse, particularly that the circle of desire is tightened around it through the wager, functions as a safe outlet and a method of containment for masculine desire. Standing in as a fetish for the homosocial group as a whole, it insures the possibility of the statement, '*I* (a man) *love him* (a man)' – which it implicitly encourages – from being uttered, instead offering 'I love *her* (the horse)', or 'I *will be* him (the owner of the horse)'.[4] At the same time, the horse is '*lotna*', that is, 'swift' or 'fleeting', but also 'evanescent'. Were it to be true to its name and disappear, what would become of homosocial masculine desire? It is, in the end, only a thin screen that separates man from man.

Yet the horse also symbolises death ('to ride her is certain death', says Wodnicki in the opening sequences). Indeed, at the conclusion of the cavalry charge sequence the narcissistic regime of male identification is shaken. First of all, the cavalrymen, unlike the tank crews, are armored only in the spectacular aura of performance and are brutally cut down by the shells and bullets of the tanks. Yet their bodies and those of their horses continue, again in narrative excess, to be objects of spectacle for the camera. Indeed, as it focuses in detail on the death and mutilation of the riders, pausing to record with agonising slowness the crushing of a dead horse and rider by the treads of an oncoming tank, it is as if the spectacle of annihilation of the body is more satisfying than the spectacle of the body's seeming invulnerability. Further, as the remaining riders regroup behind a dune following the debacle of the charge, we see a close-up of Jerzy's face, which, as he gazes at the saber he has uselessly shattered on the barrel of a tank, registers not the hopeless despair we might expect after witnessing such a total rout, but joy that he has 'blooded'

Virgin soldier on white horse: *Lotna*

himself in battle. Jerzy's broken saber, read – as Wajda himself will authorise us to do below – as a symbolic castration, encapsulates the significance of the broken bodies of the dead cavalrymen. Yet this radical demonstration that the national subject does *not* possess the phallus is recoded as pleasure, not only in Jerzy's eyes, but also in those of the young boys, who eagerly scamper out of from behind the bushes, where they have just witnessed the whole scene, to snatch the trophy of the German officer's hat that Jerzy carelessly discards. Indeed, the elation is, as it were, exponentially increased the greater the disfigurement, with the greatest exhilaration being perhaps death itself: as mentioned, Jerzy will ultimately die trying to unite his body with the fleeing white horse, beautiful, but all too vulnerable as a physical target for the German aircraft guns.

Why is this? Because in Wajda's cinema, catastrophe eliminates the thin barrier separating male desire from other men and allows the homosocial bond to be (re)eroticised. This is very delicately and fleetingly marked in this film, which is still a part of the early cinema, from a period when Wajda was yet working his way towards a therapeutic film language. When Lotna appears dragging the dead captain's body, Wodnicki disentangles the corpse, composes it in the sand, and lies down on top of it. Furthermore, the desire not to *be* a man, but to *have* one, will be coded in these sequences as a desire to consume.

The captain's body is brought into a butcher's hut, where animal carcasses are being hacked apart with an axe. The captain's body is explicitly juxtaposed in a single shot with the dead animals, and is then carried into the dining room where it is *placed on the table*, as if it were some bizarre meal to be consumed. Indeed, this metaphoric ingestion of the male body has already been suggested in the enigmatic shot of the gasping, dying fish in the peasant kitchen, itself an ingestion by Wajda into his film of an image by his deceased friend, Andrzej Wróblewski. Furthermore, the opening sequences of the film have juxtaposed the cavalrymen on horseback to images of the fragmented statues of nude female bodies, evoking feminisation, a hint at the later fragmentation of their own bodies, and an image for aesthetic consumption.

Let us summarise before moving on. On the basis of these examples from *Lotna*, we see that the male (national) subject is enjoined to produce the spectacle of the masculine, but is then forced to witness the annihilation of the material support of that spectacle, his own body or that of another man. In fact, for Wajda, the actual production of the masculine is not achieved *until* the moment of mutilation occurs. To be a *true* man can only mean *to once have been a powerful man*. Furthermore, as we have known from Maciek's spectacular murder and subsequent embrace of Szczuka in *Ashes and Diamonds (Popiół i diament,* 1958), Wajda's cinema strives to put two (wounded) men in one another's arms; but the path to that point is sewn with death and destruction. Why?

In a 1968 interview Wajda proposed an unusual thought experiment:

Nowadays when I look back on [my earlier films] from a mature perspective, I often wish that instead of some of the traditional national symbols – the saber, the white horse, the red poppies, the rowan tree – I had used erotic symbols from Freud's textbook. But I wasn't raised on Freud's textbook and I can't change that. I discovered Freud too late to be able make use of his ideas. (in Wertenstein 2000: 47)

Three questions pose themselves on the basis of this quote: why *Lotna* (and it is clear from the 'traditional national symbols' that *Lotna* is the film he has in mind)? Why *erotic* symbols? And why Freud? My tentative answers to these questions will be, in brief: 1) *Lotna*, because this film, as is known, has been regarded by Wajda as his most personal; 2) *Lotna* comes closest to representing the structure of adolescent desire of Wajda's pre-war childhood, itself organically linked to the psychosocial and political structures of the late 1930s, and so violently rewritten in September 1939; and 3) Freud functions here as a signifier of Wajda's career-long intent to develop a therapeutic language that would represent the psychosexual trauma of the war years.

I want to emphasise that the underlying narrative of desire behind the images of Wajda's films is not necessarily an *obvious* one. On the contrary, it surfaces fleetingly, in many cases as seeming excess, occurring in scenes sometimes tangential to the forward motion of the plot, realised most often in the *mise-en-scène* and disappearing quickly from the spectator's consciousness, quite often forgotten. Indeed many spectators of his films with whom I have spoken do not even recall the presence of some of the scenes I discuss, nor, if they do, has that aspect of it struck them. Yet Wajda himself had not explicitly alluded to a twin underlying erotic and therapeutic thrust to his films. From this perspective part of the challenge of Wajda's cinema is, as he states above, that he was not 'raised on Freud's textbook'. Unlike Western critics, who sometimes, it seems, are raised on nothing else, his cinema is an intuitive, highly idiosyncratic, and original exploration of what might be called 'cultural clinical therapy', a concept still to be fully elaborated in discursive terms. Wajda, in his ignorance of Freud is a godsend to psychoanalytic critics, because he is 'uncontaminated'. In his films the subject gives expression to the structure of its desire in a way not already directed towards another subject 'supposed to know'. On the other hand, rigorous analysis of the psychic structures in his films, with their roots in what is for most Westerners the unfamiliar contours of the post-aristocratic romantic strand of Polish culture, may force us to rethink some of the precepts of Western psychoanalytic discourse, perhaps turning some of us into – why not – 'Wajdians'.

Indeed, it is this highly original aspect of Wajda's cinema that may provide a reason for the presence of much of what the Polish film critic Alicja Helman finds objectionable in it. She writes: 'In *Lotna* we find a symbolisation that is cheap, blatant, univocal … The symbols do not suggest, but insistently scream. What *ought to be* [my italics] subtextual, merely touched on, becomes vulgar, unacceptable' (1959: 3). Helman holds up the mirror of high artistic illusiveness and ambiguity to Wajda's film and it produces at best a highly distorted reflection. Indeed the early Wajda, though appearing to utilise modernist intertextuality – the shattered piano from Norwid and the quote from Dante at the entrance to the canals in *Kanal*, the late romantic Norwid poem carved on the wall of a Gothic cathedral (!) and the appearance of the horse in the same cathedral – is far from subtle. On the contrary, as Helman recognises, he is essentially beating the viewer over the head, when not seeming to short-circuit or explode the signals he is sending. But the answer is not to announce the failure of his films. It is to rethink one's methodology and locate the significance of these images elsewhere. Wajda is not fashioning Eliotian fragments, but is attempting to create a specific psychic disposition through a network of symbols and images. In other words he is attempting to create a new therapeutic language, while at the same time identifying and evoking those to whom it will speak.

Having sketched the structure of masculine subjectivity and masculine desire in Wajda's early cinema, I want now to turn to a historical argument and speculate on its origin. In an interview, Wajda states:

> In 1939, when the Germans invaded Poland, I was 13 years old. Through the eyes of a boy I saw the horrible, crushing defeat of the magnificent army, in which my father served as an officer. Just a few years earlier, watching riders drill on horseback with saber and lance, I had seen images so beautiful they took my breath away, as if they had come straight out of John Ford's films. Now in despair I watched columns of thousands of officers being led into German captivity. (in Wertenstein 2000: 178)

The various layers in this reminiscence are so densely bound up with one another that it is almost impossible to untwine them. The disaster is simultaneously aesthetic, social, political, psychic and sexual. The 'defeat of the magnificent army' also necessarily entails the collapse of the political and social order in which it functioned and which it was unable to defend. The army is associated both with the father, who was taken not into German, but Soviet captivity (again, indirection) and was soon to be dead within in a year in the forest of Katyń. Furthermore, there is the childish desire for the image of the masculine ideal ('images so beautiful they took my breath away'). And the reference to cinema ('John Ford's films') points to an awareness of the ideal itself as a performance, as a conscious transformation of the male body into spectacle 'in the eyes of others'. But the despair is also due to the fact that this avenue of coming into existence 'in the eyes of others' has now been definitively closed for the boy.

The crux of my argument lies in a re-examination of the cult of the military and of the cavalry that flourished during the late 1930s in Poland in order to see it not as wholly continuous with the Polish romantic tradition, but as having introduced a rupture in that tradition. The post-1935 National Democratic state, responding to the socio-economic and political crises that were the lot of the countries in Central and Eastern Europe in this period, sought to compensate for these, 1) politically, by shifting radically to rightist authoritarianism and introducing proto-fascist elements into its structure, 2) culturally, by channeling unrest through mobilisation of traditional Polish patriotic sentiment in order to construct an exclusivist national unity. The unity so constructed was not in any sense the genuine return to a pre-modern wholeness it purported to be, but a modern reconstruction of the past in the image of the present, itself signaling its modernity by, among other things, the extreme aestheticisation of the symbols of the nation and, predictably, in the context of the cult of the cavalry, of the bodies of the men, who represented that nation. Now, while it is important to note the ultimate failure of the rightist authoritarian or proto-fascist project in interwar Poland,[5] it is no less important to take note of the deep inroads it made in the area of culture.

Polish literary critic, Kazimierz Wyka, referring to the policies of the National Democratic state as 'superpower ideology', neatly captures this split:

> There were few who believed in 'superpower ideology' as justification for complete political isolation, leaving Poland standing alone eye to eye with German fascism. There was, however, an area where the slogan bore fruit. And these were fruit that were very useful for the *sanacja* camp, for treating the colonels as geniuses able to assume any position of responsibility. It was precisely in the area of judgments as to the military strength of the country that the slogan bore fruit. It was quite universally believed that militarily Poland was a partner able to conduct politics in a manner which did not require taking into account at all the basic political and geographical possibilities of the country. (1985: 89; my translation)

Wyka, while registering widespread lack of support for the regime's right radical authoritarian politics, at the same time notes a success in its cultivation of a militarist, and hence masculine disposition. Indeed the popularity of the cult of the military in the late 1930s is frequently noted in historical accounts. The regime underwrote the publication of large albums constructing in words and images the exploits of the Polish cavalry from its origins, through the present day, into the future, detailing every aspect of the cavalryman's life, such as training, uniform appearance, and horse-care. The lavish aestheticism with which the entire cult was treated is reflected in a common name for horses at that time: 'Fetish'. Such albums were standard fare for many young people of the period and Wajda on one occasion recalls the influence they had on his boyhood imagination (see Wajda 1973). Important in this context is the way in which the cavalry is consistently configured as a *modern* military method of warfare. Here is, for instance, a passage from an expensive, bright red volume entitled *The Book of Polish Cavalry* (*Księga jazdy polskiej*, 1938), dedicated to the memory of Marshall Józef Piłsudski and sponsored by his self-styled successor, Edward Rydz-Śmigły, commander-in-chief of the Polish armed forces.

> It is precisely the supposed 'enemy' of the cavalry – in reality its great 'benefactor' – the engine, which has freed it from all burdens and services that weighed upon it and has allowed it to dedicate itself above all to actions on the offensive, which is after all the essential and exclusive purpose of cavalry actions in the grand style.
>
> In this way modern means of motor transport have not only not negated the meaning of the cavalry, but on the contrary, have allowed it to successfully triumph over the crisis in which it found itself for almost a century, one of the greatest crises which it ever experienced.
>
> Thanks to motorisation the most wonderful possibilities of bold and effective action have opened themselves up to the cavalry, to which it will undoubtedly prove itself worthy in any future war. (*Księga jazdy* 1938: 312–13; my translation)

Naturally, passages such as this one, following the debacle of September 1939, can only seem to be ironic, even parodic. But this was not the case for Wajda as a young boy.

> I was raised in the cavalry barracks, where I would see things like six galloping horses drawing artillery pieces come racing into the yard. And these weren't cavalrymen of the type you see now in London at the changing of the guard. They were part of a true cavalry that was to conduct warfare and destroy the enemy. These weren't marionettes but living people, whom I saw, loved and knew. How could I not accept them? (in Wertenstein 2000: 48)

Significantly, in Wajda's words, the cavalry is not an anachronism maintained out of sentiment, but a crowning achievement of modern technology. The engine, far from threatening the existence of the cavalry, has actually ended its 'hundred year crisis' not through retiring it, but by allowing it to assume the position of premier military force in a modern war. Finally, the cavalry is here characterised not in terms of the actual manoeuvres it will perform, but primarily as style, as a theatrical spectacle.

Hence, while an element of spectacle had, to be sure, always been integral to the cavalry's military performance, the aesthetic aura now acquires a status so autonomous that it dazzles the strategists into being unable to see the danger in the heavy reliance on cavalry in the context of modern warfare. Here are the elements of rupture of which I spoke. At no previous moment in his history had it been so fetishised as spectacle and on such a broad scale, and – here is the key – at no time previously was the desire of young men so successfully harnessed to the homosocial sphere of the military, while at the same time productively channeled and contained to suppress the danger of the homoerotic.[6] In a 'normal' battle situation, that is, one in which one's forces are not defeated, events may have been assumed to unfold along the lines of the reading I offered above of the opening sequences of *Lotna*, in which male desire is carefully disengaged from the bodies of women and located within the male group, but contained through the wager and the mediation of the horse.

As we have seen, the German invasion of 1939 shattered this dream of wholeness. Once again, Kazimierz Wyka concisely frames this event:

> The shock of military defeat struck society a blow in its least protected most vulnerable spot. Within the course of a few days it became clear that the military secrets had been a sheer bluff and that the army was absolutely unprepared for a modern war. And the blow had effects that were not limited to military matters alone. This was because the politicians in uniform had based their political and social platforms precisely on the uniform itself. Thus, the attitude of trust towards the ruling party, which had been forced on the people, turned out to be based on blindness, lies and irresponsibility. And for this reason in September of 1939, the blow to the uniform spread its sense of defeat over all that had led up to it. (1985: 90)

Wyka makes clear that the catastrophe was both political, but also psychosocial. While the nation may have been able to accommodate the demise of the National Democratic state, the destruction of the spectacle of the uniform – and behind the spectacle and the uniform is the body – was experienced as traumatic and unleashed a series of contradictory and complex emotions.

Let us embed this in the context of Wajda's biography, where the collapse of the state as the governing body of the fatherland coincides with the death of his own father. In fact, it is inappropriate to speak of 'coincidence' here. For the young Wajda, as we saw earlier, this is *the same* event. Clearly the first emotions are grief and despair on account of the lost father and the shattered dream of the cavalry. At the same time, the defeat is also the *failure* of the father, the revelation that the aesthetic spectacle of the masculine power was only, in the end, a hollow production, like the old nobleman at the beginning of *Lotna*, who says to the captain, 'Shake me and I'll fall apart'. Hence, at some level a feeling of contempt or derision, due to the fact that in the fall of the father, the son's future is destroyed, will compete with the despair. Furthermore, the death of the father removes the authority that deftly channelled homosocial desire into the mediations, such as the horse, that allowed the desire of men 'with the same taste', as Jerzy puts it, to mingle in a harmless context. The dialectic of rivalry and admiration is snapped. Though this homoerotic desire can still not be literally represented, it does flicker in the metaphoric images of consumption of the male body in *Lotna*, in the highly reflexive and playful scenes from the films of the late 1970s, and, as we shall see, in the 'death hug' of Maciek and Szczuka. Therefore, paradoxically, the traumatic event is also the source, in a sense, of a newfound pleasure and grief over the father's death and the contempt for the exposed fragility of his legacy, are now joined by a sense of erotic liberation.

How to give adequate and *simultaneous* expression to the conflicting emotions generated in the wake of the crisis? Through a contradictory and overcharged cinematic style that in its very excess gives body to the symptom. Of his early cinematic art, Wajda states:

> I don't think that it would have occurred either to me or to Andrzej [Wróblewski] to make ourselves into the heroes of our art. Our gaze was fixed on our fathers. We considered it the duty of our generation as sons to bear the testimony of our fathers, to recreate their experiences, for the murdered can no longer speak. (1971: 29)

As 'bearing testimony for the father', Wajda's early cinema commemorates the father, who was murdered. At the same time, 'the murdered can no longer speak' because they failed to prevent the catastrophe, their spectacular legacy proved to be a sham, and the once powerful images cannot not now emit a bitter irony. Hence, Wajda's cinema will paradoxically commemorate the father by ... murdering him again. Might this not be the origin of the incessant destruction and mutilation visited upon the male body in scene after scene of Wajda's cinema, a cinema, the hero of which is, in part, the father? But the catastrophe is also feverishly generated again and again for another reason. Symbolically eliminating the father will free homosocial desire to wander outside the circuit of narcissistic identification and rivalry. It will eliminate the fleeting mediating screen separating men from men, which like the white horse, is only a necessary illusion. But at what a cost! It is too dangerous to eroticise the powerful man in his prime; only when he has been divorced from power, psychically and physically mutilated, and often killed, can his body be loved. Finally, the father, in the role of producer of masculine spectacle, is constantly deflecting the adoration of the son into hierarchical structures (the wager in *Lotna*); his message is, in accordance with the resolution of Oedipus, *be* me, not *love* me. But the catastrophe undoes this injunction, releasing the son from the obligation only to *be*. So, once again, the murder of father is on some level motivated by love for the father, for only in generating the catastrophe that will kill the father, can the son embrace the father's body.

Maciek Chełmicki's classic murder and embrace of Szczuka in *Ashes and Diamonds* is an example of Wajda's spectacular attempt to represent trauma. This is a scene, which by disengaging narrative from image, is able to load itself literally to the bursting point (fireworks) with allegorical meaning. At plot level, Maciek and Szczuka are on opposite sides. Strictly speaking, the embrace from Maciek's perspective can signify nothing but sudden guilty sympathy for his victim, triggered by realisation that he has become a murderer. The authorial ironic commentary would be to point up the fact that Pole is killing Pole. But Wajda, in an addition to the screenplay, has given Szczuka a son. Between Maciek and the actual son an explicit parallel is drawn. In prison Szczuka's son stares as a moth bats around frantically inside a lampshade, resisting yet drawn to the glowing bulb. In front of his hotel Maciek paces fitfully before deciding to go through with the murder. As Maciek shoots, Szczuka lurches towards him, dying in his grasp. Maciek stares and the fireworks celebrating the end of the war go off directly above his head. He drops Szczuka and kneels down as the camera pans down to shoot the reflection of the descending fireworks in a puddle, so that they now reverse direction and flow upward, gently seeming to push Szczuka's body skyward. Can this not be read as a scene expressing tremendous grief at the loss of the father, grief expressed, ironically, by a son who has just murdered him? But is it not also an example of the horrific path that must be traversed in Wajda's cinema in order to bring about the embrace of two men? And finally, does the excessive addition of the fireworks to the scene not *simultaneously* signify spectacular commemoration, the release of murderous pent-up fury and rage, reflexive celebration of the cinematic signifier, and, finally – why not – orgasm?

By way of conclusion I want briefly to broach the topic of the white horse. As mentioned earlier, to sit on *Lotna* is certain death. Jerzy is warned that on the white horse he presents a far too visible target to German aircraft. At the same time, the white horse is the core of the cavalry tradition, which as Prokop remarks, depends precisely on *being seen*. Unfortunately, in modern warfare, this includes being a target. In other words, the national subject is enjoined to occupy an impossible position. The very moment that it comes into being is always also the moment of the cessation of its being. More detailed analysis would isolate similar positions in Wajda's cinema, which it would be impossible to occupy and survive. What, then, is the significance for the romantic strand of national identity that Wajda, the 'essential Pole', who is often seen as engaging in the positive project of Polish *Bildung* outside the constraints of the illegitimate state, figures the achievement of national identity, at least from a formal perspective, is a wholly negative project and is, as it were, constantly preparing the spectator for the emergence of a post-romantic subjectivity. Perhaps Wajda is mistakenly seen as guaranteeing the *continuity* of a series of positive expressions of national identity, because in constantly re-enacting 'the death of the national subject' in film after film, he has no positive program to follow it. Instead, this impossible position is inscribed, in the figure of the white horse, into the cinematic medium. The horse, like the cinema screen, is a white surface onto which fantasy can be projected, but the fantasy, like the horse, is fleeting and disappears once the projector is turned off.

Notes

1   *Jazda* literally means 'drive', or 'travel by conveyance'.
2   For the notion of the masculine as a spectacular effect, requiring effort to produce, I am indebted to the thinking of Norman Bryson, 'Géricault and "Masculinity"' (1994: 228–59).
3   Here is Eve Kosofky Sedgwick's definition of the term homosocial: 'a word occasionally used in history and the social sciences, where it describes social bonds between persons of the same sex. It is a neologism, obviously formed by analogy with "homosexual" and just as obviously meant to be distinguished from "homosexual". In fact, it is applied to such activities as "male bonding", which may, as in our society, be characterised by intense homophobia, fear and hatred of homosexuality.' Nevertheless, she 'hypothesise[s] the potential unbrokenness of a continuum between the homosocial and homosexual – a continuum whose visibility, for men, in our society, is radically disrupted' (1985: 1–2).
4   Sedgwick, on the slippages that occur when male–male erotic desire is

unrepresentable, writes: 'Freud in his discussion with Dr. Schreber gives the following list of the possible eroto-grammatical transformations that can be generated in contradiction of the sentence, unspeakable under a homophobic regime of utterance, "*I* (a man) *love him* (a man)". First, "I do not *love* him – I *hate* him"; second, "I do not love *him*, I love *her*"; third, "*I* do not love him; *she* loves him"; and finally, "I do not love him; I do not love anyone"', to which Sedgwick adds a fifth, '"I do not *love* him, I *am* him"' (1990: 161–2).

5   Here are the carefully researched and judicious characterisations of the political scientists. Edward Wynot writes: 'Poland [of the late 1930s] offers an excellent illustration of how a ruling group sought to use the outer trappings of Fascism while rejecting the real essence and extreme methods that gave this movement its dynamic character (1974: xi). Similarly, Stanley Payne writes that [Poland of 1937–39 was a] syncretic, semi-pluralist authoritarian regime, lacking a mass-based government or a distinctive new party system, which strove to develop a semi-bureaucratic semi-fascist movement from the top down, but failed in the enterprise (1995: 469).

6   For the notion of early twentieth-century radical-right authoritarianism as combining a masculine homoerotic charge with simultaneous suppression, or perhaps, shaping of that charge, see Sedgwick 1993: 50–1.

CHAPTER TEN

Wajda, Grotowski and Mickiewicz: The Dialectics of Apotheosis and Derision

Michael Goddard

In Eugenio Barba's book *Land of Ashes and Diamonds* (1999), which contextualises the publication of his correspondence with Jerzy Grotowski, Barba writes of the formative experience of viewing Andrzej Wajda's film *Ashes and Diamonds* (*Popiół i diament*, 1958) before travelling to Poland (1999: 15). In fact, as the constitutive factor in Barba's decision to pursue research into theatre in Poland, this moment is only surpassed by his eventual encounter with Grotowski. For Barba, the film *was* the image of Poland that he was seeking, an image that he would try to locate in the milieu of 1960s Polish theatre, and that he ultimately discovered in Grotowski's 'Theatre of 13 Rows'.[1] I would argue that this is not a purely arbitrary connection but an essential one, because there is a commonality to be found between the theatre of Grotowski and the cinema of Wajda. This commonality lies in a working through or re-inscription of tradition, particularly the legacy of Polish Romanticism and Symbolism in a contemporary context. Furthermore I will argue that for both Grotowski and Wajda, this tradition is valued not so much for its specific content as for providing models of subjectivation,[2] or even a heroic subjectivation capable of being transposed into the contemporary world. In the case of Grotowski this was referred to critically as 'a dialectics of apotheosis and derision', and it is this critical conception that I will examine first in relation to Grotowski before assessing its applicability to Wajda's cinema. This will be done in order to elaborate a framework through which to approach Wajda's own relations to Polish Romanticism, rather than constituting a thorough engagement with Grotowski's theatre itself.

The Dialectics of Apotheosis and Derision in Grotowski's Theatre

The above phrase was first used as a critical evaluation of one of Grotowski's productions, significantly Adam Mickiewicz's *Forefathers' Eve* (*Dziady III*),[3] but it was soon adopted by Grotowski and his collaborators for the programmatic texts accompanying their performances (Kumiega 1985: 38). While it can also refer to Grotowski's transgression of the rules of naturalistic theatre through experiments in theatrical space, or his unique method of actor training, it primarily refers to Grotowski's way of re-working canonical theatrical texts. From the beginnings of the 'Theatre of 13 Rows', Grotowski rejected the use of avant-garde texts, preferring instead to stage transgressive versions of canonical texts by European playwrights such as Calderon, Marlow and Shakespeare and especially those of the Polish 'national poets' including Mickiewicz's *Forefathers' Eve*, Juliusz Słowacki's *Kordian* and Stanisław Wyspiański's *Akropolis*. The transgressive treatment of these texts, however, through deformations of theatrical space and performer-audience relations, innovative actor training and the breaking up of the unity of the original text, was the key site of Grotowski's theatrical experimentation.

But how did this experimentation constitute 'a dialectics of apotheosis and derision'? Grotowski treated literary texts not as unified wholes to be represented, but as a type of raw material to be transcoded into a coherent system of theatrical signs. In keeping with Grotowski's emphasis on theatre as a space of constantly renegotiated performer-audience relations, his treatment of literary texts was also intended to open up the relations between theatre and text without either slavish fidelity or complete abandonment. In a sense the dialectic of apotheosis and derision is a theatrical deconstruction of texts in which in a first 'derisive' phase their formal unity is broken up and then in a second phase re-inscribed in an entirely new system of theatrical signs, often using some apparently incidental element of the text as a guiding principle.

Grotowski's celebrated adaptation of Wyspiański's *Akropolis* was itself the apotheosis of this phase of his career. The phrases in the original play, 'the cemetery of the tribes', and 'our Acropolis', were taken as an anticipation of the death camps, and so Wyspiański's text was broken up and transposed from Wawel to the environment of Auschwitz (see Barba 1999: 56–7). The text was interspersed with both textual accounts of the camps and the ritualised actions of the actors playing the inmates developed during rehearsals. Nevertheless, this is not merely the 'derision' of the original text since it also takes Wyspiański's examination of the mythologies of Western civilisation to an apotheosis through its relocation in the context of Auschwitz. Grotowski's method of stripping away the surface layers of the personality, or the subjective masks of the actor, to arrive at his true essence or 'the total act'[4] clearly parallels the processes of subjectivation present in Polish romantic texts such as *Forefathers' Eve* and *Kordian* in which through self-sacrifice an individual character becomes the expression of the aspirations of the Polish nation and its people. This subjectivation of the performing body clearly added to the intensity of the apotheosis of a production such as *Akropolis*. Thus when commentators like Peter Brook saw in it not so much a representation of Auschwitz but its recreation in a kind of 'black mass',[5] this was due less to the effects of innovative staging, than to the subjectivation of the performing bodies who were in a sense spoken by the text; or rather by the intertextuality of *Akropolis* and Auschwitz as expressions of a romantic subjectivation carried to extreme apotheosis.

This raises the question of whether such apotheosis and derision is merely a continuation of Polish romanticism in the modern, post-Holocaust era or whether it radically transforms this tradition, whether it deconstructs it in order to create something radically different for which romanticism is merely the inspiration. One could note, for example, that in marked contrast to Wajda's cinema, Grotowski's theatre subjects the national elements in the Polish drama to derision, in order to facilitate an apotheosis of their more universal and sacral elements. Grotowski's theatre is thus more an exploration of what it means to be human, rather than to be Polish. This universalism is not necessarily a departure from romanticism, however, but merely from the national inflections of its Polish variants and could in fact be read as an apotheosis of romanticism rather than its critique.[6] For our present purposes it is sufficient at this stage to underline the direct links between Grotowski's theatrical practice and Polish Romanticism, before moving on to an engagement with Wajda's treatment of the same tradition.

Wajda and Polish Romanticism: Problematising the Relationship

In a society such as ours, the artist does help shape opinions, and can function as a kind of conscience for the nation. In that sense, yes, we can and should play a leading role. (Wajda in Georgakas (ed.) 1983: 324)

The relationship between Wajda and Polish Romanticism is often stated as self-evident and his film-making has been described in terms that could equally be applied to Polish Romantic poets such as Mickiewicz or Słowacki:

With special exceptions, Wajda does not strain to capture universal themes so much as he strains to play upon those that relate to the nation's consciousness. Wajda hears at once the echoes of his country's history and the sounds of its life. He listens for the tones, harmonious or dissonant, and thus captures his special cinematic music. (Michałek & Turaj 1988: 133).

This relationship would seem to find its ultimate confirmation in Wajda's 1999 adaptation of Mickiewicz's *Pan Tadeusz*, which is at once the epitome of Polish Romantic poetry and a work of profound national significance. It could be argued, however, that *Pan Tadeusz*, in its use of irony and critical treatment of Polish nationalist aspirations, is a post-romantic work relative to the earlier work such as *Forefathers' Eve*. Yet on an aesthetic level it remains committed to the principle thematics of Romanticism, especially in its evocation of the mythical homeland as evidenced by the opening lines on Lithuania. So that on the level of the national at least, Wajda's treatment of romantic tradition could not be more different from Grotowski's. Rather it seems to be a much more a direct continuation of the tendencies of the Polish Romantics, and especially Mickiewicz, to link subjective and national liberation.

Before reading Wajda as the direct heir of Polish Romanticism and Adam Mickiewicz in particular it is necessary to emphasise some of the profound differences between the historical and artistic situations of Wajda as a film director in post-World War Two Poland and that of the nineteenth-century Romantic poet. Mickiewicz, for example, as a largely exiled poet at the time of the partitions, fits precisely the profile of the disenfranchised, solitary and rebellious romantic poet in an almost archetypical way.[7] Wajda on the other hand, engaged in the most collective of art-forms during the era of Communist Poland, was in a very different political and existential situation. It was one that required constant negotiation not only with his audience, which was also a key problematic of Mickiewicz's poetry, but also with the communist authorities and censors, to play the double game of the Polish intellectual analysed by Czesław Miłosz in *The Captive Mind* (1953). If Wajda saw himself as occupying, or wanting to occupy, a similar position to Mickiewicz as the voice and conscience of the nation,[8] then neither the form of national oppression nor the place of Wajda as an artist is identical to the situation of Mickiewicz. Furthermore, over a century of traumatic history separates the two artists, and Wajda's artistic engagement with this very history cannot fully hide something anachronistic in the maintenance of a romantic attitude, especially after the atrocities of World War Two, largely taking place on Polish soil.

To fully grasp the invocation of Polish Romanticism in Wajda's films it is necessary to clarify what is specific to it, particularly in the work of Mickiewicz, clearly Wajda's preferred model of the Romantic poet. This will enable us to see how Polish Romanticism is transformed in Wajda's cinema and whether as in Grotowski's theatre, this constitutes a dialectics of apotheosis and derision. To do this I will briefly examine *Forefathers' Eve*, particularly the figure of Konrad as Polish Romantic heroic persona *par excellence*, then examine the heroic personae of Wajda's *Man of Marble* (*Człowiek z marmuru*, 1976) as a reworking and splitting of this persona. This might seem a strange choice given Wajda's more explicitly romantic films such as *Kanal* (*Kanał*, 1957) or *Lotna* (1959), not to mention *Pan Tadeusz* itself. However, what I hope to show is that it is when Wajda is at his most political and 'original' rather than following literary models or obvious romantic treatments of history, his cinema has its strongest relationship to the romanticism of Mickiewicz, itself engaged directly with contemporary politics.

Mickiewicz's Romanticism: Forefathers' Eve and the Figure of Konrad

Mickiewicz's romanticism was marked from the beginning by the specificity of the historical situation of Poland and Lithuania as disenfranchised countries under the domination of the partitioning powers, particularly that of Tsarist Russia which controlled Lithuania. While he shared the Western European romantic rebellion against the norms of classical poetry and its attendant enlightenment values of reason and common sense, his work never constituted that retreat into the self to be found in the work of the English romantic poets. Certainly the figure of the rebellious poet as transcendent subject was every bit as important to Mickiewicz as to his Western European contemporaries, but the key difference was that the mere existence of such a sovereign subject was of immediate political and national significance in occupied Poland, whereas in other parts of Europe it was only of aesthetic significance. For example, the affirmation of the 'All Souls' Day' ritual in *Forefathers' Eve* parts

II and IV [9] is not merely the *mise-en-scène* for the apparition of phantoms from the other world, but an explicit critique of the complicity of the Church, with the destruction of these folk practices. More than this in re-working these rituals through poetry, Mickiewicz transformed them into a call for national redemption on a material level, rather than as mere pretexts for examining the tortures of the romantic subject: these tortures are certainly there in the figure of Gustav, but their solution will not be found solely in the realm of the spirit, but in concrete forms of national redemption.

This political redemption would be most fully expressed in *Forefathers' Eve*, which concerns the transformation of the romantic hero into a political visionary, who is no longer merely acting for himself but for his nation. It is therefore looking more closely at this subjective metamorphosis and why it is so significant for contemporary Polish art and culture. In the prologue of *Forefathers' Eve*, Gustav is imprisoned in Wilno and having fitful dreams in which he is visited by his Guardian Angel who tells him that he will be free (see Segel 1977: 81ff). Gustav interprets this not in personal but in national terms, rejecting any freedom that his jailers could grant him: 'Striking the fetters from my feet and hands/To rivet on my spirit heavier bands!/An exiled singer, now condemned to go/[Among] foreign and inimical throngs' (1977: 82). This is a clear expression of Mickiewicz's own fate as an exiled poet and a demonstration of how close the character of Gustav is to the poet himself. This heightens the significance of the celebrated metamorphosis which follows in which Gustav dies to be reborn as Konrad, enacted by inscribing this death and rebirth on the prison walls. This is both a pagan rite of passage and a metaphor of the power of poetic creation, but it is also a distinctly modern assumption of a collective rather than individual identity, in which the trials of Gustav as a romantic individual pale into insignificance next to the trials of his nation. This does not mean that subjective states are of no importance, but rather that visionary consciousness is no longer an individual phenomenon but tied to national and historical aspirations: the poet has been transformed into a national prophet.

It is in this context that Konrad's 'great improvisation' (Segel 1977: 100–11) can be understood, a fact that is underlined by its emergence out of a collective retelling of Russian atrocities by his fellow prisoners. Konrad, after having a vision of himself as an Eagle, the national symbol of Poland as well as a more general representation of prophecy, is then almost engulfed by a raven representing the dark forces of oppression. Out of this experience the improvisation emerges at the height of which Konrad challenges God himself and demands equal powers: 'I would have power o'er souls no less/Than you in heaven here possess' (1977: 106). This demand to become a poet-ruler, or even a God in his own right, which seems to prefigure Nietzsche's Zarathustra, is an apotheosis of Polish Romanticism, which takes it to a level that is at once political and metaphysical. What is so remarkable about it and what distinguishes it from other varieties of Romanticism is not its metaphysical aspirations, but the grounding of these aspirations firmly in the political setting of occupied Poland. Konrad does not want to usurp God for his own purposes but for his nation, which God has allowed to be subjugated. In fact the climax of his improvisation, which he cannot utter himself, is that God has already been usurped by the pure evil that is manifested in the form of the Tsar: 'My voice shot throughout creation/From generation unto generation/ Shouts you are not the father ... (Voice of the Devil) But the Tsar' (1977: 109). This alignment of good and evil with the concrete political realities of the subjugation of Poland and Lithuania by Russia is, of course, what has given the play its efficacy as a demand for rebellion against occupying powers up until the communist era, and this political symbolism is certainly present throughout Wajda's cinema.

This is a partial and narrow reading of a very complex work, but it serves to draw out the key features of the poetic persona of Konrad as one specific to Polish Romanticism, and one which was highly influential on the work of Wajda. This is not to say that Wajda's films are literally populated with Konrad-like figures, but rather that the idea of the transcendent or monumental subject, undergoing a metamorphosis to a national consciousness is a key feature of his cinema in its political forms. As such, what Wajda, like Grotowski, extracts from Polish Romanticism is not so much its content as its insistence on individual metamorphosis, in the context of and, as Michałek and Turaj have argued, *against* the tides of history. In other words what both Grotowski and Wajda extract from the legacy of Polish Romanticism is a model for heroic subjectivation, in the former in order to attain to a universal human essence, while in the latter in order to become the embodiment of the aspirations of the nation itself. This already throws some doubt on whether Wajda's engagement of this tradition can in any way be a critique or has any element of derision in relation to its key works. However if derision and apotheosis are understood abstractly as processes of breaking down and extracting elements from a tradition, then intensifying them through re-inscription in a new context, in other words as a creative deconstruction, then their application to Wajda's cinema becomes more apparent. What is most interesting here is the way Wajda constructs romantic personae in his films, despite the fact that they occupy for the most part an entirely modern world, markedly different in terms of recent traumatic history, political systems and artistic media than that of Mickiewicz. For this reason I will not be dealing with Wajda's adaptations of particular canonical texts such as *The Wedding* or *Pan Tadeusz*, but rather with perhaps his most strikingly modern work, *Man of Marble*, which is no less marked by these processes of romantic subjectivation. I will therefore read this film intertextually in relation to Mickiewicz's *Forefathers' Eve*, which though not an explicit model for the film certainly provides an implicit model for its processes of individual and national subjectivation.

Man of Marble: A Contemporary Forefathers' Eve?

Perhaps the most immediate similarity between *Man of Marble* and *Forefathers' Eve* is the dramatic act of artistic self-transformation. Prior to these works Mickiewicz and Wajda were already seen as 'national artists'. Nevertheless these works were for both dramatic breaks constituting their strongest political – if not aesthetic – statements. While Wajda had established himself as a film-maker of national importance, especially through his 'war trilogy', he had not been able for some time since to occupy a position as 'critic and conscience of the nation'.[10] *Man of Marble* was therefore a dramatic breakthrough restoring Wajda to his former significance as an artistic and political voice, ironically through the re-examination of the very period in which he had first come to prominence. But the similarities between *Man of Marble* and *Forefathers' Eve* do not stop at their significance in their creator's biographies. They also concern the creation of personae that operate on both a historical and mythical level. Significantly here *Man of Marble* was one of Wajda's few films *not* based on literary adaptation, while no less rooted in the legacy of Polish Romantic literature.

At first glance the figure of Birkut, the Stahkanovite bricklayer at the centre of the film, has little similarity with any type of romantic hero. First, he is not a rebel but a hyper-conformist, who embraces the oppressive system he is under rather than seeking to reject or even evade it. Furthermore, he is presented as a construct of the system, the product of socialist realist aesthetics and political policies, presented through newsreels that underline the artificiality of his heroic status. This impression is misleading however on several counts, which have to be taken into consideration. Birkut's conformity is based on a real and simple faith in the system rather than the cynicism that may have characterised the architects of this system. He may be on the wrong side politically, but he displays the romantic qualities of faith and loyalty even if it is to the 'phantom' of the ideal socialist society. This naïveté is presented in such a touching way that it contrasts sharply with the cynicism of all those around him.

Of course given this naïveté and also his historical situation as a worker, he cannot be an unmediated stand-in for Wajda himself, who was even in the 1950s a self-aware cinematic artist and a member of the intelligentsia. To deal with this problem Wajda embeds his story in a double temporal structure, as being the research of the contemporary film-maker Agnieszka, who will be discussed shortly, and presents a series of mediators who narrate different parts of Birkut's story from different perspectives. In a manner resembling *Citizen Kane* (Orson Welles, 1941),[11] the initial newsreel presentations of Birkut as socialist realist hero are complicated and questioned by layers of subsequent stories, none of which provide the whole truth of Birkut but only a fragment from a particular perspective. The first of these mediators, Burski, the film-maker who made the newsreels depicting Birkut and who filmed the bricklaying record, is of particular significance, since as a veteran film-maker of the era of Socialist Realism and still a popular film-maker in the present of the film, he is clearly a stand-in for Wajda himself, a fact underlined by Wajda's name appearing on the credits of one of his newsreels as his assistant director.

This complex structuring allows for a kind of metonymy between Birkut as romantic hero, Burski as the film-maker's artistic stand-in and Wajda himself. It is as if Wajda is claiming that the true 'heroes' of the Stalinist era were not the intellectuals like himself who criticised it but the ordinary people who really believed that they were building socialism and devoted or even sacrificed their lives to this ideal as epitomised by Birkut's participation in the celebrated bricklaying record. Furthermore, Birkut, like Gustav, goes through a radical transformation, although of a very different type. On this point it may be even harder to recognise the kind of metamorphosis enacted in *Forefathers' Eve* as the form it takes is radically different. Nevertheless, a certain mythic transformation can be identified in the passage between Birkut as model worker to Birkut as political martyr as is implied by the end of the film, and then made explicit in its sequel, *Man of Iron* (*Człowiek z żelaza*, 1981). Whereas Gustav, the tortured romantic, is transformed by his experience of imprisonment into a national prophet, Birkut begins not as a true individual but a generic image of the ideal worker. Nevertheless Gustav's transformation in *Forefathers' Eve* is not merely from the individual to the collective but rather from the generic individual of his time, that is, the tortured romantic, to the absolutely singular, the prophet, who is nevertheless in profound connection with the collective, or the soul of the nation. Similarly Birkut begins as the false generic image of the 'hero of the masses' and becomes genuinely heroic, both through the development of an individual consciousness, and a real rather than artificial relation to the people. Like Gustav, it is Birkut's expanding awareness of political realities, epitomised by his imprisonment for his insistence on trying to assist his workmate, that opens up the possibility of metamorphosis from an individual to a national consciousness, even if this passes principally through a 'dark night of the soul' of political disillusionment. In the film the destruction of the false image of Birkut is given most emphasis as he progressively becomes aware of the injustices of the system both in his own treatment and the treatment of others. Much of the film is devoted to this process, in which Birkut passes from collective hero to has-been, whose only social connection seems to be with the band of Gypsy musicians he pays to follow him through the streets of Kraków. The power of his persona derives precisely from the fact that he does not begin as a rebel, but as a true believer in the system, who can only respond in a sincere way to what he experiences. He therefore can only become profoundly disillusioned with the system which had used him to construct its own self-image and then discarded him when he began to question rather than confirm that image.

Birkut has to start from a very different place to Gustav. Only over time does he become the tortured, disillusioned individual that Gustav begins as, and finally, it is hinted, a revolutionary who may not lead his nation but certainly sacrifices himself for its liberation. However, the romanticism of *Man of Marble* does not stop with Birkut, but is also expressed through the figure of Agnieszka, the young film-maker who is researching Birkut's story. Agnieszka's development is similar to Birkut's in that she begins with ignorance about both Birkut's and her own era, and through passion and sincerity comes both to know the oppressions of the system and to be committed to resisting it. In some ways Agnieszka is even more significant as a romantic persona than Birkut, not only because as a film-maker she is an unmediated stand-in for Wajda, but also because she is the one who is able to become the prophet of the overthrow of the system through her activity as a relentless film-maker and researcher. Unlike the investigative reporter, Thompson, in *Citizen Kane* who is little more than a figure of the film's reflexivity, Agnieszka is a dominant character in *Man of Marble*, and functions metonymically as an allegory of artistic and political subjectivation in a similar way to Konrad in *Forefathers' Eve*. There is a particularly strong relation between Agnieszka and Burski, the older film-maker as artistic personae of Wajda, with Burski operating as a kind of self-critique of the film-maker he has been in the past, and Agnieszka as the younger generation of politicised film-makers that he would wish to align himself with. This is a clear example of the dialectics of apotheosis and derision in *Man of Marble* on the level of artistic personae. This was, of course, a very controversial self-representation with critics such as Paul Coates arguing that, in his representation of Agnieszka, 'Wajda's misogyny and his crabbed envy of youth come into strange and messy contradiction with his identification with the young film-maker' (1985: 148).

Apart from the gender issue of Wajda representing himself through the figure of a young woman, there is the way she is presented iconically, as both highly aggressive in her filming role and her passage through cinematic space where distorted lenses and camera-angles stress her figure's height and angularity. However, it is misleading to subject this representation to a merely sociological analysis of gender relations; as a cinematic persona she is not merely 'a woman' or 'a young film-maker', but a visionary and allegorical figure who is attempting to do nothing less than to redeem the past, and thereby the present. Her relentless striding across the frame whether pacing the corridors of the television station, or racing to the abandoned backrooms of the museum is the expression of a desire to get outside the frame of censored perceptions and controlled movements of the socialist state, to literally get to the edges of the image and to discover and redeem the abandoned detritus of the system and its history, in this case the discarded hero Birkut. The sheer energy and intensity of her presence in *Man of Marble* makes her a crucial figure, and a romantic hero in the full Mickiewiczian sense of a political visionary who will not rest until the truths she has discovered are fully acknowledged, which of course would only be possible with the overthrow of the system. This poetic persona is largely constructed through Wajda's orchestration of her extreme mobility through cinematic space.

Finally, in a sense cinema itself is the hero of *Man of Marble,* through its power to forge a link with the past capable of troubling and destabilising the order of the present. The intertextuality with *Citizen Kane* is important in this respect for the way it complicates Wajda's relation to the tradition of Polish Romanticism. While *Man of Marble* is fully embedded in Polish political and aesthetic history, it is also fully engaged with the history of cinema to the extent that the 'dialectics of apotheosis and derision' operates as much in relation to cinematic models. The complex narration in the film does not just repeat the strategy of *Citizen Kane*, which itself was both a critique of Hollywood cinema and an attempt to take it to an apotheosis in which its tarnished ideals as a mass art would be realised. Rather it attempts to show the complex interweaving of cinematic forms with political oppression and acts of resistance, including that performed by the film itself. Rather than resulting in an open-ended questioning of the relativity of truth as in *Citizen Kane*, *Man of Marble* attempts to show truth as being graspable through an attention to cinematic logics. On the edges of the frame it is as if the cinema in its very act of concealing political truths has attained the capacity to reveal them when viewed from the perspective of engagement. In other words the film is very much a dialectics of apotheosis and derision in relation to the history of cinema; derision in relation to cinema's use for ideological purposes and apotheosis in re-discovering cinema as a tool for political subversion and national liberation. Certainly film is also shown to be a vehicle for propaganda and power in the form of socialist realist newsreels, but even here it is implied that behind these deceptions, a viewer willing to see it can nevertheless glimpse the truth. Furthermore, in the guerrilla film-making tactics of Agnieszka, a vision of film-making emerges as both a poetic and revolutionary activity, capable of forging a redemptive link between the present and the past, in much the same way that Mickiewicz envisaged the prophetic power of poetry. This is most forcefully expressed in the scene in which Agnieszka grabs the camera from the reluctant camera operator and films Birkut's statue while straddling it; this is not merely a mastery of the lessons of the past but an erotic relation to it that is able to extract not only facts but also the poetic truths of the life of the past as it was lived.[12] When Agnieszka is questioned early in the film about her interest in Birkut and replies that for her he is like the 'knights of old', this is not merely an expression of her naïveté. It also demonstrates this poetic and erotic engagement with the past, which reaches a kind of actualisation through her relationship with Birkut's son in *Man of Iron*.

The question remains, as in the case of Grotowski's theatre, to what extent *Man of Marble* simply repeats Romantic strategies, and to what extent it reworks them through the modernist or reflexive complications of its personae and of narrative structure. Does Wajda's cinema constitute a dialectics of apotheosis and derision in relation to Polish Romanticism, and if so does this go beyond the aesthetics of Mickiewicz and the other Polish Romantics? Or does it merely relocate them in a different historical era by means of a radically different medium? These are complex questions: certainly in some statements by Wajda there is a definite irony in relation to Polish national aspirations, a caution about their delirium, also evident in his adaptation of Wyspiański's *The Wedding*. Nevertheless, one could also find this type of irony not only in the work of Wyspiański, but even in that of Mickiewicz, notably in *Pan Tadeusz*, leading to the possibility that Polish Romanticism itself is marked by a dialectics of apotheosis and derision, or in other words is self-deconstructive.

Furthermore, it is perhaps even more questionable to what extent Wajda could position himself as a 'national prophet' in the full Mickiewiczian sense, given the different political realities his work is confronting, even if he would still like to occupy the more modest romantic position of the critic and conscience of the nation. Yet it is clear that *Man of Marble* was indeed prophetic about the emergent politics of resistance to the communist regime that would culminate in the Solidarity movement; hence the extreme difficulty the censors faced in knowing what to do with a film that was, in a similar sense to *Forefathers' Eve*, an aesthetic time-bomb. It can certainly be argued that the modernist, reflexive aspects of *Man of Marble,* especially its double temporality and questioning of narrative truth, are essential revisions of Polish Romantic aesthetics without which the film would have been bombastic and anachronistic. In this sense it is both a critique and an apotheosis of Polish Romantic aesthetics. In contrast to Grotowski's theatre the critique is aimed more at the aesthetic form of romanticism *vis-à-vis* the complexities of contemporary experience, while its political dimension of transcendent subjectivation *vis-à-vis* national aspiration is what is taken to apotheosis. In other words, both Grotowski's theatre and Wajda's cinema can be seen as Neo-Romanticisms that contest and continue the tradition of Polish Romanticism, whether re-territorialised through the body of the performer as universal self-sacrificing subject or the figure of the subversive film-maker as embodiment of national aspirations for liberation. In both cases it is the process of visionary subjectivation, originating in Polish Romantic texts, that forms the basis for this neo-romantic aesthetics. For an aesthetics that departs from the legacy of Polish Romanticism altogether, it is necessary to look elsewhere. Such a modernist aesthetics can be found in the work of Witold Gombrowicz and Stanisław Witkiewicz in literature, Tadeusz Kantor in theatre, and, arguably, Andrzej Munk, Wojciech Has, Walerian Borowczyk and Jerzy Skolimowski in cinema.

Notes

1   This is the original name of Grotowski's theatre, at that time located in Opole, which would subsequently be renamed the 'Theatre Laboratory' and be relocated to the city of Wrocław.

2   'Subjectivation' is used here to refer to the constitution of subjectivity as a dynamic process, particularly following its use by Felix Guattari. See 'On the Production of Subjectivity', in Guattari (1995) *Chaosmosis: An Ethico-Aesthetic Paradigm*, trans. Paul Bains and Julian Pefanis. Sydney: Power

Publications.

3 For a translation of this crucial work of Polish Romanticism, see Harold B. Segel 1977: 73–176.

4 For Grotowski's formulation of the 'total act', see 'Statement of Principles', in Grotowski 1975: 211–18.

5 Brook makes this comment in his introduction to the filmed performance of *Akropolis*. See Jerzy Grotowski (1988) *Akropolis* (Videorecording). New York: Arthur Cantor Films.

6 Jan Błoński, for example, reads Grotowski's later theatrical experimentation as directly linked to both a Rousseau-type naturalism and German romanticism. See Błoński 1979: 67–76.

7 On the poetry of Adam Mickiewicz and Polish Romanticism see Czesław Miłosz 1983: 195–280, esp. 208–32. See also Harold B. Segel 1977: 21–71.

8 As is expressed in numerous statements by Wajda such as the one cited at the beginning of this section.

9 The numbering of these parts is fairly arbitrary as there is no Part I, and Part III was written considerably after Part IV; this can be seen as a Romantic strategy of fragmentation used against the enlightenment principles of rational order and logic.

10 See Michałek and Turaj 1988: 129–38 for an account of how Wajda's first four films established his reputation as a film-maker committed to carrying out 'a settlement of accounts on behalf of his nation, its aspirations, disappointments, in short its history' (1988: 137).

11 Another Polish film-maker, Andrzej Munk, a contemporary of Wajda's from the 1950s, had already used this kind of technique in his film *Man on the Track* (*Człowiek na torze*, 1956), also in order to question the current political order; it is likely that this film was just as influential on *Man of Marble* as was *Citizen Kane*.

12 This is a vision of history resonant with that of Walter Benjamin, especially as expressed in his 'Theses on the Philosophy of History', through the concept of the 'dialectical image'. See Benjamin 1968: 253–64.

CHAPTER ELEVEN

Andrzej Wajda's Vision of 'The Promised Land'[1]

Ewelina Nurczyńska-Fidelska

When Andrzej Wajda adapted Władysław Stanisław Reymont's novel, *Promised Land* (*Ziemia obiecana*), originally published in 1899, he reminded Poles of one of the great novels in their literature that had been strangely forgotten and overshadowed by *The Peasants* (*Chłopi*), for which Reymont won the Nobel Prize. Having signed the contract for the novel with his publishers, Gebethner and Wolff, Reymont spent a few months in Łódź in 1896 but he wrote the book far from the city – in France, between 1897 and 1898, when it was serialised in *The Daily Courier* (*Kurier Codzienny*), a newspaper belonging to the publishers. The circumstance of the novel's genesis confirms that Reymont possessed an unusual sense of observation and excellent memory, although the image of Łódź the novel produced is not mimetically faithful, descriptively objective or detailed. Yet Reymont himself characterised the essence of the city's image:

> This life and the world of Łódź thrill me because of the variety of elements, lack of stereotypes of any kind, unleashing of instincts, total disregard for everything and their nearly elemental powers. It

is a chaos of dirt, dregs, wildness, thieving, defeats, victims, struggles and downfalls; it is a sewer down which everything flows; it is a wild fight for the rouble, a great saraband by the altar of the golden calf – it is disgusting, but at the same time horribly powerful and great. (in Kocówna 1966: 1)

Such an image of Łódź, emerging from the pages of the novel, fascinated Andrzej Wajda, who – having found great material for a screenplay – realised that he could not only draw out the natural elements of cinema but also intensify the sensuality and emotions within the text. Wajda knew that the power of Reymont's novel did not lie in its realism: for its realist conventions were founded on illusion. Kazimierz Wyka has pointed out this feature of the novel:

Considering the details and the realism of representation, *Promised Land* possesses visionary qualities and is based on artistic qualities which are diametrically opposed. Its construction is full of *real phantasms* [my italics]. The work as a whole seems to reach beyond its time and realistic foundations. (1979: 113–14)

The extraordinary mix of literary styles conveying Reymont's vision is also a feature of Wajda's cinematic vision. It shapes the aesthetic expression of the 'here and now' rooted in his vision of Łódź in the nineteenth century. Moving still further than Reymont from the paradigm of realist convention, Wajda also charged his film with signifiers that universalise the evil powers of money.

Wajda probably noticed yet another unusual value of the novel – namely, its filmic qualities; *Promised Land* possessed the value of a practically ready-made screenplay. Yet Julian Krzyżanowski had pointed out the filmic qualities of the novel as early as 1937:

Reymont … construes his novel in an almost filmic way, setting the scenes one after another, scenes which could be reset in a different order without disturbing the whole composition but which, on the other hand, could not be eliminated without harming the work as a whole. (1937: 47)

A similar opinion was expressed half a century later by another eminent theoretician of literature and cinema-lover, Kazimeirz Wyka:

Reymont's literary technique in *Promised Land* persistently brings to mind various filmic procedures of the earliest phases in the development of cinematography – bright, torn and quivering. The comparison is justified inasmuch as the registering of reality by film and the registering of reality by Reymont took place almost simultaneously at the end of the last decade of the nineteenth century, between 1890 and 1900. (1979: 91–2)

We can assume, therefore, that Wajda felt the novel contained the plot construction of a potential film and that the internal organisation of scenes within the plot possesses a style and dramaturgy characteristic of film narrative. Thus in adapting the book Wajda was left only with questions of selection: first, the selection of plot-lines and characters from a vast gallery; second, a founding style for the whole work, bearing in mind Reymont's literary style registered 'life itself' but also surprised the reader with unrealistic creations and its huge tendency to the mythic and the poetic. In the film many of the plot lines and characters were either cut down or eliminated. Feature film narrative could not cope with the epic dimensions of the original with its gallery of almost eighty characters. But these choices had other consequences – the composition of the film plot revealed different filmic features than those in the novel. Wajda appointed his three main protagonists – Karol, Moryc and Maks – to the role of guiding the plot. It was their 'guidance' that allowed

Special seats for bosom friends: *Promised Land*

him to place in film language all those motifs and locales to which they are intimately connected.

Different versions of the screenplay for *Promised Land* and Wajda's notes[2] show the film organisation of the plot included many characters at first and that it was not easy for the director to part with some characters and subplots. The final discarding of so many subplots and characters, plus the decision to focus the action around the characters of Karol, Moryc and Maks proved a dramatic and temporal necessity. This in turn led to a different principle of plot composition. Reymont's 'filmic' narrative technique, using character-guides to aid the viewer through various subplots and different locales, constantly adding new characters, turned out in fact to be dysfunctional. The film narrative had to become even more dramatic. The key to dramatisation came through the classic method of building the story along the axis of the central plot: the friendship of 'three Łódź brothers', a friendship established with one aim only, to build a factory as a symbol of success in a city where the only yardstick of success was wealth and possession.

Reymont, a writer of the naturalist and modernist period, fell under the spell of the myth of the monster-city. At that time an indispensable element of this myth was to be found in the genre conventions of the crime novel and the horror romance, which had replaced the adventure plots of the first half of the nineteenth century. Such a fiction paradigm was used by Eugene Sue in his *Mysteries of Paris*, although similar motifs had appeared earlier in works by Balzac and Charles Dickens. However Magdalena Popiel points out that

> contrary to the mystery novel, in order to reveal the criminal world of Łódź one does not have to penetrate dark city bystreets, as poverty-stricken districts do not hide any dark secrets. There are no isolated territories of the criminal underworld here. In *Promised Land* the whole city is infected with fraud and crime. The novel's skeletal structure, Borowiecki's career, grows around a romantic and criminal intrigue. The amazing discovery of a telegram containing news about a rise in customs duties forms the starting point of the action, while the news of bankruptcies of foreign firms, stable until that point, which spreads quickly among the theatre audience results in a series of fires and suicides. We are also offered prostitution and murder: the subplot of 'the fallen' Zośka Malinowska and family vendetta culminates in the symbolic scene of the death of victim and oppressor caught in the cogwheels of a factory machine. Such financial frauds like those committed by the Grünspans or Grosman against insurance companies,

or Welt's swindling of banker Grosglik's money [Grünspan's money in the film], take place here on a daily basis ... Swindles, frauds and crimes set action in motion, enhance its tempo, introduce the element of surprise and strengthen the suspense. (1966: xliii–xlix)

The film portrait of Karol Borowiecki replaces the somewhat dull image (in the novel) of provincial seducer and morally torn *Lodzermensch* (as the inhabitants of Łódź who built the city were called). As played by Daniel Olbrychski, he takes on the features of a big city gangster. His factotum – Moryc Welt, brilliantly played by Wojciech Pszoniak – is not only a ubiquitous merchant and stock exchange player, but also a man capable of a great fraud: a poker game scam that would be the icing on the cake for any gangster screenplay. The film version of the scam, though based on the original in concept, refers to a different genre tradition. Wajda stylises Moryc, who in his own way is a kind-hearted fellow, by means of clothes, gestures and behaviour as a gangster figure from classic movies of that genre. The director and actor both know they are playing a game with their viewers. So as not to leave any doubt Moryc Welt winks at the camera in the final shot of this splendid sequence, waving to the audience and thus reminding us that gangsters and gangster stories were not made up by the Americans, that mobsters also lived in Łódź of 1885.

The character of Maks Baum, played by Andrzej Seweryn, is also related to the conventions of a gangster movie. More often than not in the organised crime gang there appears the figure of a 'more honest' man with moral scruples. Maks becomes exactly such a character. The friendship of 'three Łódź brothers', stripped in the film version of all elements of betrayal, also belongs to the convention of a gangster film: friendship based on common business interests is a typical pattern. Lucy Zucker, a beautiful and sentimental Jewess, ensnares Karol in a trap of her own making but only in the film does this romantic subplot assume the form of a rapacious passion where feeling is subordinate to sexual desire. The culmination of their passion takes place during an orgiastic scene in a luxurious train carriage, an innovation that was Wajda's.[3]

Reymont's use of contrast in forming his romantic subplots is made visible in the novel by the character of Anka, Borowiecki's fiancée. However, in Wajda's film this contrast is stressed more deeply. The enhanced expressiveness of passionate Lucy Zucker is underlined by an almost mythicised image of Anka – an ideal model of a beautiful and marriageable girl from a country manor house and this quality in the character was stressed by the physical appearance of the actress – Anna Nehrebecka. Elimination or reduction of subplots forced Wajda to fuse characters from the novel or to present them with features that acted as symbolic shorthand for ideas the novel had expressed at great length. It can be seen in the tactical reduction of Jewish characters where, for example, Grünspan is left in solely in order that Moryc Welt can play his great game, and Zucker is there only so that the climax of the main plot, the burning down of the factory as an act of revenge, can take place. These two characters form an ambient image of the world of wealthy Jews in Łódź, an image greatly limited in range when compared to the novel, but a compressed image that still remains highly expressive.

The subplot of Stanisław Trawiński is the only significant step away from the course of the novel's narrative. Undoubtedly under the influence of nationalist and democratic ideology Reymont describes the successes of Polish factory owners such as Trawiński with enormous satisfaction. Wajda, 'condemning' Trawiński to suicidal death, subverts the idea of success through honest endeavour among Poles, and in this way undermines the novel's faith in nationalist values. Trawiński's suicide also adds to the plot elements of suspense, anxiety and romance intimately connected to Karol Borowiecki's plight. For the latter's own choices are direct responses to his colleague's suicide, his either/or: either I die like Trawiński or marry Mada Müller.

Incarnate horror and evil have many representatives in *Promised Land*. A German, Herman Bucholc – the 'lord' of Łódź – is the most crucial figure here. It is Bucholc who gains the name of 'the ringleader of the thieves of Łódź' and a 'rogue'. The film devotes most attention to this figure, and not only because at the threshold of his career Borowiecki works for Bucholc who values him greatly as an engineer and factory manager. The film about a monster-city could not do without such a protagonist, so the viewer enters the castle/palace of 'the ringleader' and his kingdom – the factory. The lord presiding over them is haughty, cruel, ruthless, and devoid of any human features which some of his lesser rivals possess. The uncanny nature of Bucholc (Andrzej Szalawski) is also underlined by the circumstances of his death – he dies in 'the mortal grasp' of the factory. In the film, the ride of his wheelchair – an empty throne, pushed across the factory yard by his humiliated valet, August, gains unusual powers of symbolic expression.

In order to enhance the sensational and romantic subplot Wajda makes quite a significant change in the main plot. In the novel there is no suggestion that it was Lucy Zucker's husband who set fire to the factory in revenge; Borowiecki accuses Moryc Welt. The different figure that Moryc becomes in the film (intelligent but not the unambiguous conniver and swindler of the novel) and the friendship of the three *Lodzermenschen* in the foreground has to result in key changes in the main plot axis. Thus Bum-Bum sets fire to the factory on Zucker's orders and this act of revenge on the part of a betrayed husband not only concludes the plot but also enhances its sensational and romantic convention.

The expressiveness of Reymont's characters is made more concrete by Wajda's actors because in many cases they become archetypal models of romantic and action film narratives – a gangster and his gang, a ringleader, a profiteer, a usurer, a hired killer, a *femme fatale*, a lyrical beauty. These elements from action and romantic genres in film show that Wajda was not afraid of intensifying the literary elements of popular genre by referring to the tradition of the cinema. In another instance, however, there is a key divergence. Reymont's novel has filmic qualities because the author often breaks with linear and causal narrative to be episodic and use his three main characters as narrative guides for the reader. Wajda's adaptation 'betrayed' these filmic values, however, because it returned to the tradition of closed composition in which the plot itself was made the diegetic dominant, constructed according to the rules defined by the given film genre, in this case, a sensational and romantic film. The mystery of how the conventions of this type of film were transgressed is hidden in *Promised Land* not on the level of plot, but of expression.

Andrzej Wajda wrote in his memoirs:

Promised Land is a unique novel in Polish literature – it is an exception. Its realism wonderfully harmonised with the spontaneity of the cinema, which is the photographic description of the world. The dialogues, too, turned out to be an almost phonetic record of the speech of the people that Reymont observed. The characters speak in their own language, expressing in Polish thoughts translated from German, Russian or Yiddish, creating linguistic opulence not found in other Polish novels of the end of the nineteenth century. (1996b: 35)

So an extraordinary quality of the literary original is the individualisation of language of individual characters which, considering their national and environmental differentiation, additionally enhances the opulence of the novel's values. Generalising the features of the language of individual protagonists one can say that Reymont was not only a sharp observer of the inhabitants of Łódź, but also that he was an acute listener. That is why the characters of his novels speaking Polish speak at the same time different languages. In the broken Polish of the Germans and Jews we can 'hear' elements of German and the influence of Yiddish, while the Poles speak the language of the gentry and intelligentsia-turned-middle class, as well as the vernacular of those few protagonists who are peasants or belong to the working class. Reymont also introduces into the dialogues elements of the specific language of the *Lodzermenschen* who created the singular local vernacular, connected mainly with the world of business they conduct.

However, the film introduces new qualities, impossible to express in literature, which are, of course, connected with the phonetic aspect of the spoken language. All shades and colours of the spoken language, performed by the representatives of all social classes and nationalities, flow from the screen. Enriched by the gestures and facial expression of splendid actors they create cognitive and aesthetic values that are out of reach of the literary text, even though they are rooted in it.

Another very interesting aspect of the film is the way in which Wajda presents descriptive parts of the novel on the screen – images of Łódź, its factory landscape, streets, interiors of factories and their surroundings, palaces and banking-houses. This nineteenth-century material substance of the city Wajda and his director of photography, Witold Sobociński, found in contemporary Łódź and they 'photographed' it in a spirit of enchantment.

Again in his memoirs, written years after the making of *Promised Land*, Wajda wrote:

> I had known Łódź before. I had lived there for four years during my studies, but I never liked this city and I was never really interested in it, but now Łódź was taking its revenge for my contempt and indifference in those years […] We started shooting in summer and that is when a wonderful adventure with this city began, the city, as it turned out, I did not know, the city which unveiled before us new fragments of its existence every day … The eye of the camera, it seemed, could cover unlimited space. Making a historical film one usually builds the set or adapts existing buildings and constructs large fragments of the set around them in order to hide contemporaneousness. But nineteenth-century Łódź still existed in our Promised Land, along with its giant factories, unchanged since the beginning of the century, complete with train stations and warehouses making up whole cities, isolated from the rest of the world by brick walls. And all of this cost us nothing, we could use it, it was just there, ready, as if waiting for a film. (1996b: 33, 39)

In the finished work this 'photography' of the city did not have a merely historical function, a function of a *de facto* documentary registration or of a simple background of the story told. Neither was it a simple equivalent of Reymont's literary descriptions whose essence was created by the expressive effects of horror and fear woven into the story. Wajda endowed his narrative with phantasmagorical elements through the way in which he filmed the city as locale. In the realistic space of the city a mythical reality is born – the myth of the city and the people possessed by this city. The inhabitants of the 'promised land' live in the space of authentic reality, but their story grows beyond the realism of description and the narrative, taking on precisely the shape of myth and parable.

Wajda avoids simple metaphor and symbolism here. The mythic and poetic power of his film is hidden not in the detail of symbolic images (like, for example, the cog-wheel which kills both oppressor and victim during their deadly struggle), but in the total vision of the city and its inhabitants. That is why the death of Karol's father becomes symbolic only indirectly. His son's factory is on fire, but in reality the fire confirms that the world represented by old Borowiecki must pass away. The fire will ultimately justify Karol's choices: he will get rid of all his moral scruples and forever reject the system of values cherished in his family household.

The colour coding of filmic images in *Promised Land* is also extremely rich, ranging between the impressionistic colours of the Kurów landscape and the cold, torpid shades of Łódź landscapes at dawn, interiors of factories and their yards. In many sequences, the Expressionistic use of colour is an aesthetic of shock: in the theatre, the orgy in Kessler's gardens, the scene of the deaths of Kessler and Malinowski, and the sequence of the burning factory. Colour rarely appears in this film with a neutral function. The semantic values of colour are often enhanced by the deformation of human faces as stylistic signifiers of moral evil. This semantic and expressive use of colour is reinforced by clusters of natural sound; sonority forms an unusually strong expressive quality of this movie.[4]

The world of natural sounds is composed in *Promised Land* from a few main motives – the thunder and clatter of machinery, the squealing of winches and the wheels turning in the factories, their concentrated whisper, the whistling of factory sirens and fire-engines, crackling of fire and the hiss of steam, sounds of the train station and the train on the tracks, the clutter of wooden clogs in the factories and streets, the sound of horseshoes on the cobbles and of footsteps in the interiors of the palaces, and finally the incomprehensible hum of conversation and the sounds of nature in Kurów and during Lucy's and Karol's meetings outdoors. These main sound motifs constantly change in pitch: they are either intensified or silenced. They gain various rhythmic qualities and as a result speed up the action or slow it down – they are everywhere in the background. One can understand what the 'pulse' of the world of sounds is when one *listens* to that film. We also ought to risk saying that it is not frame editing but sound editing that creates the accelerated, nervous rhythm of narration in *Promised Land*. Through harmonious editing of the world of images and the world of sounds Wajda controls the perception of the viewer who, as if habitually, points mainly to the stream of images as the source of the impression of unusually dynamic narration. In *Promised Land* the richness and creation of a world of sounds seems to be decisive in this aspect of the film.

Unusual effects, achieved thanks to the idea of using natural sounds, is additionally reinforced by Wojciech Kilar's music which does not compete with them but co-exists creatively and harmoniously. The most clear-cut example of this co-existence is the second sequence of the film – 'morning in Łódź' – in which music becomes one with the natural pulse of the city; devoid of any melodic line it seems a 'mechanistic' element of the images, a musical stylisation of machinery at work and the sounds of the waking city. There are no 'quiet' scenes or sequences in this film. Even in the lyrical life in Kurów, consciously juxtaposed with the images of the city, anxiety lies under the surface. Its source is a sense of impending finale and the destruction of the old at the expense of the new. The sequences where the tempo of the action is suspended, as in the Łódź apartment of Mr Adam and Anka, are a time of expectancy, of what will soon happen to disturb an illusionary tranquillity. The rest is motion. Even the scenes of Karol's and Lucy's meetings pulsate with the anxieties of passion and threat, and culminate in the brutal sequence of the orgy on the train.

Movement, rhythm and unusual human energy are also present in the factories and in such enclosed spaces as the infernal restaurant or the theatre where propriety is expected – but not in Łódź, where the live performance in reality takes place in the audience. Even Bucholc's funeral is a circumstance that reveals the power of the mechanisms that govern the 'public' gathered for the occasion. The energetic bustle of the film's main protagonists possessed by their common idea forces the rhythm of the whole story. Its climax is the horror of the burning factory; the fire becomes the essence of motion, and then its suppression and freezing. However, a moment later the three friends gathered in a bachelor's apartment, will re-ignite this motion in a fight – 'I have nothing. You have nothing. Which means we have enough, just about enough!' In the epilogue the rhythm of events is intensified slowly, while the *polonaise* sounds gradually more and more ominously. The camera showing these events goes through the deformation of the interior's perspective and human faces, then stops on Borowiecki's enlarged ('bloodied') hands. Then the order 'Fire!' is heard, and after that the camera discovers a figure of a worker shot dead. This image 'stops' the movie.

Much has been written about the ideological ambiguity of Reymont's novel. On the one hand it is fascinated by the 'mystical power' of the city and the energy of the people who create it: on the other hand there is fear of the destructive force of this energy, both a moral degeneration and biological destruction. This anti-industrial fear clashes with the open fascination for the city and its inhabitants is the novel's first internal contradiction. The second one may be seen in the image of the characters, participants in the great process of the country's industrialisation and the representatives of three nations. Moral degeneration seems to touch all of them just they take part in the creation of the monster-city. However, Reymont shows Polish capitalists in a different, better light than the 'aliens'. In the context of the whole social spectrum he is not very convincing. He attributes to the Borowieckis, Trawińskis and Kurowskis higher moral values. They turn out to be more honest in business, pay their workers better wages, etc. Undoubtedly Reymont portrayed Polish characters in his novel in such a way because he was under the influence of contemporary Polish nationalists – which may have seemed justified when Poland was under partition.

Especially Karol Borowiecki's story proves how ideology overwhelms acute observation of the success mechanisms in the world of the *Lodzer-menschen*. A seducer and reckless gambler, a man who quite consciously rejects his past of a representative of the gentry and sells his soul to the 'golden calf' suddenly feels exhaustion and dullness when he achieves the peak of his precious career – he feels that he has wasted his life. Borowiecki's moral 'conversion', naïve, sentimental and lacking in truth in the context of the whole novel, shows that the simple division into 'our people' and 'aliens' was only the writer's ideological dream, contradicting, in truth, the image of the world he presents. Reymont was describing a life as lived: for Wajda the film was a return to the past. What terrified Reymont and made him ask questions about where things were heading, Andrzej Wajda could narrate from the distant perspective of time and historical knowledge. History is the main theme and protagonist in nearly all of Wajda's films (see Nurczyńska-Fidelska 1996a). *Promised Land* is no exception: the main theme of reflection is the relation of history and the world of values.

Apparently the film version of *Promised Land* shows only an 'evil' history, the aggressive reality that carries the triumph of money and power and the principle of *homo homini lupus*. Wajda rejected Karol Borowiecki's moral rebirth. In the film's epilogue film he introduces a different history whose symbol is a red banner in the workers' hands. National history is viewed from a different perspective here than in the Romantic tradition of the Polish struggle for independence. The dramas of Wajda's 'Romantic' protagonists, often described with bitter irony and despair in his other films, were replaced in *Promised Land* by a story of characters from a different world. These characters personify 'evil', but they were raised and protected by history whose global verdicts turned out to be irreversible. The world of these characters had to pass away, and this process was started by the order: 'Fire!' Michał Komar writes:

> The ending of the film tends, in contradiction to persistent symbolism and historical knowledge, to an aesthetic rather than thematic solution: a leading Łódź *gründler*, Karol Borowiecki, gives the order to fire at the workers more in the name of History than his own name. His historical Self was veiled by Wajda's fascination with History in the making. (1975: 122)

The film version is an apparent 'betrayal' of the original where the proletariat had been a silent force, mere background to Reymont's main focus of interest. A creative adapter, an interpreter of a classic text, written 'here and now', could not do anything else – he had to have the courage to reject the writer's illusions and let History speak. Changing the ending of the novel, Wajda silenced one of its internal contradictions. He treated another one of those analogically, namely the one which is connected with the division of the characters into 'our' good people and evil 'aliens', so obvious in the original. In the interpretation of the world shown in the film, the world governed by the one and only power – money – there is no division into less or more moral people; or at least this morality is not divided among the representatives of any given nationalities, 'ours' or 'others'.

'Our people', represented also by Staś Wilczek and Karczmarek-Karczmarski, are figures presented without the specific sympathy exhibited towards them in the novel and have become rather bleak and disgusting characters. Thus 'our people' in Wajda's film have not been presented in a much better light than the 'aliens'. The film portrait of the multinational society of Łódź also lacks sympathy towards the Germans, evident in the original. Even the most ignoble of them all, Herman Bucholc 'the ringleader', is not a swindler of the kind that the novel's Jews represent. Wajda sharpens the portraits of the Germans; he makes Bucholc more brutal and strongly 'eroticises' Kessler, who is an intellectual partner for Poles in the book; he makes Müller more primitive, and von Horn more naïve. Portraying the 'wolfpack' of Łódź, Wajda neglected the quasi-demonic image of the Jewish community to which Reymont attributed a style of conducting ruthless business transactions. Such a portrait of the Jews was probably drawn also under the influence of nationalistic ideology. Though Reymont endowed this group with many general features, the book contains a multitude of detailed images of their workings in factories and banks, of descriptions of their family lives and of the attitudes of their millionaire children.

From the gallery of the novel's Jewish protagonists Wajda chose only four – the passionate Lucy Zucker and her betrayed husband, Grünspan (whose portrait was not exaggerated) as a specific synthesis of many Jewish characters and, of course, Moryc Welt, a completely different hero in the film. Other Jews move around in the backdrop of streets, banking-houses, restaurants and theatre. The film contains none of Reymont's malice towards the Jewish community. That is why it seems amazing that in Wajda's memoirs we find the following fragment:

> For the first time in my life I made a film about money and people who go after it at all costs. I've always wanted to make such an 'American' film. No wonder that an Oscar nomination raised hopes for the popularity of the film in the US. However, I was quickly disenchanted. The press conference in Hollywood was reduced to a discussion about Polish anti-semitism and ended in a completely absurd way. A certain journalist from Israel who criticised my film most severely, answered, when asked if he had seen *Promised Land*: 'I don't have to see the movie at all, as far as I am concerned it's enough that it came out of Poland.' (As late as ten years later I was trying to convince the guy who bought *Promised Land* that I would cut out the scenes they were opposed to. He thought for a long time and finally pointed to Müller as a caricature of a Jew. But Müller in my film is German.[5]) It was then that I understood that the tragic legacy of the Jewish Holocaust on Polish soil no film could erase, and certainly not a Polish film. I also understood that nothing would ever change such opinions. Jews in the United States do not want to be associated with those ruthless businessmen who created

'the promised land'; they rather want to be seen as the descendants of the kind fiddler on the roof. (1996b: 41)

So, in the interpretation of the world governed by cruel and ruthless money-talk, Andrzej Wajda's film does not spare anyone or any nationality – they all play the same game, and if they differ slightly as to the tactics it is either because of their different starting points or individual traits of character. The image of Łódź of the end of the nineteenth century is pure Grand Guignol, a shocking *teatrum* of pseudo-culture ruled by the powers of evil, crime, corruption and ruthless baseness. The world created by Reymont contained chinks of light through which goodness and hope have filtered, even if they are elements of the writer's utopian vision. Wajda's world, except for the friendship plot carried over from a different movie, is darker and shows us only images of *nouveau riche* decadence, trash values and vulgarity, images of an aggressive struggle for a place at the top, and finally images of inevitable downfall and degeneration confirmed by the film's epilogue.

(Translated by Maciej Świerkocki)

Notes

1   The object of interpretation is Wajda's film *Promised Land* and its version which premiered on 21 February 1975. In 1975 and 1976 Polish Television broadcast a series, *Promised Land*, composed of eight one-hour episodes. On 9 October 2000 a premiere of a partly re-edited *Promised Land* with new Dolby Digital sound recording took place (relevant references can be found in the text of the article).
2   Materials from Andrzej Wajda's archive.
3   In the version of the film re-edited in 2000 Wajda toned down the scene greatly, in honour, he claimed, of the actress Kalina Jędrusik who had died a few years earlier.
4   This function of the sound aspect of the film was enhanced in the 2000 version by the Dolby Digital system.
5   In parentheses, a fragment of handwritten notes, from the collection in Andrzej Wajda's archives, published by permission of the author.

CHAPTER TWELVE

As the Years Pass, As the Days Pass...
– An Ironic Epic

Tomasz Kłys

a game of whist, a dinner party,
close friends, and good companions.
As years go by, as days go by,
this one has died, that one's not there.
    – Stanisław Wyspiański, *The Wedding* (*Wesele*), act 3, scene 12

One of the greatest, but least well-known, artistic achievements in Andrzej Wajda's oeuvre is the television series *As the Years Pass, As the Days Pass...* (*Z biegiem lat, z biegiem dni...*). Produced in 1980 for Polish Television, it was an adaptation for television of the famous spectacle from Stary Teatr in Craców, realised two years earlier with essentially the same cast of actors. This spectacle, performed either as an all-night marathon, or during three consecutive nights[1] enjoyed enormous popularity with the audience and great acclaim from the critics. The script of both spectacle and television series was based on nine literary works (six plays, two novels and one novella), created between 1883 and 1919 by several Polish Modernist writers: Michał Bałucki, Gabriela Zapolska, Jan August Kisielewski, Zygmunt Kawecki and Juliusz

Kaden-Bandrowski.[2] Those works were ingeniously conjoined; the basic device providing coherence for the heterogeneous narrative material was blending several characters from different works whom scriptwriter Joanna Ronikier had perceived as representing the same psychological type or the same attitudes despite superficial differences, thus creating a new amalgamated character. For example, a central – and arguably the most important – character in the series, Mrs Dulska, is a blend of the title character from Gabriela Zapolska's play *Mrs. Dulska's Morality* (*Moralność pani Dulskiej*), famous and proverbial in Polish literature and culture as a personification of smug hypocrisy, greed and stupidity; of Kamila from Michał Bałucki's comedy play *Open house* (*Dom otwarty*); and of the heroine of Zapolska's novel *Seasonal love* (*Sezonowa miłość*), Tuśka Żebrowska. Similar 'syntheses' also account for other characters in the series.

The eight-part series narrates the story of two Craców families, the Chomińskis and the Dulskis, during the forty-year period between 1874 and 1914. The members of those families share the fate of the Polish people under foreign rule, more precisely the Austrian occupation in Galicia, regarded as enjoying more political freedom than the other provinces of Poland partitioned between Prussia and Russia. We are thus presented with an epic in which the vicissitudes of a small group of people metonymically reflect the life of a community as seen against the background of important historical events (in the series, those events include the revolution of 1905 and the outbreak of World War One, important milestones on the road to Poland's independence; two Polish uprisings, of 1830–31 and 1863–64, are referred to in the dialogues).

The plot also makes references to the cultural and artistic scene of the period (no less important in an occupied country than political and military governance). The cultural events, variously presented in the series, are of two very different kinds. The first group includes patriotic ceremonies and anniversary celebrations of a political-national character, such as the requiem mass in the cathedral for the poet Wincenty Pol; the performance of tableaux inspired by the national epic, *Pan Tadeusz*; work on the monumental historical painting by Jan Matejko, *The Battle of Grunwald* (*Bitwa pod Grunwaldem*); patriotic enthusiasm after the publication (by the magazine *Life* (*Życie*), in 1898) of Stanisław Wyspiański's play *Warszawianka*; the patriotic spectacles of 1914 animated by the hope for independence. At the other extreme there are references to the achievements of a group of modernist artists, known in the Polish cultural tradition as Młoda Polska (Young Poland), the followers of Stanisław Przybyszewski, and to their provocative behaviour: their scandalising lectures and 'decadent' lifestyle characteristic of artistic bohemians at the turn of the century. Other cultural facts made use of in the series include the creation by Stanisław Wyspiański of the extraordinary Art Nouveau stained-glass windows in the Craców Franciscan church, the enthusiastic reception of Gerhard Hauptmann's *Weavers* at the time of the revolutionary unrest, the performances of *Green Balloon* (*Zielony Balonik*), a cabaret based at the legendary coffeehouse, *Jama Michalikowa*; the first successes of Tadeusz Żeleński – nicknamed 'Boy', an outstanding critic and translator of French literature.

Perhaps the most important of the artistic events referred to in the series is the premiere, in 1901, of Stanisław Wyspiański's play *The Wedding* (*Wesele*). It is a work both extremely novel in its form, which seems to exemplify the essential aesthetics of Polish modernism with its predilection for symbolism and magic realism, and one that provoked national discussion because of its claim of the futility of Polish aspirations to independence. A large part of the fourth episode of the series is devoted to the controversies around this play, which 'the whole of Craców' went to see. The quote from *The Wedding* which heads this chapter are the words of the Journalist, one of the play's characters. In the series, the sentiment was voiced by Tadeusz 'Boy' Żeleński, who had just arrived from Paris, in reply to someone's question of 'How do you find Craców?'. The writer found a comment fitting his own situation in this remark of the journalist (see Wyspiański 1958: 183). Making use of it, Wajda subtly signalled not only the source of the title of the whole series, but also its pervading spirit, which might be called 'the spirit of *The Wedding*'. It is worth noting that both the Journalist's remark adopted by Boy, and the title of the series, have to do with time, and more exactly capture the painful fact that human life on earth is both an individual and a collective passing away.

This issue has been considered in depth by Paul Ricoeur in his monumental work *Time and Narrative* (1984–88). I do not mention this fascinating work here only to point out that Wajda's series illustrates its ideas, since this could be said of virtually any narrative text. The point is, rather, that Wajda's series, through its thematisation of time, signalled already in the title, its aesthetics, and also its function in the social context at the moment of its creation, brings out very clearly some of the fundamental ideas of the French philosopher. Particularly striking is the fact that the series quite clearly illustrates the mechanism, described by Ricoeur, of construing history as a kind of narrative, as a story, created *ex post facto*, when the events experienced by someone facing an unknown and uncertain future can be ordered in longer temporal perspective, into a coherent and clear plot giving meaning both to the past and to another 'currently experienced' moment (when we construct or read and relive the story while reading). According to Ricoeur, man's 'plotting' activity is a very important means of resolving the existential tension between an individual's subjective experience of time as 'being-towards-death' (that is, its perception as finite and limited), and cosmological time, conceived in 'long perspective' (this objectivist conception of time has been adopted by physicists and historians). The *emplotment* (*mise-en-intrigue*, narrative, *récit*, plot, or, as Aristotle calls it in his *Poetics* – mythos (Arystoteles 2001: 583–4)), thus gives expression to two otherwise incompatible poles of experiencing time: the objective time, in which one is 'immersed', which has to have passed to be narrated and presented as a coherent whole, an order; and the subjective time, the time of activity which causes events, activity which propels history, simply the time of life in the process of becoming, full of chaos and suffering (cf. Ricoeur 1984–88, vol. 1: 31–51).

The two great domains of emplotment are artistic fiction (mainly, but not exclusively, literary fiction), and history (historiography). The narrative rendering of time – both cosmic and human, social and individual – by written history and artistic fiction is possible thanks to the mutual borrowing between these domains, a unique 'feedback' between the 'historical' and the 'fictional' mode of narrative activity (which is also illustrated by the film series). The historical intention construing the narrative of the actual past must use the devices of fictionalisation worked out by narrative imagination (such as the paradigmatic tropes of metaphor, metonymy, synecdoche and irony; the model narratives of romance, epic, tragedy, comedy and satire).[3] In turn, the intention to create fiction achieves its aim of presenting the actions and experiences of fictional characters only through a parallel strategy: the assimilation and emulation of the devices of 'historicisation', consisting in the attempts to reconstruct the actual past from all kinds of traces, records, documents and archives. This feedback and interplay between the historicisation of the fictional narrative and the fictionalisation of the historical narrative results in something that may be called 'human time' – graspable, comprehensible and acceptable by human individuals – which is nothing else but 'narrated time'.[4]

Defusing the dramatic tension between cosmic/historical time and personal, phenomenological time, all stories, plots and written narratives at the same time build up the 'narrative identity' of both individuals and communities. Both the individual and the collective self are constituted or rather consolidated through emplotments. The former kind may be exemplified by the 'cases', described by psychoanalysts (for example, Freud): during the process of therapy, fragments of personal history, previously incomprehensible and unbearable, come to form a coherent and acceptable story, in which the subject may recognise his identity and stable essence. In turn, the nation of Israel provides a good example of the collective identity constituted by emplotment. Providing a narrative account of the events that were believed to lie at the foundation of its history, the Biblical Israel became a historical community. It was a circular process – the historical community called 'the nation of Israel' gained its identity thanks to its adoption of the narratives it had produced earlier. As Ricoeur has put it, 'subjects recognise themselves in the stories they tell about themselves' (1984–88, vol. 3: 247).

Considered as a whole, Wajda's oeuvre seems to be a similarly clear example of creating the historical identity of the Poles through emplotment,[5] from his 1954 debut film, *A Generation*, (*Pokolenie*) to his 1999 adaptation of *Pan Tadeusz*, a literary epic that includes elements of Romance, Comedy and Satire (to use the terms employed by Frye and White), a work essential in the formation of Polish national identity. This role of the director is evidenced particularly clearly by his films made between 1972 and 1981, his great artistic achievements, which won both critical and popular acclaim: *The Wedding* (*Wesele*, 1972), *Promised Land* (*Ziemia obiecana*, 1974), *Man of Marble* (*Człowiek z marmuru*, 1976) and *Man of Iron* (*Człowiek z żelaza*, 1981). The series discussed here also belongs to this group. It was made in 1980 – the last year of Edward Gierek's decade in office, the year of the great explosion of the Solidarity movement. It is no accident that in Wajda's filmography it occupies a place between *Man of Marble* and *Man of Iron*: these two finely-tuned works exemplifying tragic mythos are separated by an ironic epic, no less important in shaping the collective consciousness of the Polish people at the close of Gierek's 'reign' than the other two films.

Wajda's series is an epic; at the same time, it has an undertone of irony, which produces a fascinating dialectic of the sublime and the trivial, of exalted affirmation and caustic satire, of authentic emotion and buffoonish affectation. This dialectic is played out not only at the level of the presented events. The image of a stagnant, politically enslaved community, pondering over their failed uprisings or trying to forget about them, a community more excited by cultural than by political events, trying to live 'normally' in an abnormal political situation, and not quite conscious of the importance of the impending explosion which will permanently alter their lives – that image must have been received by the viewer living in the People's Republic of Poland in 1980 as a mirror of his own situation and state of mind. In this case Ricoeur's thesis that 'subjects recognise themselves in the stories they tell about themselves', and that this fact both constitutes their identity and plays a therapeutic function on the personal and social levels, finds a particularly good exemplification.

The series is an equally clear illustration of the claim of the French philosopher that constructing history by means of an emplotment involves both historicising the fictional narrative and fictionalising the historical narrative. Presenting the story of fictional characters against the background of actual historical events (revolution, war) and making them interact with a number of well-known historical figures (such artists and writers as Boy, Przybyszewski, Bałucki, Matejko, Wyspiański) is a rather obvious device, familiar from almost any historical novel. However, the subtler feeling of the presence of history and the documents of the past, results from the use of art works, places, streets and architectural landmarks unchanged in a century, in all their materiality, impossible to be rendered in literature or theatre, but almost palpable and moving in the film medium. The role of such documents historicising fictional events is also played by the literary works whose plots were used in constructing the script of the episodes; coming from the historical period presented in the series, they necessarily reflect its true spirit. This concerns not only time, but also place. The *genius loci* of Craców (and in the second episode – of Zakopane) is strongly present in the literary originals of the particular episodes: in Michał Bałucki's comedy *Open House* (1); Gabriela Zapolska's novel *Seasonal Love* (2); in Jan August Kisielewski's dramatic diptych *In the Net* (*W sieci*) (3) and *The Last Meeting* (*Ostatnie spotkanie*) (5); in the same author's play *Caricatures* (*Karykatury*) (4); in Juliusz Kaden-Bandrowski's novel *Arch* (*Łuk*) (8). As regards the literary originals of episodes 6, 7 and the second half of part 8 (i.e. Zygmunt Kawecki's *Kalina's Drama* (*Dramat Kaliny*, 1902), *Mrs. Dulska's Morality* (1907) by Gabriela Zapolska, and her *The Death of Felicjan Dulski* (*Śmierć Felicjana Dulskiego*, 1911)), their action takes place in Lvov, but transferring it to Craców does not seem to have had much effect on the 'spirit of the place', if we remember that in the case of both cities it was the same unique 'spirit of Galicia'.

In turn, the fictionalisation of the historical narrative consists in such ordering of historical events that there emerges a 'model plot', a mythos in Aristotle's and Frye's terms. Though from a 'bird's-eye', or global, perspective, it may seem to be the mythos of the Epos, or Epic, the trope of irony permeating this epic turns its plot into the mythos of Satire. This takes place, however, at the level of the whole series; the mythos of the individual episodes seems rather to take the form of the more 'naïve' model plots – Romance, Tragedy or Comedy. The transformation into Satire occurs largely when Romance, Tragedy and Comedy recede in time – when they become the past, which elevates the sublime, valuable and creative elements to the status of the Epos, and attends to the trivial, superficial, and base aspects only to denounce, unmask and deride them. In Frye's typology, the trope of irony and the mythos of Satire, the most conscious and devoid of the illusions of the more naïve models, are associated with the most melancholic and 'joyless' season – winter. Perhaps it is not an accident that the action of all the episodes (except the last one) takes place either in winter or in almost equally gloomy and dreary late autumn (note that in Frye's typology, autumn is associated with the mythos of Tragedy). The last part of the series begins with the images of the spring of 1914 (more precisely – the turn of spring into summer), the images of marching Polish troops and of the enthusiastic, 'improperly dressed' Hesia Dulska, who barges, carrying flowers, into her father's stuffy office. These signals of the impending destruction of the old order are also signs of the coming of 'spring' on the historical and political plane (the hope that Poland will regain its independence) and in the ethical sphere (the end of the prevailing 'morality of Mrs Dulska'). Another significant choice (though perhaps not quite consciously made by the script-writer and the director for its implied symbolism) is the change of the time of action from summer in the novel *Seasonal Love* to winter in the adaptation. Though the place of the action remained the same (Zakopane), the novel's choice of summer as the temporal background for its plot gave it the status of Comedy (or Romance), while winter, with its connotations of lifelessness and inertia and the fact that the heroine cannot get rid of her awkward layers of warm clothing, quickly turns the Comedy/Romance into Satire, which immediately disqualifies Dulska as a romantic character (though her equivalent in the novel, Tuśka, was the heroine of a romance, at least for a short time, and not only an object of satire).

The mutual subversion in the film series of the 'Epic' and irony (though irony does not wholly destroy the elevated quality of the Epic, it does undermine it) takes place on several planes: the time and place of the action, the image of the political events, the personal life of the heroes, the art scene of the period, and the composition of the series and its relationship with the literary originals of its parts. Here I will only discuss the last-mentioned issue.

The series is essentially composed of nine moments (shown as if blown up and dramatised) chosen from among many on the time axis – and more precisely, from the history of the Chomiński and the Dulski families, some aspects of which parallel national and social history. The presentation of each of those moments is usually based on one literary work, whose action originally takes place in roughly the same period, though not necessarily in the same year (which has no serious consequences).[6] Though the series consists of only eight episodes, there are nine such moments, because the last episode presents two moments from 1914: the day on which the Craców newspapers bring news of the assassination of the arch-prince Ferdinand (28 June) and one day in mid-summer when the War is already raging . Each of the nine episodes covering the forty years of history takes the simple form of a play characterised by the unity of time, place and action. This should not be too surprising if we consider the essential structure of the composition and plot of the originals, all dramatic works regardless of their genre. Three of the nine originals, formally belonging to the genre of the narrative (novel, novella), have more dramatic than narrative character in their 'deep structure'. The world of Zapolska's novel *Seasonal Love* seems to be a projection of the outwardly inhibited and secretly sensuous personality of the protagonist, Tuśka Żebrowska, and the action develops around the 'love-affair', presented as if in a 'well made play', with elements of both melodrama and comedy. The novella *The Death of Felicjan Dulski* begs to set on the stage; the main place of action is the living-room, which various people enter and leave, and the hero dies 'in the wings', forgotten and instrumentally treated by the other characters. The first two chapters of Juliusz Kaden-Bandrowski's novel, inspiring the first part of the eighth episode, are particularly 'dramatic' because of the multitude of dialogues and the interweaving of various people's stories within the confines of a limited space (a Craców cafe, the streets of Craców at the verge of the war).

The decision to base the episodes of the series on dramatic works and compose each of them like a play rather than, for example, a novel (theoretically, a possible choice) seems to be wise and well considered in the case of a work which thematises time in all its aspects (already evident in its title). To return to the remarks of Ricoeur, inspired by Aristotle's *Poetics*: the time of the subject, of activity which provokes events, which propels history; simply the time of life, full of disharmony and suffering, time in the process of becoming, of bestowing actuality on various potentials, ruled by tension and expectation because of the uncertain future lying ahead – such time can be rendered artistically only in a work employing dramatisation to present actions, words and thoughts of various agents, actors, subjects or just people. However, the 'current' moment, ungraspable when experienced and only realised after the fact, passes inevitably and imperceptibly, becoming the past, being transformed on the time axis into a moment of time separated from the subject, objectivised as historical time (still human, but no longer personal), or cosmic time (wholly non-human). This past time can, however, be narrated, turned into an narrative (it is not an accident that we talk of the 'narrative past tense'), which transforms the chaos of the emerging present into the order of history by its panoramic *ex post* outlook, and gives meaning to once seemingly meaningless details. In the perceptive formulation of Kierkegaard, if life must be lived forward, it can only be understood backwards.[7]

As already noted, Andrzej Wajda's series evidences this mechanism of producing an epic out of dramatised moments. Each of the episodes, from the second to the last, features, against the background of the opening credits, a narrator's commentary reminding the viewers of the most important events from the previous episodes. This might be regarded as a 'non-filmic' solution, a certain shortcoming of the script, but perhaps necessary, considering the multitude of the literary sources of the plot. I believe, however, that taking into account the basic theme of the series – showing how everyday life, often trivial, banal, boring, disgusting or pitiful, is turned into History – the use of the narrator's commentary is truly revealing. It is perhaps worth quoting such an introduction to one of the episodes (I have chosen episode 6):

> It's been 31 years since two sisters, a young wife Janina Chomińska, and Aniela, today Mrs Dulska, then unmarried, were looking forward to a *soirée dansante*, which was to introduce some excitement into their monotonous life. Craców, then a dull, provincial town, has changed considerably over these years. The two sisters, now advanced in age, hate all those new fads invading their lives, those emancipations and secessions, decadence and socialism, cabarets and revolutions. They also find it increasingly difficult to understand their own children. Mrs Dulska cannot understand why her son, Zbyszko, loiters in the company of artists instead of thinking of a career in an office. Mrs Chomińska, her sister, recovering after the hard times given to her by her 'crazy' daughter Julka, now wrings her hands over her son Józio, who has taken to heart the ideals of the 1905 revolution and joined the socialists.

This introduction does not just remind the viewer of what happened, but gives meaning to those events, builds up their hierarchy, creating orienting points in the chaos for both the viewer and the characters themselves, making them project their activities onto the history of their community. As regards social history, these orienting points are here the 'decadence and socialism', 'cabarets and revolutions', and in the private history of the Chomińskis and the Dulskis – problems with the 'crazy' Julka (presented in episodes 3 and 5), or the memorable *soirée dansante* during the carnival season of 1874, recurring in the introduction to every episode; it is in fact the 'founding event' of Wajda's 'ironic epic', mythical both for the characters and the viewers, and increasingly mythologised as it recedes in time both from the characters and the viewer.

Reflection on time is also thematised in the action of the particular episodes, in the various scenes or statements uttered by the characters. One example is Boy's quote from *The Wedding*, cited at the beginning. The cruelly true prediction of Michał Bałucki, a playwright forgotten and spurned by his contemporaries: 'Time does not spare anyone! You too will grow old! Only then will you see how painful this is, how terribly painful!' is really moving, especially if one knows that it was uttered shortly before Bałucki committed suicide. The dance-leader Fikalski, at the height of his popularity in 1874, but old and worn out in 1902, with a raspy voice, tries to go on entertaining the guests at a soirée, who not only ignore him, but tell the ex-star: 'Grandpa, you're in the way, we want to dance!' Mrs Chomińska, impoverished and forced to relinquish her apartment to her despotic sister, sorts out her possessions before the removal, deciding, with bleeding heart, to get rid of some memorabilia, documents of her personal history. Those provide another set of orienting points in time; the narrator's comment reminds the viewer of their history. The objects which land on 'the rubbish heap of history' include the memorabilia of Mrs Chomińska's children: a portrait of the poet Boreński painted by Julka, Fredzio's toy sword and cap – very important elements of the plot of Wajda's epic. In the last episode, while Mr Dulski is dying in the next room, the two sisters, Mrs Dulska and Mrs Chomińska recall their dresses, a pink and a willow green one, respectively, which they wore at the *soirée dansante*. Various memories are also evoked by the piano in the Dulskis' living-room: Mrs Chomińska often recalls how her sister used to play it out of tune together with her husband; and Wicia, Józio and Misia, exalted by watching a regiment of young Polish soldiers marching below their window, are inspired to recreate a 1898 scene of joint recitation and singing of the patriotic song *Warszawianka*.

Some scenes seem to be crucial for the composition of the series. They bring together, in the same space and time, the greatest possible number of characters, condensing various subplots in one place, and presenting many opposing viewpoints. One of the four such scenes is the 1898 scene mentioned above; another is the *soirée dansante* of 1874; there is also a scene in a café from the carnival season of 1902; and the real dramaturgical masterpiece – a scene from the summer of 1914, taking place in the Dulskis' living room, with Mr Dulski dying in the next room, and History happening outside. It is a deeply symbolic scene, representing the end of an era, both in the family's history and on the national scale. The various plots and characters, until then largely separate, come together in a living room of a Craców apartment, which becomes an 'open house' where 'the door never closes' for only the second time in the past forty years – a fact angrily noted by its present owner, Mrs Dulska.

Wajda's 'ironic epic' is surprisingly coherent if we consider the number and variety of its literary sources. This coherence results not only from the ingenious technique of building fictional characters and mixing them up with historical figures, but also from the ideological homogeneity of the literary works which capture part of the 'spirit of the age'. Though the list of the adapted works from the Young Poland period does not include the most important of them – *The Wedding* – we should not forget about Wajda's earlier adaptation of this extraordinary play by Wyspiański, which had determined the aesthetics of the 'ironic epic': projecting the text of the play over the background of the time-honoured edifices and streets of old Craców, Wajda created a strikingly real material context for the conflicting ideological attitudes and points of view presented at the wedding reception in a Bronowice cottage. In the series, similarly, the Chomińskis' and the Dulskis' living rooms and the coffeehouses where most of the characters meet function just like that cottage,[8] and the context of the city is now most abundantly present – if only because of the length of the series. We should not forget about the intra-narrative presence in the series of the premiere of *The Wedding* in 1901 as an important historical event, about the influence of the play on the characters' attitudes, about their lacing their conversations with quotations from that play, and last but not least, about the fact that the very title of the 'ironic epic' is a quote from it. This fascinating journey in time, 'as years go by, as days go by', through the narrow streets, stuffy apartments and historical memorabilia of old Craców, is truly permeated with the spirit of *The Wedding*.

(Translated by Alina Kwiatkowska)

Notes

1   *As the Years Pass, As the Days Pass... A Dramatic Tale for One Night or Three Evenings (Z biegiem lat, z biegiem dni... Opowieść teatralna na jedną noc albo trzy wieczory).* Part 1: *Evviva l'arte!*; Part 2: *Oh I Need Some Fresh Air! (Ach powietrza, tchu!)*; Part 3: *What Was Distant Is Now Close (Co dalekie było – blisko).* The premiere: Stary Teatr, Craców – 29,

30, 21 March, 1 April 1978. Staged by Andrzej Wajda, directed by Anna Polony.

2   Strictly speaking, Michał Bałucki, whose comedy *Open House* (*Dom otwarty*) is the literary source of episode 1, is not a modernist writer, but rather one who represents the aesthetics of realism (or 'positivism', as this period is termed by the Polish literary theorists).

3   See White 1973: 5–11, 29–39. The typology of narrative archetypes, used by White, had been outlined by Northrop Frye in is classical work *Anatomy of Criticism* (1957: 33–67, 158–239). Frye employs the term mythos (taken directly from Aristotle) to refer to a 'model' or 'archetypical' plot.

4   It is not an accident that the word 'history' in many languages denotes both the course of actual events, an account of those events (i.e. historiography) and a story – a narrative of fictional events. See Ricoeur 1984–88, vol. 3: 101–2.

5   This is pointed out by Ewelina Nurczyńska-Fidelska in her articles on Wajda (1996a: 7–17; 1996b: 229–49).

6   The date of publication of the literary sources of each episode and the year in which the action is supposed to take place in the series are as follows: Episode 1 – 1874, *Open House* – 1883; Episode 2 – 1886, *Seasonal Love* – 1905; Episode 3 – 1898, *In the Net* – 1899; Episode 4 – 1901 (the year of *The Wedding!*), *Caricatures* – 1899; Episode 5 – 1902, *The Last Meeting* – 1899; Episode 6 – 1905, *Kalina's Drama* – 1902; Episode 7 – 1907, *Mrs. Dulska's Morality* – 1907; Episode 8 – 1914, *Arch* – 1919, but the action of the first two parts of this novel, which inspired the series, takes place in 1914; *The Death of Felicjan Dulski* – 1911. The most essential, though not the greatest divergence, may be observed in the last case: Zapolska's novella of 1911 presents the triumph of the seemingly indestructible 'morality of Mrs Dulska' in the stagnant Austro-Hungarian Galicia; but 1914, the year of Felicjan Dulski's death in the series, marks the end of this world. Consequently, the characterisation of Mrs Dulska in the series is much less sarcastic and vituperative than in the novel, where she is presented as a repulsive and frightening figure; the series portrays her instead as pitiable, disgusting but nevertheless human.

7   This remark by Kierkegaard may be found in the monograph on Thackeray (Ray 1955: 407), in the section devoted to Thackeray's treatment of time in his *Vanity Fair*.

8   The farmhouse/cottage in Bronowice near Craców is where the action of Wyspiański's *The Wedding* takes place.

CHAPTER THIRTEEN

'Ojczyzno Moja': Adapting Pan Tadeusz

Lisa Di Bartolomeo

In Polish literature, perhaps the most important opening lines are the *laus patria*: 'Litwo. Ojczyzno moja.' ('O Lithuania. My homeland.')[1] In Polish culture, perhaps the most enduring figure is Adam Mickiewicz. In Polish cinema, perhaps the best-known director is Andrzej Wajda. Wajda's film *Pan Tadeusz* constitutes the seemingly inevitable confluence of all three. An impressionistic rendering of the greatest achievement of Polish letters, the film deserves examination as part of the same nostalgic yearning for a more beautiful time that Mickiewicz himself wove into the text. Ranging from the embodiment of the poet within the film to the sentimental evocation of Polish pastoral splendor, Wajda's adaptation captures both the spirit and the letter of the original text, and even accomplishes a *rapprochement* with Polish Romanticism. This chapter will briefly examine Romanticism in Polish literary history, Wajda's earlier adaptation of Stanisław Wyspiański's *The Wedding* (*Wesele*, 1972), his later *Pan Tadeusz* (1999), and the intersections of this film with the original, in order to illuminate the effectiveness of his adaptation.

The legacy of Romanticism, which in Poland began around 1820 as a youth movement and ended in 1863 with the disillusionment created by the last, failed Polish uprising against Russia, continues even today to influence Polish culture. A natural bridge between West and East at the heart of Europe with ties to the Roman Catholic Church, Poland's peculiar position provided fertile soil for Romantic ideas, which, in Poland, invariably blended a longing for nationhood with individualistic aspirations. In 1772, 1792 and 1794, Poland watched helplessly as neighbouring Russia, Prussia and Austria-Hungary swallowed her up and partitioned her off for themselves. Although the successive waves of rebellions and revolutionary foment neither succeeded in liberating Poland nor drew the eyes of the world to her plight, these cataclysmic years irrevocably shaped the modern Polish consciousness, leading Poles to far-reaching conclusions for their nation: a self-perceived martyrdom, according to which the 'Christ of Nations' had fallen to less enlightened, more rapacious empires; and a recognition of their own culpability in the erasure of Poland, the ruling classes having indulged for so many centuries in selfish obscurantism, dooming their own leaders to impotence before the powerful *szlachta* (gentry). Napoleon's march across Europe sparked fiercely burning desires for the restoration of Poland, but revolt after revolt flamed up, only to be smothered by the overwhelmingly superior ruling imperial forces. Languishing under external oppression, Poland's social and political conditions were naturally bound to exacerbate the patriotic and revolutionary features of Romanticism. In a land no longer sovereign, poets such as Mickiewicz (and, to a lesser degree, Juliusz Słowacki and Zygmunt Krasiński) filled the void among a people hungering for spiritual as well as political leaders.

Partly a reaction to the Enlightenment, with its faith in the rational progress of civilisation, Polish Romanticism envisioned a dualistic, inadequate *świat* (world) which must be overthrown or left behind, opposed to the *zaświat* (world beyond), which might be metaphysical, religious, or simply located on the margins of civilisation. The harmonious, measured and well-proportioned world, as formerly contemplated, became discordant, extreme and chaotic. The Romantic focus on man's inner life came to share attention with the outside world, with the agenda of the salvation of the nation in the forefront. Polish Romantic literature, as Charles S. Kraszewski asserts, 'far from being an empty Prometheanism glorifying the "supernature" of a certain individual, directs its energies outward – toward millions of individuals – in an attempt at transforming them into the heroes who should bring independence to their nation' (1998: 10). The political character of Polish Romanticism thus arose in particular national and political circumstances. The tendency of Romantics elsewhere in Europe to seek the folk roots of their respective national cultures seemed all the more imperative in partitioned Poland, where

Polish culture was threatened with the same extinction political Poland had suffered. In Poland, anti-establishment themes characteristic of Romantic works took on a singular urgency and expressiveness, where the establishment was an evil, foreign force. The Romantic cult of youth and nationalism spread like wildfire through Polish cities and country estates thirsting for action, self-expression and self-determination; the Romantic embracing of revolution stirred the Polish soul.

Enter the messiah of Polish culture, Adam Mickiewicz (1798–1855). Mickiewicz implicitly announced the arrival of Polish Romanticism with his first book of verse *Ballads and Romances* (*Ballady i romanse*, 1822). Even more, he lived the Romantic life: he was arrested within a year of his first publications, imprisoned and exiled to Russia. His friendships with suspect elements (including ex-soldiers of Tadeusz Kościuszko's campaigns, and the Russian poets Zhukovskii and Pushkin), combined with his youthful fervor, not only marked Mickiewicz for the authorities but also provided him with the credentials necessary to assume a position at the forefront of Polish letters and the Polish people. His own childhood in the Wilno-Kowno (now Vilnius) area spurred his interest in local folklore (such as the Belarusian tradition known in Poland as *zaduszki*, which merged with later, Christian 'All Saints' Eve'), expressed in such works as *Forefathers' Eve* (*Dziady*) and *Ballads and Romances*. An ill-fated love affair of his own, *à la* Werther, led him to write of unrequited love, while his own political aspirations and vision led him to compose works such as *Konrad Wallenrod*, a seditious piece wherein treachery serves the cause of the nation: the hero plots the downfall of the Teutonic Knights from within. Mickiewicz's works inspired his contemporaries who saw *Konrad Wallenrod*, in particular, as a call to arms. His disillusionment upon his return to Poland in 1831, fast on the heels of the failed November Uprising of 1830, expressed itself in various works from 1831–34, including the final part of *Forefathers' Eve*; the huge, almost Biblical *Books of the Polish Nation and Polish Pilgrimage* (in which he refers to Poland as the 'Christ of Nations'); and, perhaps most important, *Pan Tadeusz* (1834).

An epic verse tale (it is indeed difficult to define precisely its genre) against a bucolic background, *Pan Tadeusz* lovingly treats an aristocratic family feud peopled with eccentric characters, young lovers eventually united and uniting two families, rebellion against Russian domination, and a mysterious figure (Robak/Jacek) who manipulates events from behind the scenes. The plot follows young Tadeusz as he returns home to his family's country estate, welcomed there by his Uncle Soplica, an attractive older woman (Telimena) with whom he has a brief affair, and quarrelsome neighbours who contest possession of a certain castle and lands. The family feud eventually comes to violence, which in turn brings Russian intervention and punishment. Further battle erupts, this time with the families united against the foreign oppressors. Such a small victory, however, is not enough to change political reality, and the participants in the rebellion are forced into exile from Poland. By this point, Tadeusz has fallen in love with the lovely young Zosia, whose token he keeps with him throughout his trying years beyond Poland's soil. Abroad, many of the insurrectionists join Napoleon's military march across Europe, and only return home a few years later. When Tadeusz finally returns home, he and Zosia are married, thus tying the two feuding families together and christening a new era of pastoral happiness. Written in Polish Alexandrines (rhyming couplets of thirteen-syllable lines), the tale describes 1811–12 Lithuania – the Lithuania of Mickiewicz's childhood – with a unique attention to quotidian detail. These very details serve as the focus of the work, showing the lost world Mickiewicz looks back on, the last days of Lithuania's ethnically Polish gentry. For Mickiewicz, *Pan Tadeusz* is a work of pure love, which a contemporary, Stanisław Worcell, described as 'a tombstone laid by the hand of a genius upon our Poland' (in Miłosz 1983: 228–9).

Influencing his oeuvre profoundly was Mickiewicz's own self-image as the *wieszcz* (bard or seer), who chronicles the nation's history, recounts its myths and narratives, and sees the nation's future. In *Pan Tadeusz*, Mickiewicz sets out to preserve the customs, language and lore of a time already only dimly recalled even in the 1830s; in it, he also expresses the Romantic notions of escaping this world (*świat*) into another world (*zaświat*), here envisioned not as death, but rather as the cozy, gentrified country world of the Soplicowo estate, where young Tadeusz, his friends and family interact. Mickiewicz not only allows his fellow Poles to comfort themselves with an escape to a better world, a more hopeful time, but also points the way for the future, toward a more unified Poland, strengthened by the resolution of petty differences and cooperation among the gentry and the peasants.

The simplicity and familiarity of the plot of *Pan Tadeusz* raises an immediate question: why is this work worthy of consideration as Mickiewicz's masterpiece? The tale follows star-crossed young lovers, separated by an old family grievance; political intrigue against a foreign occupant; machinations by a mysterious figure whose true identity is only revealed on his deathbed; such melodramatic elements had become commonplace by the time Mickiewicz composed his poem. Additionally, as even contemporary critics (most famously, Juliusz Słowacki) noted, the abundance of quotidian detail and banal objects (odes to coffee, rabbits, mushrooms, etc.) seems to debase the work itself, dragging the poetry into the morass of everyday human existence. But through its complete recreation of setting and its magical poetry, *Pan Tadeusz* beautifully transcends what might otherwise seem a rehashed pastiche of Byron, Walter Scott or Goethe simply relocated to the Polish countryside.

If we consider, as Dudley Andrew does, 'that the task of adaptation is the reproduction in cinema of something essential about an original text,' or that 'we have a clear-cut case of film trying to measure up to a literary work, or of an audience expecting to make such a comparison' (1984: 100), then Wajda had a daunting task before him in bringing *Pan Tadeusz* to film. It might be considered the duty of every Polish citizen to have read Mickiewicz's work. Only Henryk Sienkiewicz's historical trilogy (*Ogniem i mieczem* (*With Fire and the Sword*), *The Deluge* (*Potop*) *Fire in the Steppe* (*Pan Wołodyjowsk*)) or his *Quo Vadis* could rival the centrality of *Pan Tadeusz* within the Polish popular literary canon. Inevitably, when adapting a work of such primordial importance to a national literature, one faces difficult choices. The length and complexity of a literary work must somehow be condensed to fit a conventional theatrical run of two or three hours; the language may be outdated or even incomprehensible to modern viewers; the social and historical contexts may seem strikingly unfamiliar. A comparison might be made to the classic Shakespeare films of Laurence Olivier, to Derek Jarman's more subversive *The Tempest* (1979) and Peter Greenaway's *Prospero's Books* (1991), or even to the recent spate of Shakespeare adaptations, such as Baz Luhrmann's *Romeo + Juliet* (1996), or Kenneth Branagh's many Shakespeare films. As Neil Sinyard notes, although 'it is often said that Shakespeare would have made a great screenwriter and that many devices he uses in his plays are very "cinematic"', Shakespeare 'is our greatest verbal dramatist, relying on the associative metaphorical power of words to trigger the imagination' (1986: 3). Sinyard goes on to posit two possibilities when filming Shakespeare: jettison the text or use it closely (1986: 4–5). One might compare certain Shakespeare adaptations' (Olivier's and Branagh's, specifically) implicit postulation of 'national purpose and national identity: Britishness of one sort or another' (Anderegg 2000: 161–2) with the centrality of 'Polishness' to *Pan Tadeusz*; one could also suggest that a great adaptation of Mickiewicz would resemble a great adaptation of Shakespeare: 'a fusion of great literature, cinema and theatre, and ... reverential [to the author] in the only way an interpreter can be truly reverential: they do him justice' (Sinyard 1986: 23).

Whereas adaptations of Shakespeare, as the largest figure in Anglophone literature, serve primarily as timeless classics whose thought-provoking themes and dramas require no introduction and only a nodding acquaintance with the original work's historical circumstances, filmic adaptations of Polish literary works require the same knowledge of Polish cultural and political history as the original texts. One cannot hope to understand a film based on *Pan Tadeusz* without knowing something of the partitions and the Russian occupation, as well as Poland's complex relationship with Napoleon, both as historical personage and as myth. In the case of *Pan Tadeusz*, a director may rely on his native audience's familiarity with the historical background. Similarly, the language, characters and setting are so well-known to and beloved by generations of Polish readers that the obstacle of comprehension virtually fades away. In fact, this may be the central issue in Wajda's adaptation: the work is *so* familiar and *so* beloved as to make it possible to elide certain portions without sacrificing the flavour of the original. The basic premise behind Wajda's adaptation seems to have been this: we all know and love this work; let us now embody it, envision it, relive it, welcome it again.

If we consider only one of the many other adaptations comprising Wajda's oeuvre, *The Wedding*, we may uncover a subtle dialogue within Wajda, a polemic he carries on both with himself and with Polish culture, over the lasting influence of Polish Romanticism.[2] Written by Stanisław Wyspiański (1869–1907, in equal measure playwright, revolutionary stage director, artist), *The Wedding* (1901) consists of rhyming couplets with a 'dominant eight syllable line … which varies … from six to ten syllables' (Kapolka 1990: 9). The play also typifies the artistic movement of the early twentieth century in Poland known as 'Young Poland' (Młoda Polska). The term 'Young Poland' is used to suggest many concepts and styles within the movement: a decadent modernism, symbolism, naturalism, impressionism, and Neo-Romanticism, to paraphrase Czesław Miłosz (1983: 322–9). At the heart of Young Poland lay a crisis of faith, and those experiencing it felt a deep sense of futility and loss; 'the universe was a self-perpetuating mechanism with no room for pity and compassion' for which 'somebody had to be accused, so they accused God, with a nearly Manichean intensity, and their bitterness at times sounded like a renewal of the Byronic revolt' (Miłosz 1983: 327). Young Poland rebelled against scientific rationalism, determinism, and the trampling of the Polish countryside by capitalist interests. Its works concentrated on individual experience, moving away from the idea of the artist as a social or political leader. Young Poland valorised the Other World – less benign here than in Romanticism, not the 'other world' of Catholic cosmology but instead of occult, perhaps even Satanic, origin. As Miłosz observes, 'Art that creates values in a world deprived of values became for "Young Poland" an object of worship…'

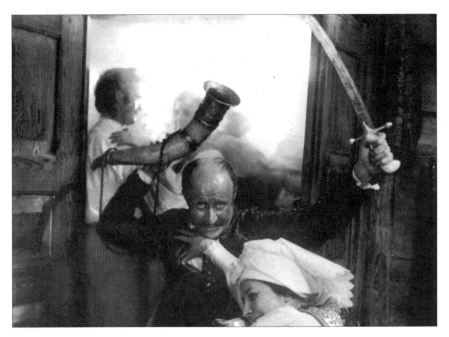

Here comes everybody: *The Wedding*

(*ibid.*). This was not art meant to comfort a people languishing in captivity; it was an elite experience, esoteric and self-indulgent. If the artist had a mission for the nation, it was to elevate others by extension, by coming into close contact with and sharing impressions of 'the ineffable essence of reality … redeem[ing] all those who do not dare to reach deeper than the superficiality of the daily grind' (*ibid.*). This was Young Poland's new twist on elitism.

Wyspiański's play is based on historical reality: his urban poet friend married a peasant girl in the fall of 1900, and the wedding celebration perforce brought together a strange mixture of intellectuals and farmers, nobles and paupers, reformers and conservatives – in fact, the same jumble of discordant characters surfacing in the play. The character called the Poet was himself emblematic of Young Poland, as a man who does not believe in political, military or Positivist actions, but only in his own words. The clearly allegorical *dramatis personae*, the set of studied, symbolic artifacts grounded in a peasant cottage, the clear literary origin of the action in the Polish *szopka* (Christmas puppet play), all add to the heady, symbolic atmosphere. In fact, the characters seem constantly to battle past texts – engaging with historical incidents, literary works, stereotypical images, and even newspaper reports, in a polemic that drives the play to the point of immobility. The play leaves no hope for revolution or triumph, as everyone is eventually trapped in the final dance of paralysis, the lulling music played by the *Chochoł* (strawman), whose demonic power stays the hands poised for action and for cooperation between the peasants and the nobles or intelligentsia. Wajda's film incorporates the synaesthesia of the *Chochoł*'s music in a visual, verbal and musical stasis in motion, a hypnotic, sinister repetition, an eternal round and round suggesting an inescapable trap for Poland. Clearly in Wyspiański's mind were the words (here implied and ironised) from *Pan Tadeusz*: 'Kochajmy się!' ('Let us love one another!'), that are as nationally symbolic as the wedding itself. The wedding as concept is foregrounded, as well. Whereas in *Pan Tadeusz* the wedding serves as a unifying force both for families and for social groups, in *The Wedding* the two families and groups of people come together only to have their differences delineated for them. The wedding that ends *Pan Tadeusz* liberates the dancers, a liberation expressed symbolically as the participants move out into nature. *The Wedding*'s lulling dance implicitly refers to *Pan Tadeusz*, giving it an ironic twist, particularly if one considers the *Chochoł* as a force of nature as well as a poetic figure for Polish society. In *Pan Tadeusz*, nature unifies the action in one golden, homogeneous whole; in *The Wedding*, everyone is entranced by the mulch, an ignoble character who transforms the wedding into the final symbol of the stasis of Polish society, a disquieting negation of the call to 'love one another' and an ominous portent for the future.

That Wajda chose to make *The Wedding* in 1972, in the early years of the so-called 'cinema of moral anxiety' ('kino moralnego niepokoju'), is telling. The disillusionment that marked this period may perhaps have found reflection in Wajda's choice of material. After 1968, when prominent professors, many of them Jewish, were expelled from Poland, intellectuals felt betrayed by the workers, who not only did not join them in protest, but instead even joined the authorities' denunciations. For people of Wajda's generation, and even more for many of his younger colleagues (such as Krzysztof Kieślowski and Agnieszka Holland), the disillusionment became an object lesson on personal moral responsibility as well as on the inefficacy of public protest. The historic rift between noble and peasant, intelligentsia and worker, seemed too broad to be bridged. As we may surmise from Wajda's adaptation of *The Wedding*, even such a hopeful symbolic event as the union of peasant and poet inevitably ended in paralysis and inaction. The Polish nation was doomed forever to dance the dance of stasis under foreign hegemony, unless a means could be found truly to bring together the disparate elements of Polish society.

Whether Wajda eventually found some small hope in the establishment of the third Republic of Poland, or, more likely, he felt the need to eulogise Poland's irretrievably lost past, he chose finally to adapt Mickiewicz's nostalgic *cri de coeur*. Rather than reiterating *The Wedding*'s polemic with Romanticism, *Pan Tadeusz* gently pokes fun at Romanticism while still maintaining its inherent hope for unity and improvement. Poland, the first to cast off the heavy cloak of totalitarian dominion, is poised for reintegration with Europe. However, even as it looks forward, Poland must inevitably look back at what has been lost. In this sense, Mickiewicz's work assumes an even deeper symbolic importance. Wajda's film is in many ways a new Romantic take on what has been lost: the gentle, gentry past to which Poland can never return. This is just what Mickiewicz intended: a note in a bottle for future generations.

For Wajda, the film version is his monument to the old world, a fitting film to come near the end of a director's career. This sense of the 'old world' extends even to geography. Lithuania was joined dynastically to Poland in 1386. The Polish-Lithuanian Commonwealth, as it became known for generations, came to figure among the great powers of Europe, and Lithuania itself became a recurring motif in Polish literature, even after Lithuania became part of the Russian Empire following the third partition. Mickiewicz, born, raised and educated in Lithuania, considered it an integral part of Poland, despite the separation. However, Mickiewicz was not alone in his fixation on Lithuania; the works of Czesław Miłosz, in particular, demonstrate the continued presence of Lithuania in the Polish national psyche. The idea of exiles predominates, as Lithuania comes to stand for a sort of paradise lost, a pastoral haven of natural beauty and poetic inspiration. Lithuania comes to embody the lost ideals and lifestyle of a past generation, a genteel time of civility and closeness to the land. Although Wajda did not grow up in Lithuania as Miłosz did, he nevertheless keenly feels the loss of the lands long associated with past Polish glory.

Wajda's expression of Mickiewicz's escape to another world begins by overturning expectations. Rather than beginning predictably, with the poet's invocation (known even to Polish school children):

> Litwo! Ojczyzno moja! ty jesteś jak zdrowie;
> Ile cię trzeba cenić, ten tylko się dowie,
> Kto cię stracił. Dziś piękność twą w całej ozdobie
> Widzę i opisuję, bo tęsknię po tobie.

> [O Lithuania, my country, thou
> Art like good health; I never knew till now
> How precious, till I lost thee. Now I see
> Thy beauty whole, because I yearn for thee.][3]

...Wajda begins with the Epilogue. The camera wordlessly expresses the plaintive longing of the first few lines of the Epilogue, decrying the noise and filth of Paris streets, implicitly recalling for the audience the sharp self-rebuke 'Biada nam zbiegi, ześmy w czas morowy/Lękliwe nieśli za granicę głowy!' ['Alas for us who fled in times of pest/And, timid souls, took refuge in the west!' (578, 579)][4] For a Polish audience in 1999, wondering perhaps whether their country's chosen path – leading westward toward capitalism, NATO, and harsh economic realities – was indeed the right one, this silent visual quotation may elicit some introspection. Might we even infer a longing for Poland's isolation from the responsibilities of fledgling membership in the European Union as the poet suggests we shut the door on the lure of Europe? From the street we move indoors, to the darkened refuge of the poet himself. The stark décor and harsh, blue lighting suggest a spiritual isolation, a winter of the soul – a dominant motivation behind Mickiewicz's work, and perhaps even of Wajda's homage. But the poet is not alone in his exile: as the camera pans around the rooms, we see as yet unknown figures, faces which will soon become endearingly familiar: Tadeusz, Zosia, the Judge and others. Wajda physically embodies these characters from the poem within the poet's rooms, as though they were keeping him company in the long, cold years of exile in Paris. Wajda makes visually manifest the lines: 'Jedyne szczęście, kto w szarej godzinie/Z kilku przyjaciół usiadł przy kominie,/Drzwi od Europy zamykał hałasów' ['One happiness remains: when evening greys,/You sit with a few friends and lock the door,/And by the fireside shut out Europe's roar'] (580, 581) as he depicts the poet among his characters, kept company not merely by his memories of time past, but by the artistic creations of his imagination. Memory is central to Mickiewicz's verse, a retrospective from without, as the poet looks back on the long-lost world of his youth from his exile; Wajda enhances this sense of the work as a memory film by positing the poet himself as present, recalling his past even as he pens his lines.[5]

Lest he dwell visually or narratively too long in Mickiewicz's cold poetic world, Wajda implicitly follows the next lines of the text ('Chciałem pominąć, ptak małego lotu/Pominąć strefy ulewy i grzmotu/I szukać tylko cienia i pogody,/Wielki dzieciństwa, domowe zagrody' ['I longed to fly, a bird of feeble flight/Beyond the thunder and the stormy zone/And seek the sunshine and the shade alone,/The homely plot and endless childhood days'] (579, 578) and takes us into the sunny, warm Lithuanian countryside in which the action is to unfold. The visuals sweep across the golden fields and verdant trees, as Tadeusz's carriage and horses lead both him and us to the hearth and home that beckon. The effect of the cold, Parisian opening is important: we must first see the world in which Mickiewicz found himself, the better to understand his aching need to return, even if only in his mind and verse, to that warm, welcoming countryside he knew and loved. For us, too, the opening transition from cold city to warm country comes as a visual respite; we see the true depth of the poet's creative power in the contrast between the world in which he lives and the world whose image he conjures up before our eyes.

The constant reiteration of the Polish-Lithuanian countryside becomes an independent visual motif in the film. The camera lovingly plays over various scenes of pastoral beauty, including the mushroom gathering in the forest, when Telimena denigrates the Lithuanian wood compared to the views of Italy. In the original text, the narrator and Tadeusz both defend the native forests and trees; in the film, Tadeusz's words of praise are accompanied visually by the setting in a lovely wood, silently but powerfully proving his argument. Placing nature at the center of his vision, Wajda elides the poem's long bear-hunting scenes. The bear hunt, an entire chapter, or 'book' in the original, is shortened to a mere two minutes of screen time, condensed to a brief but frenzied preparation and the tense moments when the bear threatens Tadeusz and the Count before being shot dramatically by the Bernardine monk Robak. The bear-hunt scenes are framed by panning shots of the forest and a brook, lasting nearly as long as the hunt itself. These sylvan moments complete with rays of sunlight slanting in among the dark leaves and peacefully flowing water, flank the violence of the bear hunt. Whereas Mickiewicz intersperses the descriptions of the forest among the stanzas treating the bear hunt, in Wajda's film the two are divorced, with the film concentrating more intently on the portrayal of nature than on its disruption by man. The poet similarly suggests the impenetrability of the forest, of which he writes: 'Myśliwiec krąży koło puszcz litewskich łoża,/Zna je ledwie po wierzchu, ich postać, ich lice,/Lecz obce mu ich wnętrzne serca tajemnice:/Wieść tylko albo bajka wie, co się w nich dzieje' ['The huntsman skirts the forest and no more,/And only sees their face, the outward part,/Nor knows the secret mysteries of their heart;/What happens there to fable's only known'] (177, 176). In Wajda's film, the bear hunt becomes less about the hunt than about nature.

Nature also becomes an externalised expression of mood and emotion. In the text, a storm follows the battle between the *Moskale*[6] and the *szlachta*, helping to obscure the evidence and postpone discovery of the uprising:

W takim dniu pożądany był czas najburzliwszy;
Bo nawałnica, boju plac mrokiem okrywszy,
Zalała drogi, mosty zerwała na rzece,

Z folwarku niedostępną zrobiła fortecę.
O tym więc, co się działo w obozie Soplicy,
Dziś nie mogła rozejść się wieść po okolicy,
A właśnie zawisł szlachty los od tajemnicy.

[The storm was fortunate, for it concealed
As with a dusky shroud the battlefield,
And flooded all the roads, and bridges breached.
The farm was cut off and could not be reached,
And so the news of all the strange events
In Soplicowo could not travel thence;
On secrecy would hang the gentry's doom.] (432, 433)

Wajda transports this meteorological event forward in the action, to accompany the dramatic departure of Tadeusz, the Count and others into exile. The atmospheric expression of the storm is precisely placed to coincide with the tumultuous emotions contained within the Soplica household. Tadeusz must part with Zosia, whom he has come to love, and with Telimena, whom he has come to dread. In the next room, Robak lies dying, unwilling to admit his true identity to his son, Tadeusz, but he finally confesses his misdeeds to Gerwazy, who eventually forgives Jacek/Robak. The tension of the storm, the electricity in the air, dissipates with the physical departure of Tadeusz and the spiritual departure of Jacek/Robak.

When later the men-folk return triumphantly home, the landscape again becomes verdant and warm. Book XI, entitled 'The Year 1812,' begins with an ominous description of the spring's portents, declaring, 'Ogarnęło Litwinów serca z wiosny słońcem/Jakieś dziwne przeczucie, jak przed świata końcem,/Jakieś oczekiwanie tęskne i radosne' ['The hearts of Lithuanians in that Lent/Were filled with strange presentiment,/As though the ending of the world were nigh,/With joy and yearning and expectancy'] (485, 484). But the film avoids any hints of ill fate. The sudden appearance of troops is accompanied by the voice-over narration of Mickiewicz, who declares not 'Wojna ! Wojna! Nie było w Litwie kąta ziemi,/Gdzieby jej huk nie doszedł,' ['War! War! On every side the roar of war/Through all the land of Lithuania!'] (487, 486) but rather:

O wiosno! kto cię widział wtenczas w naszym kraju,
Pamięta wiosno wojny, wiosno urodzaju.
O wiosno, kto cię widział, jak byłaś kwitnąca
Zbożami i trawami, a ludźmi błyszcząca,

Obfita we zdarzenia, nadzieją brzemienna!
Ja ciebie dotąd widzę, piękna maro senna!
Urodzony w niewoli, okuty w powiciu,
Ja tylko jedną taką wiosnę miałem w życiu.

[O spring of springs! Who could forget that spring,
That spring of war, that spring of harvesting.
Who could forget how thou didst blossom then
With corn and grass and glittering of men,
Abounding in events and with hope teeming!
I see thee still, fair phantom of my dreaming!
In slavery born and bound in swaddling chain,
I never saw a spring like that again.] (489, 488)

Over the glittering troops, a crane flies, and the camera tracks its flight. The crane, a sign of spring in Poland, seems to bestow his blessing on the military men marching below him, mingling with the blossoming landscape. Indeed, far from the rather foreboding picture of war found in the text, the film strives to capture the martial majesty of the assembly. The camera lingers over the uniformed men and their steeds, weapons and battle regalia. The only hint in the film of ill portent seems to be the final long shot of the troops, with a brilliant sunny sky in the foreground, but dark clouds lurking on the distant horizon. The pairing of the military with the cranes as signs of spring suggests that nature itself blessed the men who fought to free Poland.

Tadeusz returns home, and the story soon ends with the outdoor festivities of his wedding to Zosia. The wedding guests celebrate with an elaborate Polonaise, moving in pairs out of the courtyard of the Soplica house into the nearby fields, rich with ripe vegetation. The complex interweaving motion of the dance is soon matched by an interweaving of the dancers with the grain in the field. Humans and nature mix and blend in this final visual image of Tadeusz, his friends and his family. Even the final image of the film is one of nature: the camera follows a crane, flying over a field, across a blue sky with fluffy white clouds, finally coming to land in its nest with its mate. This last, loving shot reiterates the text's and the film's primary purpose of praising and immortalising that lost world of pastoral beauty and harmony, and the fantasy of finally coming home, if only in one's dreams.

As much as the film focuses on nature in its depiction of the lost world of *Pan Tadeusz*, Wajda never loses sight of Mickiewicz himself. By inverting the order of the text and beginning with the Epilogue, Wajda saved the best for

Young love, classic history: *Pan Tadeusz*

last. The immortal opening lines' ode to Lithuania are reserved for the grand finale. After the peaceful, undulating movements of the wedding guests' dance into the field, a cut returns us to Mickiewicz's cold, blue rooms in Paris. But he is not alone. As Mickiewicz declaims what are perhaps his most famous lines, the camera pans slowly around the room to the assembled company listening to the poet's composition. But the faces we see are no longer unfamiliar as they were in the film's opening shots: we recognise Tadeusz, drinking what one can only hope is Polish coffee, Zosia bent over needlework, and the Count, as always, busily sketching. As Mickiewicz moves about the room, reading from his work, we see not only him but also emblems: a replica of the Ostra Brama icon of the Most Holy Virgin Mary, Mother of God, a symbol of Poland mentioned explicitly in the text, serving to highlight Poland's history and cultural heritage; and a quill pen, symbolising the poet's profession. The camera then shows the same room in Paris, seemingly empty, suggesting a time that has flown away and been lost forever. Again, the cold blue lighting and the deserted *mise-en-scène* hint at the spiritual and perhaps creative death of exile. But the film immediately reminds us what it is that has been lost, what it is that warms the soul and inspires the poet: the radiant, springtime landscape of Poland-Lithuania, and the herald of renewal in the crane's flight.

Not only does Wajda's film capture much of glory of nature in the original, it expresses much of Mickiewicz's gently ironic treatment of Romanticism, of nearly all the characters in the work, and even of certain national character quirks. For example, Grażyna Szapołowska's seemingly overstated performance renders perfectly the ironic 'seriousness' of Telimena; Szapołowska seems consciously to employ her own stature in Polish cinema to evoke her character's aging beauty and struggle to maintain her power over men. Similarly, Daniel Olbrychski's portrayal of Gerwazy as a self-important, quarrelsome fussbudget enacts the implicit critique of his old-world values Mickiewicz plants in the original. Wajda also maintains the implicit polemic with Romantic values that Mickiewicz adds to his text. Tadeusz might seem at first to be the young Romantic hero but in fact his affair with Telimena enacts a biting and ironic parody of romantic love. Along similar lines, Tadeusz ends up happily married to the girl he loves, in direct contrast to the Romantic trope of suicide after an unrequited love affair. Only Jacek/Robak seems to have been created within the framework of Polish Romanticism, with his dramatic death after confessing his sins, and his mysterious and checkered past, including self-imposed exile and cutting himself off from his son. It seems noteworthy that Jacek/Robak is quickly forgotten in the joyous reunions at the film's end.

Mickiewicz's narrator steps back at the work's closing, deliberately ending his tale before the clouds, looming on the horizon, move any closer, and stresses his belief that youth should not attempt to be the seer or *wieszcz*, but should instead wear Zosia's floral wreath, sing songs, and generally enjoy life. He knows what is to come, and tells his audience that Poland is in her grave; but about this painful, fresh wound he will not – cannot – speak. The narrator chooses instead to rhapsodise about the golden summers of his youth, dwelling in fantasy rather than admitting painful reality. Wajda's camera similarly prefers to linger on more hopeful images, moving from the wedding to the crane rejoining its mate; politics and division have no place in this visual poem of longing and memory.

But Wajda's romantic and Romantic depiction of the Polish countryside – nearly always seen in 'past tense' in his films – seems also to evoke a world of the more recent past, replaced during the Soviet era by polluting factories, sprawling towns and ugly architecture. Mickiewicz's longing and nostalgia for the countryside of his own youth coincides with Wajda's, although for a child of World War Two, such a safe and cozy depiction of the rural past is no doubt more a product of imagination than memory. The elegiac quality of *Pan Tadeusz* fits well with the idea of a grand finale for Wajda's career: adapting the greatest work of Polish literature as a lasting tribute both to one's nation and to one's culture.

Perhaps Wajda has come to see himself as something of a *wieszcz*, much like Mickiewicz did, imparting his vision and art to a nation and a new generation who may not yet understand their own destinies. The concept of a nation as an absolute value surely resonates with post-Communist Poles enjoying the freedom of the nation they regained after 1989. If Wajda is *wieszcz*, then what he foresees for Poland would be a golden time of unity and harmony, perhaps momentarily disrupted by petty squabbles and personal differences, but sunny and clear nonetheless. Or perhaps Wajda sees himself as Wajdelota from Mickiewicz's *Konrad Wallenrod*, preserving the folklore of a nation and reminding his young charge of the ultimate mission: the nation's liberation. Then again, perhaps Wajda is more akin to Jankiel, whose public dulcimer performance (in Wajda's version, at the wedding) forms the centerpiece of *Pan Tadeusz*, a meta-textual statement on the role of a nation's art. If anything, *film* has been Poland's art in the last fifty years, and Wajda has been instrumental in the dissemination of Polish cinema throughout the world, crowned by his honorary Oscar on 26 March 2000. In his speech to the Academy, Wajda refers to the award as 'not a personal tribute, but as a tribute to all of Polish cinema', and thanks 'the American friends of Poland and my compatriots for helping my country to rejoin the family of democratic nations, to rejoin Western civilization, its institutions and security structures', and concluding with his 'hope that the only flames people will encounter will be those of the great passions of the heart – love, gratitude and *Solidarność* (Wajda 2000b: 13). The paralysis ending *The Wedding* has finally been liberated – the dance at Tadeusz's wedding winds its way outdoors, weaving together families and nature. Wajda himself makes this explicit:

> We Poles have achieved something that had always seemed impossible. The emergence of *Solidarność* stopped that hobgoblin's [*chochoł's*] dance of ours, with everyone only for himself. Wyspiański would've been proud if he could see us [sic]. We understood the message contained in *The Wedding* and the intelligentsia chose to stand on the right side. The blemish, the stain that is so present in Polish art, had been overcome. (2000b: 29)

If the world of 1811–12 Adam Mickiewicz portrayed in *Pan Tadeusz* was gone even as he penned his alexandrines, the pastoral beauty of *Pan Tadeusz* existed only in the realm of imagination for twentieth – and now twenty-first – century Poles. The film version created by Andrzej Wajda maintains the verse, the characters and their interrelation, the geographical, socio-cultural context, and even the 'degree of participation of the storyteller' of the original in his film (Andrew 1984: 100). This fidelity to the letter of *Pan Tadeusz* enhances Wajda's film, rather than enslaving it to the hallowed text. More remarkable is Wajda's stunning fidelity to the spirit, tone, imagery and rhythm of the original. As a result, the film is neither diminished by nor diminishing of Mickiewicz's masterwork. The skill and sensitivity with which Wajda has embodied the greatest icon of Polish literature may help ensure that his film be almost as universally remembered as Mickiewicz's salutation to Lithuania.

Notes

1   My translation of Mickiewicz's opening lines in *Pan Tadeusz*.
2   Among Wajda's 34 feature films, only 8 – *Innocent Sorcerers* (*Niewinni czarnodzieje*, 1960), *Love at Twenty* (*L'amour à vingt ans*, 1962), *Everything For Sale* (*Wszystko na sprzedaż*, 1968), *Man of Marble* (*Człowiek z marmuru*, 1976), *Rough Treatment* (*Bez znieczulenia*, 1978), *The Orchestra Conductor* (*Dyrygent*, 1979), *Man of Iron* (*Człowiek z żelaza*, 1981) and *Korczak* (1990) – are based on original screenplays.
3   Book One, 'The Farm' (Księga pierwsza, 'Gospordarstwo,'), p. 2 and p. 1. All citations found herein are taken from the dual language version

of *Pan Tadeusz* translated by Kenneth R. Mackenzie (1986, New York: Hippocrene Books: 1–2), unless otherwise noted.

4   The translation, 'in the west' fits the rhyme scheme, but 'abroad' more precisely fits the original and does not so dangerously suggest to the modern reader Cold War associations.

5   The sense of Wajda's *Pan Tadeusz* as a memory film suggests a fresh link between Wajda and Orson Welles, whose influence can be felt most pointedly in *Man of Marble*. Welles' *The Magnificent Ambersons* (1942), as a nostalgia film, may also have influenced the tone of *Pan Tadeusz*.

6   *Moskale*, or 'dirty Muscovites', is an extremely pejorative Polish term for Russians.

FILMOGRAPHY

A Generation (Pokolenie) 1954
Starring: Tadeusz Łomnicki, Urszula Modrzyńska, Tadeusz Janczar, Roman Polański. Sc.: Bohdan Czeszko from his novel. Ph.: Jerzy Lipman. B&W. 90 min.

Kanal (Kanał) 1957
Starring: Wieńczysław Gliński, Teresa Iżewska, Tadeusz Janczar, Emil Karewicz. Sc. Jerzy Stefan Stawiński from his short story. Ph. Jerzy Lipman. B&W. 97 min.

Ashes and Diamonds (Popiół i diament) 1958
Starring: Zbigniew Cybulski, Ewa Krzyżewska, Wacław Zastrzeżyński, Bogumił Kobiela, Adam Pawlikowski. Sc. Jerzy Andrzejewski from his novel, and Andrzej Wajda. Ph. Jerzy Wójcik. B&W. 108 min.

Lotna 1959
Starring: Jerzy Pichelski, Adam Pawlikowski, Jerzy Moes, Mieczysław Łoza. Sc. Wojciech Żukrowski from his novella, and Andrzej Wajda. Ph. Jerzy Lipman. Colour. 90 min.

Innocent Sorcerers (Niewinni czarodzieje) 1960
Starring: Tadeusz Łomnicki, Krystyna Stypułkowska, Wanda Koczewska, Zbigniew Cybulski. Sc. Jerzy Andrzejewski, Jerzy Skolimowski. Ph. Krzysztof Winiewicz. B&W. 87 min.

Samson 1961
Starring: Serge Merlin, Alina Janowska, Elżbieta Kępińska, Tadeusz Bartosik. Sc. Kazimierz Brandys from his novel, and Andrzej Wajda. Ph. Jerzy Wójcik. B&W. 117 min.

Siberian Lady Macbeth (Sibirska Ledi Makbet) 1962
Starring: Olivera Marković, Ljuba Tadić, Miodrag Lazarević, Bojan Stupica. Sc. Sveta
Lukić from the short story by Mikolai Leskov. Ph. Aleksandar Sekulović. B&W. 94
min.

'Warsaw' (Warszawa) in *Love at Twenty (L'amour à vingt ans)* 1962
Starring: Barbara Kwiatkowska-Lass, Zbigniew Cybulski, Władysław Kowalski. Sc.
Jerzy Stefan Stawiński. Ph. Jerzy Lipman. B&W, 20 min.

Ashes (Popioły) 1965
Starring: Daniel Olbrychski, Pola Raksa, Bogusław Kierc, Beata Tyszkiewicz. Sc.
Aleksander Ścibor-Rylski from the novel by Stefan Żeromski. Ph. Jerzy Lipman.
B&W. 233 min.

The Gates to Paradise 1967
Starring: Lionel Stander, Ferdy Mayne, Jenny Agutter, Mathieu Carrière. Sc. Jerzy
Andrzejewski from his novel, and Andrzej Wajda. Ph. Mieczysław Jahoda. B&W. 89
min.

Everything For Sale (Wszystko na sprzedaż) 1968
Starring: Andrzej Łapicki, Beata Tyszkiewicz, Elżbieta Czyżewska, Daniel
Olbrychski. Sc. Andrzej Wajda. Ph. Witold Sobociński. Colour. 105 min.

Hunting Flies (Polowanie na muchy) 1969
Starring: Małgorzata Braunek, Zygmunt Malanowicz, Ewa Skarżanka, Hanna
Skarżanka. Sc. Janusz Głowacki from his short story. Ph. Zygmunt Samosiuk.
Colour. 108 min.

Landscape After Battle (Krajobraz po bitwie) 1970
Starring: Daniel Olbrychski, Stanisława Celińska, Tadeusz Janczar, Aleksander
Bardini. Sc. Andrzej Brzozowski & Andrzej Wajda from short stories by Tadeusz
Borowski. Ph. Zygmunt Samosiuk. Colour. 108 min.

The Birch Wood (Brzezina) 1970
Starring: Daniel Olbrychski, Olgierd Łukaszewicz, Emilia Krakowska, Marek
Perepeczko. Sc. Jarosław Iwaszkiewicz from his short story. Ph. Zygmunt Samosiuk.
Colour. 99 min.

Pilate and Others (Pilatus und Andere – Ein Film für Karfreitag) 1972
Starring: Wojciech Pszoniak, Jan Kreczmar, Daniel Olbrychski, Andrzej Łapicki. Sc.
Andrzej Wajda from the novel by Mikail Bulgakov. Ph. Igor Luther. Colour. 94 min.

The Wedding (Wesele) 1972
Starring: Daniel Olbrychski, Ewa Ziętek, Andrzej Łapicki, Wojciech Pszoniak. Sc.
Andrzej Kijowski from the play by Stanisław Wyspiański. Ph. Witold Sobociński.
Colour. 110 min.

Promised Land (Ziemia obiecana) 1974
Starring: Daniel Olbrychski, Wojciech Pszoniak, Andrzej Seweryn, Anna
Nehrebecka. Sc. Andrzej Wajda from the novel by Władysław St. Reymont. Ph.
Witold Sobociński, Edward Kłosiński, Wacław Dybowski. Colour. 179 min.

The Shadow Line 1976
Starring: Marek Kondrat, Graham Lines, Tom Wilkinson, Bernard Archard. Sc. Bolesław Sulik & Andrzej Wajda from the novel by Joseph Conrad. Ph. Witold Sobociński. Colour. 110 min.

Man of Marble (*Człowiek z marmuru*) 1976
Starring: Krystyna Janda, Jerzy Radziwiłłowicz, Tadeusz Łomnicki, Michał Tarkowski. Sc. Aleksander Ścibor-Rylski. Ph. Edward Kłosiński. Colour. 165 min.

Rough Treatment (*Bez znieczulenia*) 1978
Starring: Zbigniew Zapasiewicz, Ewa Dałkowska, Andrzej Seweryn, Krystyna Janda. Sc. Agnieszka Holland & Andrzej Wajda. Ph. Edward Kłosiński. Colour. 131 min.

The Young Ladies of Wilko (*Panny z Wilka*) 1979
Starring: Daniel Olbrychski, Anna Seniuk, Maja Komorowska, Stanisława Celińska. Sc. Zbigniew Kamiński from the short story by Jarosław Iwaszkiewicz. Ph. Edward Kłosiński. Colour. 116 min.

The Orchestra Conductor (*Dyrygent*) 1979
Starring: John Gielgud, Krystyna Janda, Andrzej Seweryn, Jan Ciecierski. Sc. Andrzej Kijowski. Ph. Sławomir Idziak. Colour. 102 min.

As the Years Pass, As the Days Pass... (*Z biegiem lat, z biegiem dni...*) TV. 1980
Starring: Anna Polony, Jerzy Bińczycki, Izabela Olszewska, Jerzy Stuhr. Sc. Joanna Ronikier. Ph. Edward Kłosiński, Witold Adamek. Colour.

Man of Iron (*Człowiek z żelaza*) 1981
Starring: Jerzy Radziwiłłowicz, Krystyna Janda, Marian Opania, Bogusław Linda. Sc. Aleksander Ścibor-Rylski. Ph. Edward Kłosiński. Colour. 156 min.

Danton 1982
Starring: Gérard Depardieu, Wojciech Pszoniak, Anne Alvaro, Roland Blanche. Sc. Jean-Claude Carrière from the play by Stanisława Przybyszewska. Ph. Igor Luther. Colour. 136 min.

A Love in Germany (*Eine Liebe in Deutschland – Un Amour en Allemagne*) 1983
Starring: Hanna Schygulla, Piotr Łysak, Armin Müller-Stahl, Daniel Olbrychski. Sc. Bolesław Michałek, Agnieszka Holland & Andrzej Wajda from the novel by Rolf Hochhuth. Ph. Igor Luther. Colour. 100 min.

A Chronicle of Amorous Incidents (*Kronika wypadków miłosnych*) 1986
Starring: Paulina Młynarska, Piotr Wawrzyńczak, Bernadetta Machała, Tadeusz Konwicki. Sc. Tadeusz Konwicki from his novel. Ph. Edward Kłosiński. Colour. 3287 m.

The Possessed (*Les Possédés*) 1988
Starring: Isabelle Huppert, Jutta Lampe, Philippine Leroy Beaulieu, Bernard Blier. Sc. Jean-Claude Carrière from the novel by Fiodor Dostoievski. Ph. Witold Adamek. Colour.

Korczak 1990
Starring: Wojciech Pszoniak, Ewa Dałkowska, Teresa Budzisz-Krzyżanowska, Marzena Trybała. Sc. Agnieszka Holland. Ph. Robby Müller. B&W. 118 min.

The Crowned-Eagle Ring (Pierścionek z orłem w koronie) 1992
Starring: Rafał Królikowski, Adrianna Biedrzyńska, Cezary Pazura, Mirosław Baka. Sc. Maciej Karpiński from the novel by Aleksander Ścibor-Rylski. Ph. Dariusz Kuc. Colour. 106 min.

Nastasya (Nastasja) 1994
Starring: Tamasaburo Bando, Toshiyuki Nagashima. Sc. Maciej Karpiński from the novel by Feodor Dostoievski. Ph. Pawel Edelman. Colour. 96 min.

Holy Week (Wielki Tydzień) 1995
Starring: Beata Fudalej, Wojciech Malajkat, Magdalena Warzecha, Bożena Dykiel. Sc. Andrzej Wajda from the short story by Jerzy Andrzejewski. Ph. Wit Dąbal. Colour. 94 min.

Miss Nobody (Panna Nikt) 1996
Starring: Anna Wielgucka, Anna Mucha, Anna Powierza, Stanisława Celińska. Sc. Radosław Piwowarski from the novel by Tomek Tryzna. Ph. Krzysztof Ptak. Colour. 98 min.

Pan Tadeusz 1999
Starring: Bogusław Linda, Daniel Olbrychski, Andrzej Seweryn, Michał Żebrowski. Sc. Andrzej Wajda, Jan Nowina Zarzycki, Piotr Wereśniak from the narrative poem by Adam Mickiewicz. Ph. Paweł Edelman. Colour. 157 min.

Vengeance (Zemsta) 2002
Starring: Janusz Gajos, Andrzej Seweryn, Roman Polański, Daniel Olbrychski. Sc. Andrzej Wajda from the play by Aleksander Fredro. Ph. Paweł Edelman Colour, 100 min.

BIBLIOGRAPHY

Adorno, Theodor W. (1975) *Noten zur Literatur I*. Frankfurt: Suhrkamp.

Ainsztein, Reuben (1979) *The Warsaw Ghetto Revolt*. New York: Holocaust Library.

Anderegg, Michael (2000) 'Welles/Shakespeare/Film: An Overview', in James Naremore (ed.) *Film Adaptation*. New Brunswick, NJ: Rutgers University Press.

Andrew, Dudley (1984) *Concepts in Film Theory*, Oxford: Oxford University Press.

Anon. (1958) Protokół z Komisji Ocen Scenariuszy w dniu 14 sierpnia 1958 r. (Unpublished document held at the Filmoteka Narodowa, Warsaw, File A 214 poz. 102).

Aristotle (1991) *On Rhetoric: A Theory of Civic Discourse*, trans. George A. Kennedy. Oxford: Oxford University Press.

Arystoteles (2001) *Dzieła wszystkie*, vol. 6. Warszawa: PWN.

Ascherson, Neal (1987) *The Struggles for Poland*. London: Michael Joseph.

Barba, Eugenio (1999) *Land of Ashes and Diamonds: My Apprenticeship in Poland*. Aberystwyth: Black Mountain Press.

Bartoszewski, Władysław (ed.) (1988) *Polish Help for the Jews (1939–45) – Documents*. London: Poets and Painters Press.

Bauman, Zygmunt (1989) *Modernity and the Holocaust*. Cambridge: Polity Press.

Benjamin, Walter (1968) *Illuminations*, trans. Harry Zohn. New York: Harcourt Brace and World.

Bielas, Katarzyna (1998) 'Jeszcze raz zaczynam.' An Interview with Andrzej Wajda, *Magazyn Gazety Wyborczej*, 3–4 July.

____ (2000) 'Moje Agnieszki' An Interview with Krystyna Janda, *Wysokie Obcasy*, June 17.

Błoński, Jan (1979) 'Holiday or Holiness: A Critical Revaluation of Grotowski', trans. Bolesław Taborski, in Bohdan Drozdowski (ed.) *Twentieth Century Polish Theatre*. London and Dallas: John Calder and Riverrun Press.

____ (1990) 'The Poor Poles Look at the Ghetto', in Antony Polonsky (ed.) *My Brother's Keeper?: Recent Polish Debates on the Holocaust*. Oxford: Routledge.

Boorman, John & Walter Donahue (ed.) (1995) *Projections 4 and a Half: Filmmakers on Filming*. London: Faber & Faber.

Borch-Jacobsen, Mikkel (1991) *Lacan: the Absolute Master*, Stanford, CA: Stanford University Press.

Borowski, Tadeusz (1967) *This Way for the Gas, Ladies and Gentlemen*, trans. Barbara Vedder. London: Penguin.

Bren, Frank (1986) *World Cinema: Poland*. London: Flicks Books.

Broch, Hermann (1955a) 'Das Böse im Wertsystem der Kunst', in Broch, *Gesammelte Werke 6*. Zurich: Rhein-Verlag.

_____ (1955b) 'Einige Bemerkungen zum Problem des Kitsches' in Broch, *Gesammelte Werke 6*. Zurich: Rhein-Verlag.

Bryson, Norman (1994) 'Géricault and "Masculinity"', in Bryson *et al.* (ed.) *Visual Culture: Images and Interpretations*. Hanover and London: Wesleyan University Press.

Caes, Christopher (2001) 'Catastrophic Spectacles: History, Trauma and the Masculine Subject in the Early Cinema of Andrzej Wajda' (Paper delivered at the 'Cinema and Theatre of Andrzej Wajda' conference, Łódź, 2001; revised version contained in this volume).

Canetti, Elias (1962) *Crowds and Power*, trans. Carol Stewart. London: Gollancz.

Caruth, Cathy (1996) *Unclaimed Experience: Trauma, Narrative and History*. Baltimore and London: Johns Hopkins Press.

Chatterjee, Partha (1993) *The Nation and Its Fragments. Colonial and Postcolonial Histories*. Princeton: Princeton University Press.

Ciarka, Ryszard (1997) 'Popiół czy diament?', *Kwartalnik Filmowy* 17.

Clifford, James (1997) *Routes. Travel and Translation in the Late Twentieth Century*. Cambridge, MA: Harvard University Press.

Coates, Paul (1985) *The Story of the Lost Reflection: the Alienation of the Image in Western and Polish Cinema*. London: Verso.

_____ (1992) 'Revolutionary Spirits: *The Wedding* of Wajda and Wyspiański', *Literature and Film Quarterly* 20, 2, 127–32.

_____ (1996) 'Forms of the Polish Intellectual's Self-Criticism: Revisiting *Ashes and Diamonds* with Andrzejewski and Wajda', *Canadian Slavonic Papers* XXXVIII, 3–4 (September–December), 287–303.

_____ (1997) 'Walls and Frontiers: Polish Cinema's Portrayal of Polish-Jewish Relations', in Hundert (ed.) *Jews in Early Modern Poland. POLIN: Studies in Polish Jewry*, vol. 10. London, Portland, Oregon: The Littman Library of Jewish Civilization.

_____ (2000a) 'Notes on Polish Cinema, Nationalism and Wajda's *Holy Week*', in Hjort & MacKenzie (eds) *Cinema and Nation*. London: Routledge.

_____ (2000b) 'Observing the Observer: Andrzej Wajda's *Holy Week* (1995)', *Canadian Slavonic Papers* XLII, 1–2 (March–June), 25–34.

Combs, James E. (1993) *Movies and Politics: the Dynamic Relationship*. New York: Garland Publications.

Curi, Giandomenico (1996/97) '*Wszystko na sprzedaż*', trans. Jerzy Uszyński, *Kwartalnik Filmowy* 15/16.

D'Agostini, Paolo (1993) *Andrzej Wajda*. Roma: Editrice Castoro Cinema.

Davies, Norman (2001) *Heart of Europe. The Past in Poland's Present*. Oxford: Oxford University Press.

Deleuze, Gilles (1989) *Cinema 2: The Time-Image*, trans. Hugh Tomlinson and Robert Galeta. London: Athlone Press.

Derrida, Jacques (1996) *Archive Fever: a Freudian Impression*, trans. Eric Prenowitz. Chicago: University of Chicago Press.

Dialogue and Universalism, 2000, Vol. X, 9–10. Warsaw: Institute of Philosophy at Warsaw University.

Drozdowski, Bohdan (ed.) (1979) *Twentieth Century Polish Theatre*. London and Dallas: John Calder and Riverrun Press.

Dyer, Richard & Ginette Vincendeau (eds) (1992) *Popular European Cinema*. London: Routledge.

Dzieduszycka-Ziemilska, Małgorzata (1999) 'Main Issues in Polish-Jewish Relations'. Available at: www.msz.gov.pl/english/publications.

Eco, Umberto (1967) 'The Structure of Bad Taste', in Trevelyan (ed.) *Italian Writing Now*. Harmondsworth: Penguin.

Eder, Klaus, Klaus Kreimeier, Maria Ratschewa & Bettina Theienhaus (1980) *Andrzej Wajda*. Munich: Carl Hanser Verlag.

Erikson, Kai (1995) 'Notes on Trauma and Community', in Caruth (ed.) *Trauma: Explorations in Memory*. Baltimore: Johns Hopkins.

Falkowska, Janina, (1996/1997) 'Kino polityczne Andrzeja Wajdy', trans. Hanna Baltyn, *Kwartalnik Filmowy*, 15/16.

____ (1996) *The Political Films of Andrzej Wajda: Dialogism in Man of Marble, Man of Iron and Danton*. Providence: Berghahn Books.

Fogler, Janusz (ed.) (1996) *Wajda. Films,* vols I & II. Warsaw: Wydawnictwa Artystyczne i Filmowe.

Foucault, Michel (1979) *The History of Sexuality, vol. 1: An Introduction*, trans. Robert Hurley. London: Allen Lane.

Freud, Sigmund (1967) *Beyond the Pleasure Principle*, trans. James Strachey, New York: Bantam.

____ (1973) *Moses and Monotheism*, trans. James Strachey, Standard Edition 23, London: Hogarth Press.

____ (1985) 'The Moses of Michelangelo (1914)', *The Pelican Freud Library 14. Art and Literature,* London: Penguin, 249-82.

Frye, Northrop (1957) *Anatomy of Criticism: Four Essays.* Princeton: Princeton University Press.

Fuksiewicz, Jacek (1973) *Polish Cinema.* Warszawa: Interpress Publishers.

Georgakas, Dan & Lenny Rubenstein (eds) (1983) *The Cineaste Interviews: On the Art and Politics of the Cinema.* Chicago: Lake View Press.

Ginsberg, Terri (2001) 'St. Korczak of Warsaw'. Paper delivered at the 'Cinema and Theatre of Andrzej Wajda' conference, Łódź.

Glenny, Misha (1990) *The Rebirth of History: Eastern Europe in the Age of Democracy.* London: Penguin.

Gordon, Mary (2000) *Joan of Arc.* New York: Lipper/Viking.

Goska, Danusha (2001) 'Jan Tomasz Gross's *Neighbours*; A Massacre in Jedwabne; One Polish American Responds'. Available at: http://php.indiana.edu/%7Edgoska.

Grochowiak, Stanisław (1968) 'Mówi do nas', *Kultura* 20.

Gross, Jan Tomasz (2001a) *Neighbours: The Destruction of the Jewish Community in Jedwabne, Poland.* Princeton: Princeton University Press.

____ (2001b) 'Poland's Shame', *New Yorker,* 12 March.

Grotowski, Jerzy (1975) *Towards a Poor Theatre*, ed. Eugenio Barba. London: Eyre Methuen.

Grzelecki, Stanislaw & Alicja Helman (1969) *Twenty Years of Polish Cinema: 1947–1967.* Warsaw: Art and Film Publishers.

Guattari, Felix (1995) *Chaosmosis: An Ethico-Aesthetic Paradigm,* trans. Paul Bains & Julian Pefanis. Bloomington & Indianapolis: Indiana University Press.

Helman, Alicja (2001) 'Dzieje jednego pokolenia w filmach Andrzeja Wajdy'. Paper delivered at the 'Cinema and Theatre of Andrzej Wajda' conference, Łódź.

____ (1959) 'Sarmata na żyrafie', *Ekran* 132.

Hochhuth, Rolf (1980) *German Love Story,* trans. John Brownjohn. Boston: Little, Brown.

Hoffman, Eva (1999) *Shtetl: The History of a Small Town and an Extinguished World.* London: Vintage.

Hübner, Zygmunt & Jadwiga Kosicka (1992) *Theater and Politics.* Evanston, IL: Northwestern University Press.

Hundert, David Gershon (ed.) (1997) *Jews in Early Modern Poland. POLIN: Studies in Polish Jewry,* 10. London, Portland, Oregon: The Littman Library of Jewish Civilization.

Insdorf, Annette (1983) *Indelible Shadows: Film and the Holocaust.* New York: Vintage.

Iwaszkiewicz, Jarosław (2001) *Prozy duże i małe. Wybór opowiadań.* Warszawa: Świat Ksiażki.

Jameson, Fredric (1986) 'Third-World Literature in the Era of Multinational Capitalism', *Social Text,* 15.

Janion, Maria (2000) *Do Europy. Tak, ale razem z naszymi umarłymi.* Warszawa: Sic!

Jankowiak, William (1997) 'Talking Love or Talking Sex: Culture's Dilemma', in Suggs &

Miracle (eds) *Culture, Biology, and Sexuality*. Athens and London: The University of Georgia Press.

Jankun-Dopartowa, Mariola (1996) 'Formy przestraszone ogniem i zapachem krwi' in Jankun-Dopartowa & Przylipiak (eds) *Człowiek z ekranu. Z antropologii postaci filmowej*. Kraków: Arcana.

____ (1997) 'Wcielone szyderstwo losu', in Jan Ciechowicz i Tadeusz Szczepański (eds) *Zbigniew Cybulski. Aktor XX wieku*. Gdańsk: Wydawnictwo Uniwersytetu Gdańskiego.

Kalinowska, Izabela (2002) 'Exile and Polish Cinema: From Mickiewicz and Slowacki to Kieślowski', in Radelescu (ed.) *Realms of Exile: Nomadism, Diasporas and Eastern European Voices*. Lanham, Boulder, New York, Oxford: Lexington Books.

Kałużyński, Zygmunt (1975) 'Czarna Łódź kolorowa', *Polityka* 8.

Kapolka, Gerald T. (1990) 'Introduction', in Stanisław Wyspiański, *The Wedding*, trans. Gerald T. Kapolka. Ardis: Ann Arbor, Michigan.

Karpiński, Maciej (1989) *The Theatre of Andrzej Wajda*. Cambridge: Cambridge University Press.

Knap, Włodzimierz (2001) 'Jedwabne, 10th July 1941: An Interview with Paweł Machcewicz.' Available at: http://wings.buffalo.edu/info-oland/classroom/j/Mach.html.

Kocówna, Barbara (1966) 'Kilka kart z życia Reymonta', *Przegląd Humanistyczny* 1.

Kolek, Leszek (1997) *Polish Culture: An Historical Introduction*. Lublin: Maria-Curie Skłodowska University Press.

Komar, Michał (1975) '*Ziemia obiecana* Andrzeja Wajdy', *Dialog* 2.

Kraszewski, Charles S. (1998) *The Romantic Hero and Contemporary Anti-Hero in Polish and Czech Literature: Great Souls and Grey Men*. Lampeter, Wales: The Edwin Mellen Press.

Krzyżanowski, Julian (1937) *Władysław Reymont. Twórca i dzieło*, Lwów: Zaklad Narodowy im. Ossolonskich.

Księga jazdy polskiej (1938) Bolesław Wieniawa-Długoszewski, et al. (ed.), Warszawa.

Kumiega, Jennifer (1985) *The Theatre of Grotowski*. London and New York: Methuen.

Lewin, Abraham & Antony Polonsky (eds) (1988) *A Cup of Tears: A Diary of the Warsaw Ghetto*. Oxford: Blackwell.

Lisiecka, Alicja (1969) '*Everything For Sale!*', *Young Cinema*, 9.

Lubelski, Tadeusz (1992) *Strategie autorskie w polskim filmie fabularnym lat 1945-1961*, Kraków: Wydawnictwo Uniwersytetu Jagiellońskiego.

____ (1997) 'Dwie ziemie jałowe: 1898 i 1974,' *Kwartalnik Filmowy* 18 (Summer).

____ (2000) *Strategie autorskie w polskim filmie fabularnym lat 1945–1961*, 2nd edn. Kraków: Rabid.

Mach, J. (2001) 'The Jedwabne Tragedy.' Available at: http://wings.buffalo.edu/info-poland/classroom/J.

Mazierska, Ewa (2000) 'Non-Jewish Jews, Good Poles and Historical Truth in the Films of Andrzej Wajda', *Historical Journal of Film, Radio, TV*, 20, 2.

Mazower, Mark (1998) *Dark Continent: Europe's Twentieth Century*. London: Penguin.

McArthur, Colin (ed.) (1970) *Andrzej Wajda: Polish Cinema*. London: BFI.

Merz, Irena (1960) 'Surrealizm czy kicz?', *Film* 579.

Michałek, Bolesław (1970) *Marzenia i rzeczywistość*, Warszawa: Wydawnictwa Artystyczne i Filmowe.

____ (1973) *The Cinema of Andrzej Wajda*, London: Tantivy Press.

Michałek, Bolesław and Frank Turaj (1988) *The Modern Cinema of Poland*, Bloomington: Indiana University Press.

Michnik, Adam (1996a) 'Conversation with Andrzej Wajda about *Holy Week*', in Janusz Fogler (ed.) *Wajda. Films*, vol. II. Warsaw: Wydawnictwa Artystyczne i Filmowe.

____ (1996b) 'Introduction', in Janusz Fogler (ed.) *Wajda. Films*, vol. I. Warsaw: Wydawnictwa Artystyczne i Filmowe.

____ (2001) 'Poles and the Jews: How Deep the Guilt?', *New York Times*, 17 March.

Mickiewicz, Adam (1956) 'Concert of concerts', *The Polish Review* 1, 4 (Autumn).

_____ (1977) *Forefathes' Eve Part III*, in Harold B.Segel (ed. and trans.) *Polish Romantic Drama: Three Plays in English Translation*. Ithaca and London: Cornell University Press.

_____ (1986) *Pan Tadeusz*, trans. Kenneth R. Mackenzie. New York: Hippocrene Books.

Miłosz, Czesław (1953) *The Captive Mind*, trans. Jane Zielonko, London: Secker & Warburg.

_____ (1980) *The Captive Mind*, trans. Jane Zielonko. Harmondsworth: Penguin.

_____ (1983) *The History of Polish Literature*. Berkeley: University of California Press.

_____ (1996) *Selected Poems*, trans. Louis Iribarne & David Brooks. Kraków: Wydawnictwo Literackie.

Modrzejewska, Ewa (1991) '"Byłbym innym człowiekiem": Rozmowa z Andrzejem Wajdą', *Iluzjon*, 1, 41.

Morris, Neil (1970) 'The Uses of History: Eastern Europe (extract)', in McArthur (ed.) *Andrzej Wajda: Polish Cinema*. London: BFI.

Mruklik, Barbara (1969) *Andrzej Wajda*. Warszawa: Wydawnictwa Artystyczne i Filmowe.

Naremore, James (ed.) (2000) *Film Adaptation*. New Brunswick, NJ: Rutgers University Press.

Nichols, Bill (1991) *Representing Reality*, Bloomington: Indiana University Press.

_____ (1994) *Blurred Boundaries*. Bloomington: Indiana University Press.

Nurczyńska-Fidelska, Ewelina (1996a) 'Historia i romantyzm: Szkic o twórczości Andrzeja Wajdy', in Nurczyńska-Fidelska (ed.) *Kino polskie w dziesięciu sekwencjach*, Łódź: Wydawnictwo Uniwersytetu Łódzkiego.

_____ (1996b) 'W kręgu romantycznej tradycji: O twórczości Andrzeja Wajdy', in Sobotka (ed.) *Mistrzowie kina europejskiego*. Łódź: STO Films.

_____ (1998) *Polska klasyka literacka według Andrzeja Wajdy*. Katowice: Wydawnictwo Śląsk.

Oleksy, Elżbieta, Elżbieta Ostrowska & Michael Stevenson (eds) (2000) *Gender in Film and the Media: East-West Dialogues*. Frankfurt am Main: Peter Lang.

Onecki, Stanisław (ed.) (1987) *Polish Resistance Movement in Poland and Abroad, 1939–1945*. Warsaw: PWN.

Orr, John *Cinema and Modernity*. (1993) Cambridge: Polity Press

_____ (1998) *Contemporary Cinema* Edinburgh: Edinburgh University Press.

_____ (2000) *The Art and Politics of Film* Edinburgh: Edinburgh University Press.

Ostrowska, Elżbieta (2000) 'Otherness Doubled: Representations of Jewish Women in Polish Cinema', in Oleksy *et al.* (eds) *Gender in Film and the Media. East-West Dialogues*. Frankfurt am Main: Peter Lang.

Parry, Benita (1997) 'Resistance Theory/Theorizing Resistance, or Two Cheers for Nativism', in Monga (ed.) *Contemporary Postcolonial Theory. A Reader*. London: Arnold.

Payne, Stanley (1995) *Fascism: A Comparative History 1900–1945*. Berkeley: University of California Press.

Peck, Abraham. J. (1999) '"The Two Saddest Nations on Earth": Poles, Jews and Memory', *The Sarmatian Review*, XIX, 1. Available at: www.ruf.rice.edu/sarmatia/199/peck.html.

Peters, John Durham (1999) 'Exile, Nomadism, and Diaspora: The Stakes of Mobility in the Western Canon', in Naficy (ed.) *Home, Exile, Homeland. Film, Media, and the Politics of Place*. New York: Routledge.

Pietrasik, Zdzisław (1999) 'Horror w zaścianku', *Polityka* 43.

Polonsky, Antony (1990) 'Introduction', in Polonsky (ed.) *My Brother's Keeper?: Recent Polish Debates on the Holocaust*. Oxford: Routledge.

Popiel, Magdalena (1966) Introduction to Władysław Reymont, *Ziemia obiecana*. Wrocław: Ossolinneum.

Prokop, Jan (1985) *Szczególna przygoda żyć nad Wisłą: Studia i szkice literackie*, London: Polonia.

_____ (1993) *Universum polskie. Literatura, wyobraźnia zbiorowa, mity polityczne*. Kraków: Universitas.

Quart, Leonard (2000) 'Wajda's Industrial Epic: *The Promised Land*', *Slavic and East*

European Performance, 20, 3 (Fall).

Ray, Gordon N. (1955) *Thackeray: The Uses of Adversity, 1811–1846*. New York: McGraw-Hill.

Ricoeur, Paul (1984–88) *Time and Narrative*, trans. Kathleen McLaughlin and David Pellauer, vols 1–3. Chicago: University of Illinois Press.

Ringelblum, Emmanuel (1976) *Polish-Jewish Relations*. New York: Howard Fertig.

Rohozinska, Joanna (2000) 'News from Poland', *Central Europe Review*, 2, 19, 15 May.

Rosenbaum, Ron (1998) *Explaining Hitler: The Search for the Origins of His Evil*. Basingstoke: Macmillan.

Rostworowski, Marek (1993) *Żydzi w Polsce*. Warszawa: Wydawnictwo Interpress.

Rotha, Paul (1935) *Documentary Film*. London: Faber.

Salmonowicz, Stanisław (1997) 'The Deep Roots and Long Life of Stereotypes', in Hundert (ed.) *Jews in Early Modern Poland. POLIN: Studies in Polish Jewry*, vol. 10. London, Portland, Oregon: The Littman Library of Jewish Civilization.

Schwarberg, Gunther (2001) *In the Ghetto of Warsaw: Heinrich Jost's Photographs*. Berlin: Steidl.

Sedgwick, Eve Kosofsky (1985) *Between Men: English Literature and Male Homosocial Desire*. New York: Columbia University Press.

____ (1990) *Epistemology of the Closet*, Berkeley: University of California Press.

____ (1993) *Tendencies*. Durham, NC: Duke University Press.

Segel, Harold B. (ed.) (1977) *Polish Romantic Drama: Three Plays in English Translation*, trans. Harold B. Segel. Ithaca and London: Cornell University Press.

Sinyard, Neil (1986) *Filming Literature: The Art of Screen Adaptation*. London: Croom Helm.

Siwicka, Dorota (1993) 'Ojczyzna intymna', *Res Publica Nowa*, 7–8.

Sørenssen, Bjørn (2001) *Å fange virkeligheten-Dokumentarfilmens århundre*. Oslo: Universitetsforlaget.

Spiegelman, Art (1987) *Maus: A Survivor's Tale I*. London: Penguin.

Steiner, George (1971) *In Bluebeard's Castle: Some Notes Towards the Re-Definition of Culture*. London: Faber.

Sulik, Boleslaw (1970) 'War and History: 1954–58', in McArthur (ed.) *Andrzej, Wajda: Polish Cinema*. London: BFI.

Syberberg, Hans-Jürgen (1982) *Hitler, a Film From Germany*. New York: Farrar, Straus, Giroux.

Szporer, Michael (1991) '*Man of Marble*: an Interview with Krystyna Janda', *Cineaste XVIII*, 3.

Śliwiński, Krzysztof (1997) 'Towards A Polish-Jewish Dialogue. The Way Forward', in Hundert (ed.) *Jews in Early Modern Poland. POLIN: Studies in Polish Jewry*, vol. 10. London, Portland, Oregon: The Littman Library of Jewish Civilization.

Toeplitz, Krzysztof Teodor (1958) 'Serce i rozum', *Świat*, 19 October.

Turim, Maureen (1989) *Flashbacks in Film: Memory and History*. New York and London: Routledge.

____ (1990) '*Le Jour se leve*: Poetic Realism as Psychoanalytical and Ideological Operation' in Hayward & Vincendeau (eds) *French Film: Texts and Contexts*. London: Routledge, 103–17.

Vinecour, Earl (1977) *Polish Jews: The Final Chapter*. New York: McGraw-Hill.

Wajda, Andrzej (1967) 'Destroying the Commonplace', in Geduld (ed.) *Filmmakers on Filmmaking*. Harmondsworth: Penguin.

____ (1971) 'Referat', in Irena Moderska (ed.) *Andrzej Wróblewski w 10-lecie śmierci: Referaty i głosy w dyskusji z konferencji w Rogalinie 4 maja 1967 r*, Poznań: Muzeum Narodowe w Poznaniu.

____ (1973) 'O *Lotnej*, domu rodzinnym, okresie wojny i studiach', *Kino 3*.

____ (1989) *Double Vision: My Life in Film*, trans. Rose Medina. New York: Henry Holt.

____ (1996a) *Wajda. Filmy*, vols I & II. Warszawa: Wydawnictwa Artystyczne i Filmowe.

____ (1996b) *Moje notatki z historii*, Part 3. (Akson Studio, for Canal+).

____ (2000a) *Kino i reszta świata. Autobiografia*. Kraków: Znak.

____ (2000b) 'My Place Was Here', *Dialogue and Universalism*, X, 9–10.

____ (2000c) *O sobie. O sztuce. O polityce*, wstęp, wybór i układ tekstów Maria Malatyńska. Warszawa: Pruszyński i S-ka.

____ (2000d) *Wajda. Films. Oscar 2000*, ed. Beata Kosińska. Warszawa: Wydawnictwa Artystyczne i Filmowe.

____ (2000e) 'The Young Ladies of Wilko', trans. Ewa Krasińska in Wajda, *Wajda. Films, Oscar 2000*, ed. Beata Kosińska. Warszawa: Wydawnictwa Artystyczne i Filmowe.

Wertenstein, Wanda (ed.) (2000) *Wajda mówi o sobie: wywiady i teksty*. Kraków: Wydawnictwo Literackie.

White, Hayden (1973) *Metahistory: The Historical Imagination in Nineteenth-Century Europe*. Baltimore: Johns Hopkins.

Wittek, Jerzy (ed.) (1973) *Polish Film*. Warsaw: The Ministry of Culture and Art.

Wyka, Kazimierz (1951) *Zarys współczesnej literatury polskiej 1884-1925*. Kraków: Panstowe Wydawnictwo Naukowe.

____ (1979) *Reymont, czyli ucieczka do życia*. Warszawa: Państwowy Instytut Wydawniczy.

____ (1985) *Życie na niby*. Warszawa: Książka i Wiedza.

Wynot, E. (1974) *Polish Politics in Transition 1918–1939: the camp of unity and the struggle for power*. University of Georgia Press: Athens .

Wyspiański, Stanisław (1958) *Dzieła zebrane*, vol. 4. Kraków: Wydawnictwo Literackie.

____ (1990) *The Wedding*, trans. Gerard T. Kapolka. Ardis: Ann Arbor.

Yerulshalmi, Yosef Hayim (1991) *Freud's Moses: Judaism Terminable and Interminable*. New Haven & London: Yale University Press

Zuckerman, Yitzhak ('Antek') (1993) *A Surplus of Memory: Chronicle of the Warsaw Ghetto Uprising*, ed. and trans. Barbara Harshav. Berkeley: University of California Press.

INDEX

Adorno, Theodor W.   18, 23
Akropolis   133–4, 145
Altman, Robert   9, 10
Anderegg, Michael   176
Andrew, Dudley   176, 188
Andrzejewski, Jerzy   20
Angelopoulos, Theo   3
Arch (*Łuk*)   165, 171
Aristotle   109, 163, 165, 167, 171
Arnold, Matthew   26
As the Years Pass, As the Days Pass...
   (*Z biegiem lat, z biegiem dni...*)   160, 170
Ashes and Diamonds (*Popiół i diament*)   3,
   5–6, 12, 15–16, 20, 22, 25, 36, 43, 47,
   49–50, 52, 61–2, 65–71, 75, 82, 106,
   122, 129, 132
Asphalt Jungle, The   5
Auden, W. H.   92

Ballads and Romances (*Ballady i*
   romanse)   174
Balzac, Honoré de   149
Bałucki, Michał   160–1, 165, 169, 171
Banach, Roman   43
Barba, Eugenio   132, 134
Bardini, Aleksander   52
Bartal, Israel   92
Battle of Grunwald, The (*Bitwa pod*
   Grunwaldem)   161

Bazin, André   51
Benjamin, Walter   26, 145
Bergman, Ingmar   7, 9
Bertolucci, Bernardo   9
Białoszczyński, Tadeusz   69
Bielas, Katarzyna   43–5
Bierut, Bolesław   112
Blue Chauffeur, The (*Szofer niebieski*)   37
Błoński, Jan   84–6, 89–91, 145
Book of Polish Cavalry, The (*Ksiega jazdy*
   polskiej)   126
Books of the Polish Nation and Pilgrimage   174
Boorman, John   5
Borch-Jacobsen, Mikkel   100
Borowczyk, Walerian   144
Borowski, Tadeusz   9, 168
Branagh, Kenneth   176
Brecht, Bertold   79
Bresson, Robert   27
Breughel, Pieter   85, 92
Broch, Hermann   23–6, 28
Brook, Peter   134, 145, 182
Bryson, Norman   118, 130
Bugajski, Ryszard   10
Bulgakov, Mikhail   23
Buñuel, Luis   3, 21, 24, 26, 79, 91
Byron, George G.   176

Caes, Christopher J.   28

Camouflage (*Barwy ochronne*)   103
Canetti, Elias   19
Cannon, Damian   91
Caricatures (*Karykatury*)   165, 171
Carné, Marcel   98
Caruth, Cathy   11, 15–16, 19
Celińska, Stanisława   10, 52, 68
Chatterjee, Partha   70
Chauffeur (*Szofer*)   37
Chronicle of Amorous Incidents, A (*Kronika wypadków miłosnych*)   31, 49–50
Chronique d'un été   34
Ciecierski, Jan   67
Citizen Kane   5, 11, 94–8, 140–3, 145
Clifford, James   66–7
Coates, Paul   70, 91, 142
Colonel Wolodyjowski (*Pan Wołodyjowski*)   33
Combe, Sonia   94
Conformist, The   9
Cries and Whispers   9
Crowned-Eagle Ring, The (*Pierścionek z orłem w koronie*)   59
Curi, Giandomenico   35
Cybulski, Zbigniew   6, 8, 21, 25, 32, 35–8, 43, 45, 50, 65

Dante Alighieri   123
Danton   2
Davies, Norman   62
Death of a President   103
Death of Felicjan Dulski, The (*Śmierć Felicjana Dulskiego*)   165, 167, 171
Decalogue 8 (*Dekalog 8*)   82
Deleuze, Gilles   97–8
Deluge, The (*Potop*)   176
Derrida, Jacques   94
Dickens, Charles   149
Direction Nowa Huta (*Kierunek Nowa Huta*)   43
Doctor 117641: A Holocaust Survivor   88
Drifters   111
Dzwonkowski, Aleksander   69

Eco, Umberto   25
Eder, Klaus   107
Eisenstein, Sergei   17
Eroica   15
Europa, Europa   10
Everything For Sale (*Wszystko na sprzedaż*)   8, 13, 21, 27, 31–6, 38–40, 42–5, 188
Executions (*Rozstrzelania*)   17, 36

Faithful River, The (*Wierna rzeka*)   63
Falkowska, Janina   39
Fall of Icarus   85
Fassbinder, Rainer Werner   3
Fellini, Federico   8
Ferdydurke   47
Fire in the Steppe (*Pan Wołodyjowski*)   176
Five from Barska Street, The (*Piątka z ulicy Barskiej*)   43
Flaherty, Robert   111
Fogler, Janusz   77, 88–9, 92
Ford, Aleksander   43
Ford, John   4, 14, 124
Forefathers' Eve (*Dziady III*)   133–7, 139–41, 144, 174
Foucault, Michel   49
Freud, Sigmund   15–19, 28, 60–1, 94, 100, 122–3, 130, 163
Frye, Northrop   164–6, 171

Generation, A (*Pokolenie*)   2, 5–6, 9, 15, 20, 30, 40, 62, 76–7, 79–80, 82, 85–6, 88, 90, 164
Georgakas, Dan   135
Gerusalemme Liberata   18
Gierek, Edward   39, 102, 109, 164
Godard, Jean-Luc   8, 11
Goethe, Johann, W.   176
Gombrowicz, Witold   47, 144
Good Person of Szechwan, The   79
Gordon, Mary   18
Great Man's Lady, The   95
Greenaway, Peter   176
Grierson, John   111
Grochowiak, Stanisław   36
Grotowski, Jerzy   132–8, 143–5
Grottger, Artur   26
Guattari, Felix   144

Hands Up (*Ręce do góry*)   34
Has, Wojciech   3, 15, 144
Hauptmann, Gerhard   162
Helman, Alicja   24, 28, 123
Heymann, Daniele   88–9
Hitchcock, Alfred   5, 13
Hochhuth, Rolf   56–9
Hoffman, Eva   91
Hoffman, Jerzy   33
Holland, Agnieszka   10, 43, 88, 179
Holtz, Witold   32–4, 39
Holy Week (*Wielki Tydzień*)   47, 76, 86

How To Be Loved? (*Jak być kochaną?*) 15
Howard, William K. 94
Hundert, David Gershon 92
Hunting Flies (*Polowanie na muchy*) 8

Ibsen, Henrik 106
Ilza Ceramic, The (*Ceramika
    Iłżecka*) 40
In the Net (*W sieci*) 165, 171
Innocent Sorcerers (*Niewinni czarodzieje*) 8,
    188
Interrogation (*Przesłuchanie*) 10, 21, 65, 93
Intimacy 7, 49, 52
Iwaszkiewicz, Jarosław 31, 63, 72
Iżewska, Teresa 49

Jameson, Fredric 60–1
Janczar, Tadeusz 6, 49
Janda, Krystyna 11, 41, 43, 62, 105, 114
Janion, Maria 47
Jankowiak, William 51
Jankun-Dopartowa, Mariola 37
Jarman, Derek 176
Jędrusik, Kalina 159
Joan of Arc 18

Kaden-Bandrowski, Juliusz 161, 165, 167
Kalina's Drama (*Dramat Kaliny*) 165, 171
Kalinowska, Izabela 45
Kanal (*Kanał*) 3, 6, 15, 20, 30, 49, 62, 106,
    123, 136
Kantor, Tadeusz 144
Kapolka, Gerald T. 177
Kawalerowicz, Jerzy 15, 103
Kawecki, Zygmunt 160, 165
Kierkegaard, Sören 168, 171
Kieślowski, Krzysztof 75, 82, 179
Kilar, Wojciech 155
Kisielewski, Jan August 160, 165
Kłosiński, Edward 11
Kocówna, Barbara 147
Kolberger, Krzysztof 44, 73
Komar, Michał 157
Kondrat, Marek 74
Konrad Wallenrod 174, 187
Konwicki, Tadeusz 31, 50, 63
Korczak 76–7, 79, 86–91, 188
Kordian 133–4
Kossak, Juliusz 26, 29
Kostenko, Andrzej 32, 34
Kościuszko, Tadeusz 70, 174

Kott, Jan 10
Kowalski, Władysław 75
Krasiński, Zygmunt 173
Kraszewski, Charles S. 173
Królikowski, Rafał 59, 65, 117
Krzyżanowski, Julian 147
Krzyżewska, Ewa 6, 50, 67
Kumiega, Jennifer 133
Kuncewicz, Maria 63
Kuźniar, Zdzisław 75
Kwiatkowska, Halina 67, 170

L'Armée des Ombres 9
Lacan, Jacques 100
Lancelot du lac 27
Landscape After Battle (*Krajobraz po bitwie*)
    8, 49, 52, 68–9, 75–6, 86
Lanzmann, Claude 86, 88, 92
Last Meeting, The (*Ostatnie spotkanie*) 165,
    171
Le joli Mai 34
Le Jour se leve 98
Lelouch, Claude 8, 34
Levi-Strauss, Claude 67
Lisiecka, Alicja 34
Lotna 16–17, 20, 23–9, 49–50, 116, 119–
    23, 127–9, 136
Love at Twenty (*L'amour à vingt ans*) 8, 188
Love in Germany, A (*Eine Liebe in
    Deutschland/Un Amour en Allemagne*)
    56, 59, 62
Lubelski, Tadeusz 22, 65–6, 68–71
Luhrmann, Baz 176
Łapicki, Andrzej 32–3, 40, 46
Łomnicki, Jacek 6, 40–1, 82
Łomnicki, Tadeusz 40, 82
Łoza, Mieczysław 117
Łysak, Piotr 56, 58

Macbeth 19
Mailer, Norman 27
Makarczyński, Tadeusz 43
Malick, Terrence 4–5
Man of Iron (*Człowiek z żelaza*) 4,
    12–14, 62, 95–6, 99–100, 107, 109–15,
    140, 143, 164, 188
Man of Marble (*Człowiek z marmuru*) 4–5,
    8, 11–14, 31, 38–45, 62, 95–6, 99–117,
    139–45, 164, 189
Man on the Track (*Człowiek na torze*) 145
Mankiewicz, Herman J. 95, 9–8

Marker, Chris 34
Markowski, Andrzej 78
Marx, Karl 9, 10, 22, 60–1
Mason, James 6
Masters of Fast Melting, The (*Mistrzowie szybkich wytopów*) 43
Mastroianni, Marcello 8
Matejko, Jan 161, 165
McCabe and Mrs Miller 9
Melville, Jean-Pierre 9
Mendelsohn, Ezra 92
Merz, Irena 26
Michałek, Bolesław 9, 22, 31–2, 64, 77, 79, 83, 135, 138
Mickiewicz, Adam 14, 31, 44, 47, 72–5, 90–2, 133, 135–9, 142–5, 172–88
Miłosz, Czesław 85–6, 105, 114, 135, 145, 175, 177, 180
Mirror 11–12
Modrzyńska, Urszula 6, 22
Moes, Jerzy 117
Morin, Edgar 34
Mrs. Dulska's Morality (*Moralność pani Dulskiej*) 161, 165, 171
Mruklik, Barbara 24, 26
Müller-Stahl, Armin 56
Munk, Andrzej 3, 15, 43, 57, 144–5
Musée des Beaux Arts 92
Mysteries of Paris 149

Nanook of the North 111
Nastulanka, Krystyna 38
Nehrebecka, Anna 47, 70, 150
New Art (*Nowa sztuka*) 43
Nichols, Bill 110, 115
Nietzsche, Friedrich 138
Night and Fog 87
Norwid, Kamil Cyprian 123
Nurczyńska-Fidelska, Ewelina 51, 71, 156, 171

Odd Man Out 5, 6
Olbrychski, Daniel 4, 8, 10, 33, 52, 57, 62, 68, 72, 150, 186
Olivier, Laurence 176
On the Banks of the Niemen (*Nad Niemnem*) 47
On the Set (*Na planie*) 32
Opalski, Magdalena 92
Opania, Marian 13
Open House (*Dom otwarty*) 161, 165, 170–1

Orchestra Conductor, The (*Dyrygent*) 188
Orzeszkowa, Eliza 47
Ostrowska, Elżbieta 75, 87
Outpost, The (*Placówka*) 47

Pan Tadeusz 14, 31, 44, 47–8, 51, 72–6, 86, 90–1, 106, 135–6, 139, 143, 161, 164, 172–80, 184, 187–9
Parry, Benita 75
Passenger, The (*Pasażerka*) 15, 57
Pawlikowski, Adam 65, 117
Peasants, The (*Chłopi*) 146
Peck, Abraham. J. 92
Personal File (*Kartoteka*) 47
Petelski, Czesław 40–1
Pieczka, Franciszek 70
Pietrasik, Zdzisław 44
Pilate and Others (*Pilatus und Andere – Ein Film für Karfreitag*) 21–2, 30
Piłsudski, Józef 126
Polanski, Roman 3, 5, 8
Polonsky, Anthony 84–5
Poor Christian Looks at the Ghetto, A 85–6
Popiel, Magdalena 141
Power and the Glory, The 94
Pre-Spring (*Przedwiośnie*) 22
Price of Concrete, The (*Cena betonu*) 41
Prokop, Jan 48, 55, 61, 117, 130
Promised Land 4, 22, 47–51, 62, 69–77, 87, 92, 146–60, 164
Prospero's Books 176
Prus, Bolesław 47
Przybyszewski, Stanisław 161, 165
Pszoniak, Wojciech 70, 150
Pushkin, Evgeni 174

Quo Vadis 176

Radziwiłłowicz, Jerzy 11, 62
Reed, Carol 6
Renoir, Jean 2
Resnais, Alain 87
Reymont, Władysław Stanisław 146–59
Ricoeur, Paul 162–4, 167, 171
Rocard, Michel 88
Romeo + Juliet 176
Ronikier, Joanna 161
Rosenbaum, Ron 88
Rossellini, Roberto 7
Rostworowski, Marek 92

Rotha, Paul 111
Rouch, Jean 34
Rough Treatment (*Bez znieczulenia*) 30, 188
Ruszczyc, Ferdynand 106
Rydz-Śmigły, Edward 126

Samson 76, 79, 86
Saragossa Manuscript, The (*Rękopis znaleziony w Saragossie*) 3
Schindler's List 87
Schygulla, Hanna 56
Scott, Walter 176
Seasonal Love (*Sezonowa miłość*) 161, 165–7, 171
Sedgwick, Eve Kosofsky 130–1
Segel, Harold B. 137, 145
Seweryn, Andrzej 47, 70, 150
Shakespeare, William 10, 133, 176
Shoah 86–7
Siemion, Wojciech 75
Sienkiewicz, Henryk 176
Silence, The 7
Sinyard, Neil 176
Siwicka, Dorota 47
Skolimowski, Jerzy 3, 8, 32, 34, 144
Słowacki, Juliusz 75, 133, 135, 173, 175
Sobociński, Witold 34, 153
Sørenssen, Bjørn 115
Spider's Strategem, The 9
Spielberg, Steven 87
Stachówna, Grażyna 63
Stalin, Josef 2, 12, 42–3, 104, 112
Starski, Allan 72
Stawiński, Jerzy 20
Structure of Crystal, The (*Struktura kryształu*) 103
Sturges, Preston 94
Sue, Eugene 149
Syberberg, Hans-Jürgen 126–7
Ścibor-Rylski, Aleksander 40, 43, 93, 95, 108

Tarkovsky, Andrei 3, 11–12
Tempest, The 176
Terekhova, Margarita 12
Thackeray, William 171
Thieves like Us 9
Three Stories (*Trzy opowieści*) 41
Toeplitz, Krzysztof Teodor 25
Touch of Evil 11
Trial, The 11

True End of the Great War, The 15
Truffaut, François 8, 11
Turaj, Frank 116, 135, 138, 145
Turim, Maureen 98

Vanity Fair 171
Vertigo 13
Viridiana 79
Visconti, Luchino 14

Wagner, Agnieszka 59
Wałęsa, Lech 13–14, 114
Warszawianka 161, 169
Waste Land, The 26
Weavers, The 162
Wedding, The (*Wesele*) 46–7, 62, 76, 80, 86, 106, 139, 143, 160, 162, 164, 169–80, 184–8
Welles, Orson 4–5, 11, 94–5, 140, 189
Wellman, William 95
Wertenstein, Wanda 21, 23, 32, 38, 41, 122, 124, 126
White, Hayden 171
Wild Duck, The 106
Wiszniewski, Wojciech 43
Witkiewicz, Stanisław Ignacy 144
Worcell, Stanisław 175
Wróblewski, Andrzej 17, 26, 35–8, 45, 122, 128
Wyka, Kazimierz 125, 127, 147
Wynot, Edward 131
Wyspiański, Stanisław 45–7, 62–3, 106, 133–4, 143, 160–2, 165, 170–2, 177–9, 188

Yerushalmi, Yosef Hayim 94
Young Ladies of Wilko, The (*Panny z Wilka*) 31, 72, 75

Zachwatowicz, Krystyna 112
Zajączkowski, Leonard 41, 43
Zanussi, Krzysztof 103
Zapolska, Gabriela 160–1, 165, 167, 171
Zastrzeżyński, Wacław 67
Ziarnik, Jerzy 32
Ziętek, Ewa 46
Żebrowski, Tadeusz 74
Żeromski, Stefan 22, 63
Żukrowski, Wojciech 29